AAT Level 3 Management Acc

# AAT LEVEL 3
# Management Accounting Techniques Book 1

AAT Level 3
Management Accounting
Techniques Book 1
(Q22 1.4)

AAT Level 3 Management Accounting Techniques

Published by Accountext

© Accountext Revised August 2024

All rights are reserved. No part of this publication may be reproduced, sorted in a retrieval system, or transmitted in any form or by any means, electronic, mechanical, photocopy, recording, or otherwise, without the prior written consent of the publishers. Cosmetic changes to this content through the alteration of names and/or numerical values are a breach of copyright.

This book may not be lent, re-sold, hired out or otherwise disposed of by way of trade in any form without the prior permission of the publishers.

The content of this pack is frequently updated but on occasion, changes to legislation or accounting standards may not be reflected until sometime after implementation.

The content of this publication is intended to prepare students for AAT examinations and should not be used as professional advice. Accountext Publishing Ltd does not accept any liability for any losses or damage suffered, directly or indirectly, as a result of the information within this text. Professional advice should always be sought.

Accountext Publishing Ltd
First Floor Unit B
Meltex House
65-67 Kepler
Tamworth
B79 7XE

www.accountext.co.uk

**Introduction**

The manual is split into chapters and contains many exercises. You should start at the beginning and work through each chapter in order. Should you become stuck at any point, ensure you review the content again – a second or third reading often helps.

The manual contains a number of icons to provide assistance along the way:

The Activity icon indicates that you have an activity to complete at that stage of the manual. Activities aid learning – have a go and then check where the answer came from.

When you see this icon, an answer to the activity you have carried out, will be displayed. Take time to appreciate how the answer was arrived at.

Where you see this icon an example is provided. This may be an illustration of a document that is used in business or an illustration of how a calculation or activity is to be completed.

Take note. This is information that is important or information that you may need for examination purposes.

This is one of the most important icons – it represents a requirement for you to complete an online assessment.

This page is left intentionally blank.

# Contents

## Chapter 1: The Purpose of Management Accounting .................... 9
Introduction .................... 10
The Difference between Management Accounting and Financial Accounting .................... 10
The Purpose of Internal Reporting .................... 11
Cost Accounting .................... 14
Ethical Principles in Management Accounting .................... 16
Cost Centres, Profit Centres and Investments Centres .................... 17

## Chapter 2: Cost Behaviour .................... 23
Introduction .................... 24
Cost Classification .................... 24
Cost Behaviour .................... 24
Variable Costs .................... 24
Fixed Costs .................... 25
Semi-Variable Costs .................... 27
Stepped Costs .................... 28
How Do Costs Behave? .................... 29
Identifying Cost Behaviour .................... 30
Determining the Fixed and Variable Parts of Semi-Variable Costs .................... 32
The High-Low Method .................... 32
Product Costs and Period Costs .................... 36

## Chapter 3: Inventory .................... 39
Introduction .................... 40
Inventory Valuation Techniques .................... 40
Accounting Entries for Materials .................... 53
Further Rules for Inventory Valuation .................... 57
Planning the Purchases of Materials .................... 60
Methods of Determining Inventory Requirements .................... 62
The 'Levels' Method .................... 63
The Economic Order Quantity (EOQ) .................... 67
Other Factors to Take into Account .................... 69

## Chapter 4: Calculating Direct Labour Costs .................... 74
Introduction .................... 76
Direct and Indirect Labour .................... 76
Comparison of the Different Systems .................... 84
Idle Time and Overtime Premiums .................... 86

    Sources of Information for Labour .................................................................................. 87

    Accounting for Labour Costs ............................................................................................ 88

## Chapter 5: Absorption Costing ............................................................................... 95

    Introduction ...................................................................................................................... 96

    Allocation and Apportionment .......................................................................................... 97

    Reapportioning Overheads from Support Centres to Production Centres ..................... 102

    Direct Reapportionment ................................................................................................. 103

    Step-Down Reapportionment ........................................................................................ 107

    Calculating the Budgeted Overhead Absorption Rate ................................................... 112

    Absorbing Overheads into Product Costs ..................................................................... 115

    Under and Over Absorption .......................................................................................... 118

    Accounting Entries for Overheads ................................................................................ 121

## Chapter 6: Marginal Costing .................................................................................. 127

    Introduction .................................................................................................................... 128

    The Need for Marginal Costing ...................................................................................... 128

    Contribution .................................................................................................................... 128

    Break-Even Analysis ..................................................................................................... 131

    Margins of Safety .......................................................................................................... 137

    Target Profit ................................................................................................................... 141

    Contribution / Sales Ratio .............................................................................................. 143

    Absorption Costing and Marginal Costing ..................................................................... 146

    Advantages and Disadvantages of Absorption Costing and Marginal Costing .............. 158

## Chapter 7: Activity Based Costing ........................................................................ 160

    Introduction .................................................................................................................... 162

    Activity Based Costing – the Basics .............................................................................. 163

## Chapter 8: Types of Costing Systems .................................................................. 173

    Introduction .................................................................................................................... 174

    Unit costing .................................................................................................................... 174

    Job Costing ................................................................................................................... 174

    Batch Costing ................................................................................................................ 177

    Contract Costing ........................................................................................................... 179

    Service Costing ............................................................................................................. 180

## Chapter 9: Budgeting .............................................................................................. 185

    Introduction .................................................................................................................... 186

What is a Budget?........................................................................................................ 186
What Budgets are Needed?....................................................................................... 187
Variances.................................................................................................................... 189
Causes of Variances .................................................................................................. 190
Types of Budget.......................................................................................................... 192
Calculating variances as a percentage flexed budget................................................ 196
Using Flexed Budgets for Different Scenarios ........................................................... 200

## Chapter 10: Cash Management.............................................................................. 205
Introduction ................................................................................................................ 206
The Cash Budget ....................................................................................................... 207
Including the Bank Balance in the Cash Budget........................................................ 207
The Working Capital Cycle......................................................................................... 215
The Working Capital Cycle and Improving Cash Flow ............................................... 218
Funding Methods for the Acquisition of Non-Current Assets ..................................... 221
Improving Cash Flow ................................................................................................. 222
Cash Flow and Software ............................................................................................ 224
Reconciling Profit and Cash ....................................................................................... 227

## Chapter 1: Activity Answers..................................................................................... 231
## Chapter 2: Activity Answers..................................................................................... 232
## Chapter 3: Activity Answers..................................................................................... 235
## Chapter 4: Activity Answers..................................................................................... 242
## Chapter 5: Activity Answers..................................................................................... 248
## Chapter 6: Activity Answers..................................................................................... 255
## Chapter 7: Activity Answers..................................................................................... 264
## Chapter 8: Activity Answers..................................................................................... 267
## Chapter 9: Activity Answers..................................................................................... 268
## Chapter 10: Activity Answers................................................................................... 274

This page is left intentionally blank.

# Chapter 1: The Purpose of Management Accounting

**By the end of this chapter, you should understand:**

- The Difference between Management Accounting and Financial Accounting
- The Purpose of Internal Reporting
- Cost Accounting
- Ethical Principles in Management Accounting
- Cost Centres, Revenue Centres and Investments Centres

# Chapter 1: The Purpose of Management Accounting

## Introduction

The role of a management accountant is to gather information on revenue, cash flow, materials, labour and other transactions to make estimations, and future forecasts and write reports that assist with decision making. The decisions can be short-term (day to day management) or long-term (corporate strategy).

Management accountants combine financial data and non-financial data to create a complete picture of the business for internal use only. This is known as **internal reporting**. In contrast, a financial accountant would prepare reports based on past performance and produce statutory required financial statements and information for users outside the business.

## The Difference between Management Accounting and Financial Accounting

**Management Accounting** – This is the branch of accounting which uses data from the business's financial transactions and other information to produce a wide range of information which supports the management of the business.

This could include:

- Costing information on how much products cost to manufacture, to help identify the best price to sell them at.

- Budgets and forecasts of future performance and the review of these to identify how well the company is performing.

- Appraisal of different potential investment projects (e.g. investment in new machinery) to identify which is the most suitable for the business.

**Financial Accounting** – This is the branch of accounting which produces a historical record of the transactions of the business. These are then used to produce important financial statements which report:

- The **financial position** of the business – how financially 'healthy' it is at a given date.
- The **financial performance** of the business – how 'profitable' the business has been over a given period of time.

These reports (known as the Statement of Financial Position or Balance Sheet, and the Statement of Profit or Loss or Income Statement), are generally prepared on an annual basis and are used by the business owners, lenders to the business and other interested stakeholders (e.g. His **Majesty's Revenue and Customs – HMRC**) to better understand how well the business is doing and how stable it is.

Financial Accounting is mostly concerned with the historical perspective – looking backwards in time at transactions which have actually happened. Management Accounting is concerned with looking forwards – using the events of the past along with other knowledge to try to accurately predict the future.

Here is a summary of the main differences:

**Financial Accounting**
- Summarised for the year at year end
- Statement of profit and loss
- Statement of financial position
- External users
- Assesses financial performance
- Required by law

**Management Accounting**
- Detailed data collected regularly e.g. monthly
- Management reports
- Internal users
- Assists in decision making, planning and control
- Future estimates and forecasting

Management Accounting is in many ways less formal than Financial Accounting. Whilst reports produced for financial accounting purposes must follow a fairly rigid structure and layout, organisations are free to prepare their management accounts in whatever format they wish, and as regularly as they find useful. Whereas financial statements are usually produced annually, management accounts are usually produced quarterly, monthly, or even weekly.

## The Purpose of Internal Reporting

We have already determined that the purpose of management accounting is to provide information for internal use within a company. This is called internal reporting.

**Internal reporting** can be used to provide information on budgeted financial reports such as:

- **Standard cost cards** – breakdown of costs of producing one unit or planned level of production.
- **Cash flow forecasts** – report that estimates cash coming in and out of the business.
- **Variance reports** – comparing what was expected to happen and what did happen (flexed budgets).
- **Segmented reports** – reports on different sectors, products or services of the business.

These can be used by the managers of an organisation to enable them to:

- **Plan** the activities of the business in the future.
- **Co-ordinate** the resources of the business - labour, material and equipment.
- **Control** the activities of the organisation, to ensure they remain in line with plans.
- **Make Decisions** about the business.

Management will need to make decisions for the **short-term** and the **long-term**. Short-term decisions usually affect the next day, week or perhaps a few months, whilst long-term decisions will impact the future direction and activities of the business for years to come.

## Chapter 1: The Purpose of Management Accounting

These decisions can be classified as **operational, managerial or strategic**.

Businesses must plan for their long-term future - it can often take many years for the outcome of a strategic decision to actually begin to happen. For example, a business may decide it wants to begin selling products in Australia. This cannot just happen overnight - the business will need to investigate the markets, ensure compliance with local regulations around product safety, licences etc, secure a distribution network, identify ways of shipping the products, market the product in Australia and so on. It could take several years before the products are physically on the shelves in Australian shops. It is the responsibility of the senior managers of a business to plan the **strategic direction** of the business and make the long-term decisions which shape the future of the business.

It is then usually the responsibility of middle management to put these strategic plans into action. This is done by breaking the strategic plans down into smaller activities. These can be allocated to the relevant manager, who has the responsibility for ensuring that part of the plan is implemented according to agreed timescales. This involves making tactical **managerial** decisions which relate to activities which may take months (or possibly years) to implement, but which are part of the bigger strategic direction.

Hence it would perhaps be the responsibility of the Sales Manager to identify possible markets, the Finance Manager to secure the necessary funds for the expansion, the HR Manager to recruit the Australian workforce and so on. Of course, these aspects of management may be allocated to teams (rather than individuals), and in smaller organisations, the senior management may also be responsible for tactical decision-making.

The day-to-day decision-making process is sometimes called **operational decision-making** - these are the kinds of decisions which enable the business to continue to operate on a daily basis.

This can be summarised as:

| | |
|---|---|
| **Strategic Decisions** | Decisions made at the top level of the organisation, and determine the organisation's overall direction. |
| **Managerial Decisions** | Decisions that are taken by middle managers to achieve the goals and objectives set by higher level management / directors. |
| **Operational Decisions** | Day-to-day decisions made by employees and lower level managers to ensure targets are met and the business is running smoothly. |

## Chapter 1: The Purpose of Management Accounting

Whichever type of decision is being considered, the role of the manager is to make the **optimal decision** - this is the decision which leads to the best possible outcome for the business, given the level and quality of information available to the manager to inform that decision. Of course, this does not always happen - managers will not always make the optimal decision as they may have incomplete or inaccurate information, or there may be unforeseen circumstances which lead to the predicted outcome not actually occurring. However, there can be no doubt that having the best information possible on which to base any decisions can only improve the probability of the manager making the optimal decision.

This information can be provided to management in a wide range of formats - spreadsheets, memos, reports, emails and meetings. Management does not always need beautifully presented reports, nor do they necessarily need absolutely accurate data - much management information is based on future estimates, forecasts and 'guesses'. Nevertheless, the characteristics of good information apply in management accounting just as they do in financial accounting.

Information needs to be:

- Fit for purpose
- Accurate
- Relevant
- Complete
- Timely
- Cost effective – the benefits of the information must exceed the cost of obtaining it.

 **Example 1.1**

Brightling Ltd are considering purchasing a new factory in Wales to expand production. The board of directors have commissioned a report which identifies the potential costs and benefits of this proposal. The directors are in negotiation with the government about the possibility of receiving a grant which would meet around 60% of the costs of the expansion, but for this to be awarded, the initial plans must be submitted and approved before 31st December 20X3. Today's date is 1st May 20X3.

The report must be received by the directors in a timely manner to enable them to decide whether to pursue the grant application and not to miss the deadline. The information within the report must be fit for purpose and relevant to the proposal - any irrelevant information will only serve to confuse the reader and obscure the relevant elements. The directors must have faith that they can rely on the data within the report - that it is accurate and free from bias or errors. They would also expect that any data contained within the report would be verifiable - that they could be checked and authenticated. The directors would also want to compare the data in the report to that from other sources, or against their own budgets and plans.

## Chapter 1: The Purpose of Management Accounting

### Cost Accounting

Cost accounting is a large part of management accounting. One of the primary purposes of costing is to establish, or calculate, what it costs the business to produce one unit of output or, in the case of a service provider, to calculate the cost of one unit of 'service' - such as the cost of one hour of bookkeeping.

You should recognise that there are many different types of business organisations. Even businesses which appear similar will have many differences – different product lines, different numbers of staff, different sales volumes, different ambitions and targets.

There are many types of organisations which need to be able to 'cost' their operations accurately. For example:

- **Manufacturing Organisations**

    It is particularly important for manufacturing organisations to be able to cost their products accurately – this enables them to set prices which are hopefully competitive but which enable the company to make a profit.

- **Service Organisations**

    Businesses which provide a service, such as hairdressers, plasterers and accountants also need to be able to cost their work accurately. In businesses such as this, there is no 'unit of output' in the same way there is in a manufacturing business. Each haircut, wall plastered and self-assessment return completed will be different, and so a slightly different approach is required – **each 'job' must be costed separately.**

- **Public Sector Organisations**

    The United Kingdom has experienced a number of years of 'austerity measures', where the amount of money made available to different public-sector organisations, has been reduced year on year. Managers in public sector organisations – including local councils, the NHS, education and the armed forces – are increasingly required to reduce their costs as 'belts are tightened' and budgets are squeezed. Only by knowing what the different elements of their services cost, can effective decisions be taken as to where to make cuts.

One thing that all businesses have in common, however, is the need to record, monitor and most importantly **control their costs**.

Costs are incurred by a business in manufacturing products (if it is a manufacturing business), marketing, selling and distributing products, and undertaking all the administrative tasks which are necessary to keep a business running smoothly. These costs represent items of expenditure incurred by the business and they therefore have the effect of reducing the organisation's profits for the period.

Of course, it would not be possible to run any business without incurring costs – they are a necessary part of the day-to-day business because without incurring these costs there would be no business. However, given that most businesses have an objective of maximising their profits, it clearly makes sense to minimise costs wherever possible and to eliminate unnecessary costs.

## Chapter 1: The Purpose of Management Accounting

To be able to control costs, businesses must first be able to accurately identify all the costs they incur. This means they need to collect data on every item of expenditure incurred by the business and find appropriate ways to collate this data in such a way that useful information can easily be obtained.

This information can then be used by the business to plan, co-ordinate work or make decisions aimed at reducing costs to the organisation. It can be seen therefore, that the techniques which have been developed to help identify the cost of a particular product or service, form great importance in a business because without knowing what it costs the business to make its products, it will never be able to make accurate predictions about the future.

You can see that there will be many areas of cross-over between collecting cost data for these purposes, and how financial information is collected for bookkeeping purposes. Costing information is not additional to financial information, it is simply the same data viewed for a slightly different purpose.

We can summarise the importance of costing in the following list:

- To record costs
- Pricing of products
- To control costs
- To determine costs and profits
- Value inventory
- Aid decision making and preparation of budgets

 **Activity 1.1**

a) Decide whether the following statements are true or false:

|  | True | False |
|---|---|---|
| Operational decision making looks at the long-term future of the business. | | |
| Information for management accounting comes from different sources than that used in financial accounting. | | |
| Management accounting is used for forecasting and budgeting for future periods. | | |
| Financial accounting is used for forecasting and budgeting for future periods. | | |
| Management accounts are used externally only. | | |

b) Which of the following are characteristics of useful information for management accounting purposes?

|  | ✓ |
|---|---|
| Relevant |  |
| Computerised |  |
| Complete |  |
| Cost effective |  |
| Absolute accuracy |  |

**Check your answers at the back of the book.**

## Ethical Principles in Management Accounting

You should be familiar with the five fundamental ethical principles of:

**Integrity**

**Objectivity**

**Professional Competence and Due Care**

**Confidentiality**

**Professional Behaviour**

These principles apply in management accounting just as much as they do in financial accounting. Management accounts are usually for internal use only, and therefore not released to external parties, although they may in some situations be made available to external parties such as banks and other lenders. However, the data is particularly sensitive as it is more current and more detailed than that available to competitors or investors. Therefore, ensuring the information within the management accounts remains confidential is a high priority. The same safeguards for confidentiality applied to financial information will also protect the confidentiality of management information. For data held in computerised systems, organisations must ensure there is adequate protection from external parties, such as firewalls and password protection. Data held on paper should be securely stored with appropriate physical protection. Care should be taken with information on desks and computer screens which can be seen by unauthorised persons such as visitors or colleagues from other departments. If information is taken outside the work environment (e.g. on a memory stick or laptop) then extra care must be taken not to leave in it a place where it could be stolen.

There is also a great need for the management accounts to be prepared with **integrity**. There may be times when a manager is tempted to manipulate figures to show his or her department in a good light, or to include or exclude, or give undue prominence to, certain data to further their own cause at the possible expense of the greater goal of making the optimal decision for the business as a whole.

# Chapter 1: The Purpose of Management Accounting

 **Example 1.2**

Barney is a manager at Hulbell Toys Ltd. He has been promised a bonus of £5,000 if his department achieves an overall cost saving of 2% during 20X2. At the moment, with just a few days to go until the end of 20X2, he is just a few hundred pounds of savings short of reaching his target. He does not have enough time to identify and implement any further cost-cutting measures; however, he realises that he could manipulate the actual figures slightly and would then meet the target and receive his bonus. He doubts that the senior management would ever check the accuracy of his report, and if they did, he could just say it was an error.

If Barney were to manipulate the figures he would receive personal gain, because he would be awarded the bonus. However, doing so would clearly lack integrity. Barney should submit the accurate, un-manipulated figures.

## Cost Centres, Profit Centres and Investments Centres

We will start by recapping knowledge gained from "Principles of Costing" at Level 2.

### Recap

A **Cost Centre** is any department or other part of a business which is capable of having costs 'charged' to it. This means that every cost centre must have a manager (of some description) who can be held accountable for any expenditure incurred by the cost centre. All costs incurred by the organisation must be allocated to the relevant cost centre. This allows the organisation to report on important measures such as:

- Actual expenditure to date
- Actual expenditure against budgeted expenditure
- Performance against key performance indicators (e.g. reduction in expenditure on agency staff in the year)

The **Cost Centres** used in an organisation will be determined by the size, nature of business and management structure of the organisation. For example, a sole trader may only have one cost centre – the business itself. However, in a large organisation cost centres could be different departments, different geographical locations or different stages in a production process. The actual cost centres should reflect the way in which the organisation wishes to collect and analyse its costs.

A **Profit Centre** is similar to a cost centre, but the manager of a profit centre has a responsibility not only for managing and controlling costs but also for generating income (and thereby generating profits).

Many departments within an organisation do not generate revenue, and so can never become a profit centre. For example, a Human Resources (personnel) department provides support to investment centres (recruiting staff, dealing with disciplinary issues, co-ordinating staff development and so on), but does not (normally) generate revenue. HR departments are, therefore, usually classed as cost centres rather than profit centres.

An **Investment Centre** has an extra layer of responsibility for its manager – not only is the manager responsible for the income and costs generated by the centre, they are also responsible for making decisions about how much to invest in machinery or other assets. They will then be held accountable for ensuring that an appropriate return is made on the amount invested. It is possible to differentiate between *internal investment* and *external investment*. Internal investment is funded out of the business's own funds, whereas external investment is funded by external finance, such as a bank loan.

**Responsibility Accounting**

The use of cost centres, profit centres and investment centres allow organisations to use **responsibility accounting** - this simply means that an individual manager is allocated responsibility for the activities of every single aspect of the business, and they are monitored on their performance and results. This allows the organisation to have a more flexible decentralised approach to management, rather than a highly centralised system which is often overly bureaucratic.

 **Example 1.3**

Highfield College is a medium sized further education college. The new principal, Kayleigh Ford, is keen to implement a change in the management structure which allocates greater responsibility to individual managers. Previously, for example, if a lecturer wanted to order some books, they would have to first place a request with the Head of School, who would then put the request to the Library Committee, which met once a term. At this meeting, the Library Committee would consider requests for new books from all Heads of School, and then decide which books would be purchased. The list of books to be purchased was passed to the purchasing department, which would locate the cheapest supplier and then place the order.

This process often meant that teachers did not receive the books they needed until several weeks or months later, by which time it was too late. It also meant they did not know whether or not their request had even been approved until several weeks later when the Library Committee met.

Kayleigh's revised structure will introduce responsibility accounting to the college. Each department will have a manager who is responsible for that department - within the School of Hair and Beauty, for example, there will be a manager responsible for the hairdressing courses and another manager responsible for the beauty therapy courses. These 'managers' will be appointed from the teaching staff within the department. The key is that each manager is then given a budget - an amount of money they are allowed to spend each year on key items such as books, stationery, trips etc. It is the manager's responsibility to ensure that the money is spent wisely on the resources that are most needed and that the total budget is not overspent at the end of the year. This should mean that departments are able to secure the resources they need quickly and efficiently, whilst retaining the control on costs which is necessary to ensure the survival of the college.

# Chapter 1: The Purpose of Management Accounting

**Segmented Analysis**

The use of internal management reports often focuses on comparing different segments of the business. This could be the comparison of different departments, different geographical areas, different product ranges etc. It is important for senior management to understand which segments of the business are performing well and which might be struggling.

**Costs** can be compared against the original budget for a segment of the business, or against the original budget for that segment.

**Profit** is also compared in the same way. However, it is often useful to look at the **profit margin** when comparing segments of the business; this looks at the profit as a percentage of the sales (effectively showing how much profit is earned for each £1 of sales). The formula for profit margin is therefore:

$$(PROFIT / SALES) \times 100$$

Another extremely common and useful measure is the **return on investment** – this measures how much profit each segment makes in relation to the amount the business has invested in it. The formula to use is:

$$(PROFIT / INVESTMENT) \times 100$$

Comparisons are usually made between different business segments at the same point in time, or with the same segment over a number of time periods.

 **Example 1.4**

Artswell Ltd is a retailer of art products such as paints and easels. The management is comparing the performance in 20X5 of the company's three retail outlets, which are based in London, Birmingham and Glasgow.

The following data has been identified:

|  | London £000 | Birmingham £000 | Glasgow £000 |
|---|---|---|---|
| Costs - Materials | 38 | 36 | 28 |
| Costs - Labour | 30 | 28 | 20 |
| Costs - Overheads | 48 | 40 | 32 |
| Sales Revenue | 208 | 198 | 176 |
| Investment | 384 | 270 | 455 |

# Chapter 1: The Purpose of Management Accounting

**Answer**

We can start by comparing the **costs** for each of the three shops. The total costs (i.e. materials + labour + overheads) are:

|  | London £000 | Birmingham £000 | Glasgow £000 |
| --- | --- | --- | --- |
| Total Costs | 116 | 104 | 80 |

The Glasgow shop has the lowest costs (£80,000) whilst the London shop has the highest costs (£116,000).

If we look at profit (calculated as Sales Revenue - Costs), the figures are:

|  | London £000 | Birmingham £000 | Glasgow £000 |
| --- | --- | --- | --- |
| Sales Revenue | 208 | 198 | 176 |
| Total Costs | 116 | 104 | 80 |
| **Profit** | **92** | **94** | **96** |

We can see that all three shops made a similar level of profit - London had (slightly) the lowest profit at £92,000 whilst Glasgow had the highest (£96,000).

If we now introduce the profit margin calculation, we can see there is a greater difference between the stores:

|  | London £000 | Birmingham £000 | Glasgow £000 |
| --- | --- | --- | --- |
| Sales Revenue | 208 | 198 | 176 |
| Total Costs | 116 | 104 | 80 |
| Profit | 92 | 94 | 96 |
| **Profit Margin (to 2 dp)** | **44.23%** | **47.47%** | **54.55%** |

Now we see Glasgow is achieving a profit margin of 54.55%, whilst London's margin is only 44.23%. This is because the Glasgow store's profits of £96,000 are achieved on a much lower sales total of £176,000, compared to London's figures of a slightly lower profit margin on a much higher level of sales revenue.

Finally, we can examine the returns on investment for each store. These are:

|  | London £000 | Birmingham £000 | Glasgow £000 |
|---|---|---|---|
| Profit | 92 | 94 | 96 |
| Investment | 384 | 270 | 455 |
| **Return on Investment** | **23.96%** | **34.81%** | **21.10%** |

The return on investment figures show a different picture. Now, Glasgow is the worst-performing shop, with Birmingham performing much better than the other two.

There may be many reasons why different business segments perform differently. In this example, the costs in Glasgow may be lower due to geographical factors (for example, lower pay rates for staff than in London). Similarly, the selling price of products may be cheaper in Glasgow than in London, which would explain (in part) why the sales revenue in Glasgow is lower. However, it could also be the case that the Glasgow store has had a recent refurbishment which would explain the higher amount invested in it. In time, this refurbishment may lead to more customers visiting and therefore sales revenue increasing. The Birmingham store, on the other hand, has had the least money invested in it and so may be due to have a refurbishment next year.

There are many reasons why the figures may vary, and one of the most important skills in management accounting is the ability to look at figures such as these and then develop explanations for them. It is often necessary to conduct further investigations to be confident of the reasons - for example, it would be quite straightforward to identify if there has been a refurbishment in Glasgow or not, or whether the selling prices of products are different. If these are <u>not</u> valid reasons for the differences, further investigations would be necessary.

## Assessment 1

You are now required to log in to your ROGO account to complete your online assessment before progressing on to the next chapter.

This page is left intentionally blank.

# Chapter 2: Cost Behaviour

**By the end of this chapter, you should:**

- Understand cost behaviour
- Be able to calculate variable and fixed costs using the high-low method

# Chapter 2: Cost Behaviour

## Introduction

You should be familiar with many of the costing techniques which underpin the work you do in this unit. One of the primary purposes of costing is to establish, or calculate, what it costs the business to produce one unit of output or, in the case of a service provider, to calculate the cost of one unit of 'service' - such as the cost of one hour of bookkeeping.

We will start by recapping the key concepts covered in Level 2, and then develop new ideas and techniques.

## Cost Classification

Cost can be classified depending on the purpose for which the data will be used.

To recap your Level 2 studies, the different cost classifications can be summarised as:

| Cost Classification | Purpose |
| --- | --- |
| By **ELEMENT** – labour, materials and overheads (expenses). | Cost control |
| By **NATURE** – direct or indirect. | Financial reports |
| By **FUNCTION** – production or non-production. | Cost accounts |
| By **BEHAVIOUR** – fixed, variable, stepped and semi-variable. | Budgeting and making decisions |

## Cost Behaviour

When organisations consider financial measures of how well they have performed, they must initially consider the **cost** of the products they have made (or the services they have provided). The reason for this is that different types of costs behave differently at different levels of activity.

We can categorise costs into four different types of behaviour:

- Variable Costs
- Fixed Costs
- Semi-Variable Costs
- Stepped Costs

## Variable Costs

A variable cost is one which increases proportionately with increases in activity (and also decreases proportionately with decreases in activity). This is because the cost per unit remains the same whatever the level of activity is.

An example of a variable cost is the cost of materials which are used in manufacturing a product. If a company makes 1,000 units, the cost of these materials will be, for example,

# Chapter 2: Cost Behaviour

£3,000 (i.e. £3 per unit). If it made twice as many units (2,000 units), the total cost would increase to £6,000, but the cost per unit would remain at £3.

If we plotted on a chart how a total variable cost increases as activity increases, it would look like this:

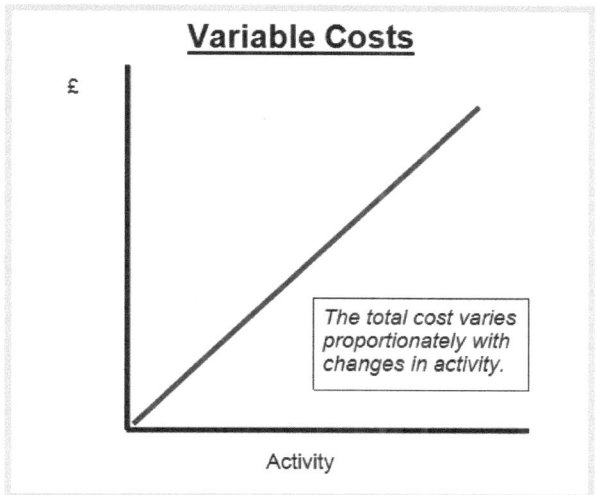

We can see that if no units are produced, then there is no cost incurred. The line representing the cost therefore 'starts' at £0 on the vertical axis, where output is zero. The gradient (the 'steepness') of the line represents the unit cost – the higher the cost per unit the steeper the line will be.

The **Cost per Unit** remains the same for a variable cost but the **Total Cost** increases in line with output.

This can be contrasted with the next type of cost behaviour – a **FIXED COST**.

## Fixed Costs

Total fixed costs do not change when activity increases or decreases. For example, an organisation may incur a cost of £20,000 for a maintenance contract for a twelve-month period. This figure will not be determined or affected by the level of output - it would not increase if production levels increase, nor decrease if it falls. It is a **Fixed Cost**.

Again, we can plot the cost behaviour of a fixed cost on a chart:

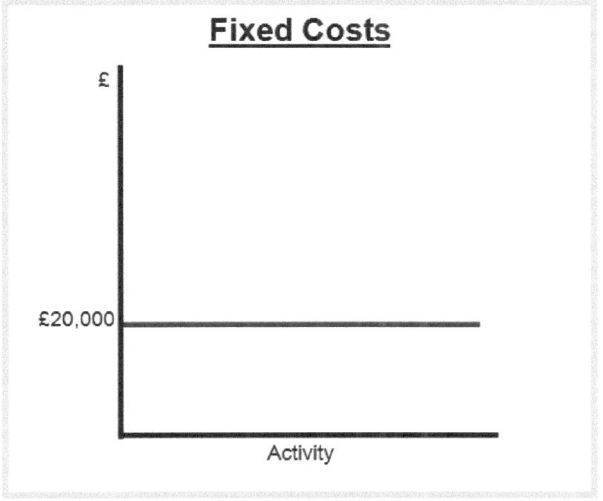

# Chapter 2: Cost Behaviour

Here, the annual cost of maintenance (£20,000) will be incurred regardless of the level of output. So even if activity is zero, the fixed cost of £20,000 will be incurred. You can see how the line starts on the vertical axis at £20,000 to reflect this. As activity increases, the total cost does not change – it is still £20,000 at any given level of activity.

The total cost is therefore fixed; however, the **Cost per Unit** for a fixed cost will fall as output increases. This is because the fixed cost is being 'spread' across more units of output. If the business made just one unit, the cost of maintenance would be attributable solely to that single unit of output:

£20,000 / 1 = **£20,000** per unit

If two thousand units were made, the total cost of the maintenance would be 'shared' between all of those units:

£20,000 / 2,000 = **£10** per unit

Obviously, most organisations would expect to make more than one unit in a year or maybe even more than 2,000 depending on the product. At higher levels of output, the cost per unit will continue to fall.

| Level of Output (units) | Total Fixed Cost | Fixed Cost Per Unit |
|---|---|---|
| 40,000 | £20,000 | £0.50 |
| 80,000 | £20,000 | £0.25 |
| 160,000 | £20,000 | £0.125 |
| 200,000 | £20,000 | £0.10 |
| 400,000 | £20,000 | £0.05 |

Businesses will therefore try to manufacture as many units of output as possible (given that there will probably be a limitation to how many they can sell) – this will reduce the cost per unit making the product more profitable.

If we plot this on the same chart as before, we can see how this happens:

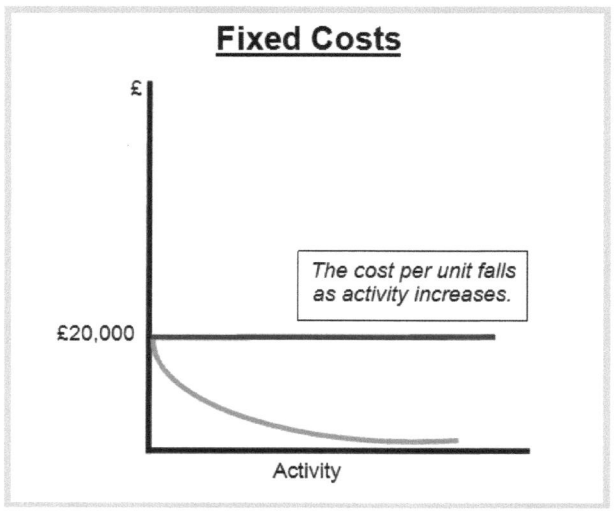

# Chapter 2: Cost Behaviour

The cost per unit falls rapidly at first and then continues to fall as output increases. The cost per unit will never reach £0, of course, but at high levels of output could come very close to it.

Some costs have both an element which is fixed and an element which is variable.

A common example of this is expenditure on items such as telephones and power, which are often made up of a fixed monthly tariff and then a cost per call (or cost per unit). This is a **SEMI-VARIABLE COST.**

## Semi-Variable Costs

A semi-variable cost is comprised of two 'elements' - a fixed element and also a variable element. The fixed element must be paid regardless of the level of activity, whilst the variable element will increase as activity increases. You should note here that activity does not necessarily relate to the number of units of output – in the case of a semi-variable cost for electricity, **the level of 'activity' is measured in terms of the number of units of electricity used** in the period.

Let us suppose that the contract stipulates a monthly fixed tariff (or 'standing charge') of £550, and the company used 4,200 units of electricity in the month at a cost of 3p per unit.

The total cost of electricity for the month is:

| | |
|---|---|
| Fixed Cost | £550 |
| Variable Cost  4,200 x 3p = | £126 |
| Total Cost | £676 |

If 5,100 units were used the following month, the total cost would be:

| | |
|---|---|
| Fixed Cost | £550 |
| Variable Cost  5,100 x 3p = | £153 |
| Total Cost | £703 |

We can look at the way in which a semi-variable cost is plotted:

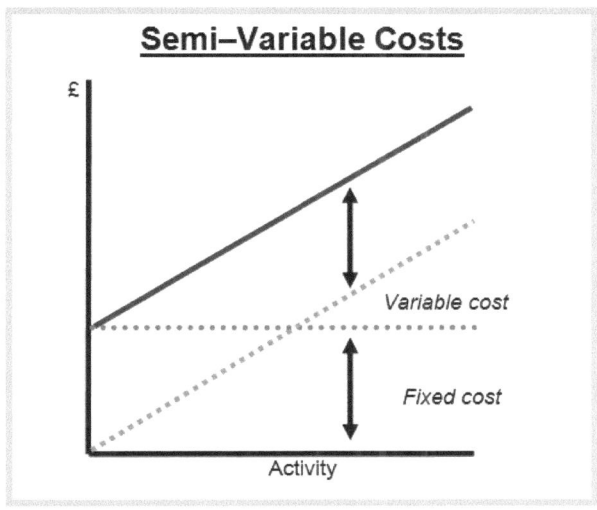

The variable cost element is shown as the sloping dotted line and cuts the vertical axis at £0.

# Chapter 2: Cost Behaviour

The fixed cost element is shown as the horizontal dotted line and cuts the vertical axis at the level of the fixed element of the cost. The **Total Cost** is shown as the sloping solid line, which is the total of the fixed and variable cost elements.

## Stepped Costs

All fixed costs will, at some level of activity, need to increase. This will be a sudden 'jump' in the cost, rather than a gradual increase.

Imagine a company which produces 10,000 units a month in its factory. The rent for the factory will be a fixed cost – it doesn't matter whether the business produces 10,000 units, 12,000, or 15,000 units a month. The rent will remain the same.

However, there will be a level of activity at which the company must start renting a second (or bigger) factory – simply because the capacity of the original factory has now been overreached.

It may be that this is currently way outside the likely activity levels – perhaps at 50,000 units per month. So long as the business is operating at activity levels of 10,000 units a month the **rent will behave as a fixed cost**. If demand for the company's product grows, activity can comfortably increase to 20,000, 30,000 or even 40,000 units per month and the rent will remain fixed in nature. However, as production starts to approach the critical level of 50,000 units, the company will need to consider renting a bigger factory, or perhaps opening a second factory.

This will lead to an increase in the cost of rent, which will then remain fixed in nature until the next 'critical' level of output (e.g. 100,000 units) is reached.

All fixed costs are therefore ultimately stepped in nature; however, this increase in cost will only be of concern to an organisation when it is approaching the critical activity level for that cost.

The critical activity level will vary for each cost; in the example above, it was at 50,000 units for rent. The company may also employ a quality assurance inspector who is paid an annual salary. This employee can only check the quality of a given level of activity each month – say 30,000 units. So, the critical output for the fixed cost of quality assurance is 30,000 units – and when this level is exceeded an additional inspector must be appointed.

The graph for a stepped cost will look like this:

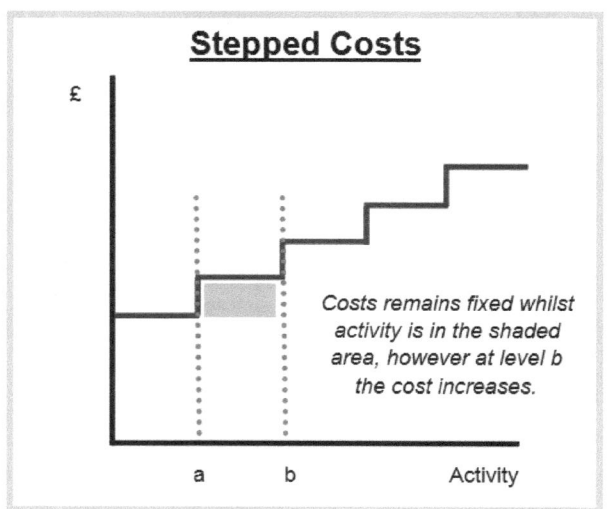

# Chapter 2: Cost Behaviour

## How Do Costs Behave?

Although there are exceptions, **direct costs** are generally **variable. Overheads** are fixed, stepped, variable, or a combination of the two, semi-variable.

Direct materials and direct labour are the costs which can be directly attributed to a unit of product. Therefore, the total cost of direct materials and direct labour is related to the level of output; as we have seen, the more units we produce the greater the total cost will be. Direct materials and direct labour, are therefore generally **variable costs**.

Overheads are incurred in order to enable the business to operate; these can be further classified as production overheads and non-production overheads. Non-production overheads, things such as admin or finance costs are not costs attributable to the production. In both cases, the costs relate to things that are not directly attributable to a specific cost unit or product. Therefore, overheads are usually **fixed costs.** However, some overheads (as we have seen) will be **semi-variable costs.** The table below shows how different types of costs will usually behave:

| Variable Costs | Fixed Costs | Semi-Variable Costs |
|---|---|---|
| Direct Materials | Rent & Rates | Telephones |
| Direct Labour (Wages) | Insurance | Electricity |
| | Marketing | Gas |
| | Maintenance | |
| | Salaries | |
| | Stationery | |

Although these are the most common ways in which costs behave, you must be careful to read any question carefully to make sure you identify any differences. For example, stationery costs are usually fixed as they do not increase proportionately when activity increases. However, if it is stationery which is used as part of the production process (such as the paper used for instructions included with each product), then it would be a variable cost.

### The Organisation's Total Costs

It is worth considering how the organisation's total costs are likely to behave. Any organisation will incur expenditure. As we have seen, some of this will be variable, some will be fixed (or at critical levels stepped) and some will be semi-variable (which is a combination of fixed and variable costs). Therefore, every organisation's **total cost** structure will be made up of a combination of these fixed and variable costs.

This is important when we consider how a business's cost structure will change as activity changes. An organisation must be aware of what proportion of its total costs are fixed, as these costs must still be incurred, even if activity levels fall. We will consider this further, later in this unit.

# Chapter 2: Cost Behaviour

 Activity 2.1

Classify the following costs of a manufacturing company into fixed, variable or semi-variable:

| Cost | Fixed | Variable | Semi-Variable |
|---|---|---|---|
| Annual salary of the finance manager. | | | |
| Cost of cooling fluid which keeps machinery cool during the production process. | | | |
| Labour cost of production staff paid an amount for each unit of production they make. | | | |
| Cost of power used to run the machines in the production process. | | | |

## Identifying Cost Behaviour

You may sometimes be required to identify different cost behaviours. You will be given different costs at different levels of activity and will need to calculate whether that particular cost is variable, fixed or semi-variable.

 Example 2.1

Herbert Ltd has identified the following costs at different levels of activity.

We can consider how each type of cost behaves in each case:

| | Variable | Fixed | Semi-Variable |
|---|---|---|---|
| a. At 2,000 units the total cost is £14,000; at 3,000 units the total cost is £21,000. | | | |
| b. At 3,000 units the cost per unit is £2.50; at 5,000 units the cost per unit is £1.50. | | | |
| c. At 1,000 units the total cost is £5,000; at 1,500 units the total cost is £7,000. | | | |

**Answer**

|  | Variable | Fixed | Semi-Variable |
|---|---|---|---|
| a. At 2,000 units the total cost is £14,000; at 3,000 units the total cost is £21,000. | ✓ |  |  |
| b. At 3,000 units the cost per unit is £2.50; at 5,000 units the cost per unit is £1.50. |  | ✓ |  |
| c. At 1,000 units the total cost is £5,000; at 1,500 units the total cost is £7,000. |  |  | ✓ |

**Explanation**

a. At 2,000 units the cost per unit is £7 (£14,000/2,000 units). At 3,000 units the cost per unit is also £7 (£21,000/3,000 units). The total cost is increasing as output rises, but the cost per unit remains the same at £7, so this is a **variable cost.**

b. At 3,000 units the total cost is £7,500 (£2.50 x 3,000 units). At 5,000 units of output, the total cost is also £7,500 (£1.50 x 5,000 units), so this is a **fixed cost.**

c. At 1,000 units the total cost is £5,000, whilst at 1,500 units the total cost rises to £7,000, so this cannot be a fixed cost. The cost per unit at 1,000 units is £5 (£5,000/1,000 units), whilst at 1,500 units the cost per unit falls to £4.67 (£7,000 / 1,500 units), as the cost per unit is not constant this cannot be a variable cost. It is, therefore, a **semi-variable cost**.

 **Activity 2.2**

Jeffrey Ltd has identified the following costs at different levels of activity. Identify the type of cost behaviour shown by each of the costs.

|  | Variable | Fixed | Semi-Variable |
|---|---|---|---|
| At 2,000 units the total cost is £9,000. At 3,000 units the total cost is £13,000. |  |  |  |
| At 5,000 units the cost per unit is £2.25. At 8,000 units the total cost is £18,000. |  |  |  |
| At 4,000 units the cost per unit is £6. At 3,000 units the cost per unit is £8. |  |  |  |

# Chapter 2: Cost Behaviour

## Determining the Fixed and Variable Parts of Semi-Variable Costs

**The High-Low Method**

If you are told that the cost of electricity for the month was £4,000 and that electricity is a semi-variable cost, can you determine how much of the electricity cost is fixed and how much is variable?

The answer is that this cannot be done. It is impossible to say how much is fixed and how much is variable when only one period's cost is available.

However, if we have two or more periods of data, then it is possible to **estimate** the fixed and variable elements of the cost, using a technique known as the **high-low method.** This is a very useful method of estimating future costs – but you should bear in mind that it is only an estimate, and may not be completely accurate.

 **Example 2.2**

Imagine we have the following information about electricity costs for two consecutive months at HT Ltd.

| Month | Usage (units) | Cost (£) |
|---|---|---|
| April | 10,300 | £762 |
| May | 10,800 | £782 |

We are also told that electricity is a semi-variable cost in relation to the number of units of electricity used.

The high-low method is based on the fact that total fixed costs do not change for an increase in activity, but **total variable costs** do change. In this example, 500 extra units were used in May compared to April, and the total cost increased by £20. None of this increase in cost could have been caused by a change in the fixed cost element (as we know fixed costs do not increase with activity) – therefore, the increase of £20 could **only** have been caused by the increase in the variable element.

**Step One:**

Rewrite the figures, putting the **higher** figure on top; like this:

| Month | Usage | Cost |
|---|---|---|
| May | 10,800 | £782 |
| April | 10,300 | £762 |

## Chapter 2: Cost Behaviour

**Step Two:**

Now subtract the lower figures from the higher figures. Subtract both the usage and the cost figures:

| Month | Usage | Cost |
|---|---|---|
| May | 10,800 | £782 |
| April | 10,300 | £762 |
|  | 500 | £ 20 |

This means that the increase in activity of 500 units led to an increase in cost of £20.

**Step Three:**

Now calculate the variable cost per unit by dividing the increase in variable cost by the increase in activity:

£20 / 500 units = £0.04, or 4p per unit

**Step Four:**

Now calculate the fixed element, by 'substituting' the variable cost of 4p per unit into **either** of the month's total costs to calculate the total variable cost for the month and then calculate the difference between the total cost and the total variable cost.

For April:

10,300 units x 4p = £412.

This means that the total variable cost for April is £412 – which means the fixed cost for April must be (£762 - £412) = £350

It is a good idea to repeat this for the other month – you should end up with the same result:

10,800 units x 4p = £432;   £782 - £432 = £350

So now we have identified how the electricity cost 'behaves' each month:

| Fixed Cost | = £350 |
|---|---|
| Variable Cost | = 4p per unit |

If we estimated the electricity usage in June to be 10,600 units, we could estimate what the total cost of electricity for the month would be:

| Fixed Cost | £350 |
|---|---|
| Variable Cost | + £424 (10,600 x £0.04) |
| Total Cost | = £774 |

This method is called the high-low method because it is based on taking the highest and lowest activity levels (and associated costs) from a range of data.

 **Example 2.3**

A business has gathered electricity costs over a period of six months as follows:

| Month | Usage (units) | Cost (£) |
| --- | --- | --- |
| July | 8,600 | £631 |
| August | 8,750 | £640 |
| September | 8,450 | £622 |
| October | 8,200 | £607 |
| November | 8,850 | £646 |
| December | 9,100 | £661 |

In this example, there are six months that we could potentially use, but we need to look for the **highest** and the **lowest** levels of activity and base our calculations on these.

The highest level of activity occurs in December (9,100 units) and the lowest in October (8,200 units). The calculation is therefore:

| Month | Units | Cost |
| --- | --- | --- |
| December | 9,100 | £661 |
| October | 8,200 | £607 |
| | 900 | £ 54 |

The increase in activity of 900 units caused an increase in the cost of £54; this means the cost per unit is (£54/900) = £0.06

In December the total variable cost is:

9,100 x £0.06 = £546

The fixed cost must therefore be:

£661 - £546 = £115

To check our answer, we can also perform the calculation for October (the 'low' month):

In October the total variable cost is:

8,200 x £0.06 = £492

The fixed cost must therefore be:

£607 - £492 = £115

## Chapter 2: Cost Behaviour

### Activity 2.3

Francis Ltd has identified the following costs associated with a number of different activity levels over the past six months.

Use the high-low method to identify:

- the fixed element of the cost
- the variable element (cost per unit)
- the forecast cost at a budgeted activity level of 5,500 units in the next month.

| Month | Activity (units) | Cost (£) |
| --- | --- | --- |
| January | 4,600 | 26,720 |
| February | 4,900 | 27,680 |
| March | 5,100 | 28,320 |
| April | 3,800 | 24,160 |
| May | 5,800 | 30,560 |
| June | 4,700 | 27,040 |

| | |
| --- | --- |
| Fixed element of the cost | |
| Variable element of the cost (cost per unit) | |
| Forecast cost at an activity level of 5,500 units | |

### Activity 2.4

Complete the table below by inserting all costs for the activity levels of 2,500 and 2,800 units.

| | 2,000 Units | 2,500 Units | 2,800 Units | 3,100 Units |
| --- | --- | --- | --- | --- |
| Variable Cost (£) | | | | |
| Fixed Cost (£) | | | | |
| Total Cost (£) | 36,600 | | | 47,490 |

# Chapter 2: Cost Behaviour

It is essential that you are confident with all of these concepts so far, as they will underpin the more complex ideas you are about to study in this unit. Please ensure you have studied and revised these key learning points thoroughly before moving on.

 **Activity 2.5**

A business has identified the following costs at different levels of activity over a six-month period:

| Month | Activity (units) | Cost |
|---|---|---|
| April | 10,500 | £85,500 |
| May | 12,800 | £99,300 |
| June | 11,850 | £93,600 |
| July | 9,420 | £79,020 |
| August | 10,120 | £83,220 |
| September | 9,950 | £82,200 |

Use the high-low method to determine:

i. The variable cost per unit.

ii. The fixed cost.

iii. The forecast cost for November, when the activity level is estimated to be 10,630 units.

## Product Costs and Period Costs

The costs that are incurred when creating a unit of output are product costs. Direct materials, direct labour and direct expenses are all clear examples of these costs. However, fixed overheads are a little trickier to classify in this way.

Fixed overheads form a large proportion of the total costs of most businesses. Traditionally, managers have tried to 'absorb' a share of the total fixed overheads into the cost of the product. However, there is also an argument which says that an alternative treatment is preferable. This is to treat the fixed overhead costs as a period cost, rather than a product cost.

Remember that fixed overheads are, by definition, fixed regardless of the level of activity. Therefore, the business must meet these costs each period before it starts to make a profit.

Let's take insurance as an example of a fixed cost. The business must pay the insurance premium each month regardless of whether it produces zero units or several thousand. Therefore, insurance is a period cost. Indeed, all fixed costs can be considered in this way.

A second approach to costing has arisen which (its proponents argue) provides more useful information to managers than the traditional approach.

 **Assessment 2**

You are now required to log in to your ROGO account to complete your online assessment before progressing on to the next chapter.

This page is left intentionally blank.

# Chapter 3: Inventory

**By the end of this chapter, you should understand:**

- Inventory Valuation Techniques
- Bookkeeping Entries for Materials
- Planning the Purchases of Materials
- Methods of Determining Inventory Requirements
- The 'Levels' Method
- The Economic Order Quantity (EOQ)

# Chapter 3: Inventory

## Introduction

You should be quite familiar with many of the ideas in this chapter from your Principles of Costing studies at Level 2. In particular, you should recall the different methods of valuing inventory and the difference between direct materials and indirect materials. This Chapter starts by recapping this essential knowledge and then develops some new techniques and ideas.

## Inventory Valuation Techniques

We will look at three different methods of inventory valuation:

- First In, First Out (FIFO)
- Last In, First Out (LIFO)
- Weighted Average Cost (AVCO)

Let's start by imagining a stores department in a manufacturing company. This department has two main functions in the smooth running of the business:

1. The stores department takes deliveries of orders of a wide range of materials from suppliers and safely stores them until they are required by the factory for production.

*Goods received from suppliers are placed in stores for safe-keeping*

2. When the factory needs the materials for the production process, the stores department then issues the materials as required.

*Materials are issued to the factory as required*

In order to keep track of all the movements of materials - both in and out - the stores department will use a stock management system, which would nowadays usually be computerised. All computerised systems still work on the same principles as a manual 'card-based' system in use for around 150 years.

# Chapter 3: Inventory

An 'inventory (or stock) record card' is created for each type of material the stores department handles. This is used to record three things:

- To record all **receipts** of the material into the stores department (i.e. deliveries from a supplier or a return of materials from the factory)
- To record all **issues** of the material **from** the stores department (i.e. issues to the factory, or returns of faulty material to the supplier)
- To record the **'running balance'** of the material in the stores department at any given time - i.e. the actual amount of material held in the stores department.

Receipts and issues of materials are recorded both in units (e.g. kilograms or litres) and also at cost (in currency). Other useful information may also be contained on the stock record card, and computerisation means the process is much simpler than before (often using bar codes or similar devices to speed the recording process up), but we will now have a look at a basic inventory record card.

| Inventory Record Card for Material HJ66 | | | | | | | | |
|---|---|---|---|---|---|---|---|---|
| Date | Receipts | | | Issues | | | Balance | |
| | Kg | Cost/Unit | Cost | Kg | Cost/Unit | Cost | Kg | Cost |
| 1/1 | | | | | | | 5,500 | £16,500 |
| 3/1 | 2,000 | £3.20 | £6,400 | | | | 7,500 | £22,900 |
| | | | | | | | | |

We can see here that on the first day of the period, 1st January, there were 5,500 kg of Material HJ66 in inventory. The total cost of these 5,500 kg was £16,500. A quick calculation shows that the cost per kg of this opening inventory is £3 (£16,500 / 5,500).

The next event which occurs is a receipt of the material from the supplier; another 2,000 kg is purchased which is placed into stores, making the balance 7,500 kg. This material cost £3.20 per kg, or £6,400 in total (2,000 kg x £3.20), making the total cost of the inventory on 3rd January £22,900.

This is fairly straightforward; it is just a case of recording the receipt and then updating the two columns on the right-hand side of the account to show the increased balance of inventory and the increased total cost.

Things get more complicated, however, when goods are issued **from** stores **to** production. The problem is caused because if we only issue **some** of the inventory to production, we must determine **which units** we have issued. This is important because (as we can see above) the inventory will have been bought at different prices (the opening inventory had cost £3 per kg, whilst the purchase on 3rd January cost £3.20).

Which stock is issued to production? It doesn't actually matter which specific units are issued - however, the organisation must apply one of the following costing methods:

# Chapter 3: Inventory

## First In, First Out (FIFO)

Under this method, we assume that any issues made to production are taken from the material which has been in inventory for the longest time - in other words, the materials are issued in chronological order moving **forward**.

 **Example 3.1**

Let's look at this in the earlier stock record card. Let's assume that on 5th January, 6,000 kg are issued to production, which will leave 1,500 kg remaining in the inventory.

| Stock Record Card for Material HJ66 ||||||||
| Date | Receipts ||| Issues ||| Balance ||
|      | Kg | Cost/Unit | Cost | Kg | Cost/Unit | Cost | Kg | Cost |
| 1/1  |    |           |      |    |           |      | 5,500 | £16,500 |
| 3/1  | 2,000 | £3.20  | £6,400 |  |           |      | 7,500 | £22,900 |
| 5/1  |    |           |      | 6,000 |        |      | 1,500 |        |

We need to calculate the cost of these materials which have been issued so that this cost can be passed on to the production department. This will also mean we are able to value the remaining material which is left in the inventory.

Under **First In, First Out**, the issue is taken from the **earliest stock possible.** Here, that would be all 5,500 kgs which were in the opening inventory, and then a further 500 kg taken from the purchase on 3rd January.

**Cost of Issue:**

5,500 kg x £3.00 = £16,500
500 kg x £3.20 = £ 1,600
6,000 kg           £18,100

The cost of the material remaining in inventory is therefore:

1,500 kg x £3.20 = £ 4,800

This is recorded in the Stock Record Card as follows:

| Stock Record Card for Material HJ66 ||||||||
| Date | Receipts ||| Issues ||| Balance ||
|      | Kg | Cost/Unit | Cost | Kg | Cost/Unit | Cost | Kg | Cost |
| 1/1  |    |           |      |    |           |      | 5,500 | £16,500 |
| 3/1  | 2,000 | £3.20  | £6,400 |  |           |      | 7,500 | £22,900 |
| 5/1/ |    |           |      | 6,000 | £3.0167 | £18,100 | 1,500 | £4,800 |

The cost per unit of £3.0167 is calculated as £18,100 / 6,000. This is not a 'nice' round number - it has lots of figures after the decimal place. In the stock record card, it is usual to round this figure to two decimal places (so would be shown as £3.02) - although you should always follow instructions given in any task. Further guidance on rounding figures is given below.

 ***An Important Note About Rounding:***

Very often the figures you will be using in these types of calculations will not result in 'nice' round numbers - there will often be many decimal places. There is a golden rule which applies here (and in other parts of your studies) - **you must not round any numbers during any calculations you carry out - you should only ever round your final figure (unless instructed otherwise in a question).**

We can see the impact of rounding too early in this example. Let's suppose that the cost per unit is calculated as £3.05333333 (this figure continues towards an infinite number of threes).

Let's imagine we had rounded this to £3.05 at this stage - after all, we are only deducting a third of a penny from the cost of a kilogram, which you might not think would make a difference. However, because we are then multiplying this cost per kg by the total number of kgs issued (which may be thousands or hundreds of thousands of units), the impact is quite significant. If we were multiplying by 6,000 units the effect would be:

**Rounded:**

**6,000 x £3.05 = £18,300**

**Not Rounded:**

**6,000 x £3.05333333333 = £18,320**

So, this simple rounding would have created an imbalance of £20 when multiplied by 6,000 kg - but imagine if it were 6,000,000 kg being issued - the difference would be £20,000!

# Chapter 3: Inventory

## Last In, First Out (LIFO)

Under **Last In, First Out (LIFO)**, the approach is similar to FIFO but in reverse; here, issues are taken from the latest stock possible - in chronological order working backwards.

 **Example 3.2**

Here is the Inventory Record Card for Material HJ66 again.

| Inventory Record Card for Material HJ66 | | | | | | | | |
|---|---|---|---|---|---|---|---|---|
| Date | Receipts | | | Issues | | | Balance | |
|  | Kg | Cost/Unit | Cost | Kg | Cost/Unit | Cost | Kg | Cost |
| 1/1/ |  |  |  |  |  |  | 5,500 | £16,500 |
| 3/1 | 2,000 | £3.20 | £6,400 |  |  |  | 7,500 | £22,900 |
| 5/1 |  |  |  | 6,000 |  |  | 1,500 |  |

You can see that the initial entry for the issue of materials is the same. However, when we calculate the cost of the issue, we do so in reverse.

Now, under **LIFO**, the issue is taken initially from the receipt on 3rd January, and only when all these have been fully issued do we then go back in time to the next most recent inventory - in this case, this will be the opening inventory.

The calculation is therefore:

**Cost of Issue:**

   2,000 kg x £3.20 = £ 6,400

   <u>4,000</u> kg x £3.00 = <u>£12,000</u>

   6,000 kg    = £18,400

The cost of the material remaining in inventory is therefore:

   1,500 kg x £3.00 = £4,500

This is recorded as follows:

| Inventory Record Card for Material HJ66 | | | | | | | | |
|---|---|---|---|---|---|---|---|---|
| Date | Receipts | | | Issues | | | Balance | |
|  | Kg | Cost/Unit | Cost | Kg | Cost/Unit | Cost | Kg | Cost |
| 1/1 |  |  |  |  |  |  | 5,500 | £16,500 |
| 3/1 | 2,000 | £3.20 | £6,400 |  |  |  | 7,500 | £22,900 |
| 5/1 |  |  |  | 6,000 | £3.0667 | £18,400 | 1,500 | £4,500 |

We can see that the cost of issues is **HIGHER** under **LIFO** than it is under **FIFO**, whilst the cost of the stock which is left in inventory is correspondingly **LOWER**. This is because when the cost of materials is rising (as it is here, with the cost increasing from £3.00 per kg to £3.20 per kg), the issues are valued at the most recent (and therefore higher) cost, whilst inventory is costed at the earliest (and therefore lowest) prices.

You should notice that, whichever method is chosen, the total cost of the issues and the cost of the remaining inventory add back to equal the total cost of the inventory before the issue:

| Under FIFO | | Under LIFO | |
|---|---|---|---|
| Cost of Materials Issued | £18,100 | Cost of Materials Issued | £18,400 |
| Cost of Materials Remaining | £4,800 | Cost of Materials Remaining | £4,500 |
| Cost of Inventory before Issue | £22,900 | Cost of Inventory before Issue | £22,900 |

### Weighted Average Cost Method (AVCO)

The third method of valuing the issue of materials assumes that, although the materials have been purchased at different prices, once the materials are received in the stores department they will all be assumed to have the same **average** cost. A good way to think of this is to imagine we are buying oil which is stored in a large tank.

The actual level of oil in the tank will of course be increased by purchases being added to it, and reduced by oil being drained out of the tank to be issued to the manufacturing department. What is more, it is impossible to say which oil is being issued at any particular time - it would be nonsensical to think of the oil being issued as being from a particular purchase as it will all be mixed together.

Under **Weighted Average Costing (AVCO)**, a new average cost of inventory is calculated immediately **before** any **issue to production.**

 **Example 3.3**

Here is the Inventory Record Card for Material HJ66 again.

| Inventory Record Card for Material HJ66 | | | | | | | | |
|---|---|---|---|---|---|---|---|---|
| Date | Receipts | | | Issues | | | Balance | |
| | Kg | Cost/Unit | Cost | Kg | Cost/Unit | Cost | Kg | Cost |
| 1/1 | | | | | | | 5,500 | £16,500 |
| 3/1 | 2,000 | £3.20 | £6,400 | | | | 7,500 | £22,900 |
| 5/1 | | | | 6,000 | | | 1,500 | |

# Chapter 3: Inventory

You can see that the initial entry for the issue of materials is the same. However, we now need to calculate an Average Cost for the materials in inventory.

**Average Cost per Kg:**

£22,900 / 7,500 kg = £3.05333333

The cost of the material issued is therefore:

6,000 kg x £3.053333333 = £18,320

The cost of the material remaining in inventory is:

1,500 kg x £3.053333333 = £4,580

This is recorded in the Inventory Record Card as follows:

| Inventory Record Card for Material HJ66 |||||||||
|---|---|---|---|---|---|---|---|---|
| Date | Receipts ||| Issues ||| Balance ||
| | Kg | Cost/Unit | Cost | Kg | Cost/Unit | Cost | Kg | Cost |
| 1/1 | | | | | | | 5,500 | £16,500 |
| 3/1 | 2,000 | £3.20 | £6,400 | | | | 7,500 | £22,900 |
| 5/1 | | | | 6,000 | £3.0533 | £18,320 | 1,500 | £4,580 |

Again, the total cost of materials issued and the total cost of the materials remaining in the inventory add up to the total cost of the inventory before the issue.

| Under FIFO || Under LIFO || Under AVCO ||
|---|---|---|---|---|---|
| Cost of Materials Issued | £18,100 | Cost of Materials Issued | £18,400 | Cost of Materials Issued | £18,320 |
| Cost of Materials Remaining | £4,800 | Cost of Materials Remaining | £4,500 | Cost of Materials Remaining | £4,580 |
| Cost of Inventory before Issue | £22,900 | Cost of Inventory before Issue | £22,900 | Cost of Inventory before Issue | £22,900 |

**A Comparison Between the Three Methods**

If we look at the results for the three methods, we can see that each will give a different cost, or value, for the materials issued and also for the materials which remain in inventory. Under normal circumstances, where material prices are rising, the highest cost of issues will be under LIFO, and the lowest will be under FIFO, with AVCO somewhere in the middle. The highest cost of inventory remaining, however, will be obtained using FIFO, with the lowest under LIFO, and, again, AVCO in the middle.

# Chapter 3: Inventory

## Which Method Should Be Used?

It may seem confusing that there are three different methods for valuing issues of materials, which give three different figures. However, organisations are free to choose whichever method they wish - so long as they do so consistently. Businesses cannot just switch from one method to another just because it suits them to do so.

However, although LIFO can be used for internal accounting (e.g. management accounts), **it cannot be used** (in the UK) as a means of valuing stock for inclusion in the company's financial statements. In this situation, the organisation would need to apply an adjustment to their stock valuations at the end of the year before including any figures in their final accounts. For this reason, most UK businesses use FIFO or AVCO as their stock valuation method. However, in countries such as the USA where LIFO is permitted in the company's financial statements, it is commonly used in high-technology industries where the value of 'old' stock is often minimal (e.g. computer games).

**LIFO will not be tested in your exam for this unit but it is still important to have a good understanding of the different methods used.**

## Example 3.4

On 1st May, Gannymede plc had 15,000 kg of Material FT34 in inventory, which had cost £2.60 per kg when it was bought.

The following receipts and issues took place in May:

| | | |
|---|---|---|
| 5th May | Receipt | 8,000 kg @ £2.75 per kg |
| 12th May | Issue | 10,000 kg |
| 18th May | Receipt | 6,500 kg @ £2.80 per kg |
| 22nd May | Issue | 9,000 kg |

You should complete a Stock Record Card for material FT34 (as shown below) using:

    a. The First In First Out (FIFO) Method

    b. The Weighted Average Cost (AVCO) Method

Show all answers for total costs rounded to the nearest whole £.

# Chapter 3: Inventory

## a. FIFO Method

| Inventory Record Card for Material FT34 | | | | | | | | |
|---|---|---|---|---|---|---|---|---|
| Date | Receipts | | | Issues | | | Balance | |
| | Kg | Cost/Unit | Cost | Kg | Cost/Unit | Cost | Kg | Cost |
| 1/5 | | | | | | | 15,000 | £39,000 |
| 5/5 | 8,000 | £2.75 | £22,000 | | | | 23,000 | £61,000 |
| 12/5 | | | | 10,000 | £2.60 | £26,000 | 13,000 | £35,000 |
| 18/5 | 6,500 | £2.80 | £18,200 | | | | 19,500 | £53,200 |
| 22/5 | | | | 9,000 | £2.667 | £24,000* | 10,500 | £29,200** |

\* (5,000 x £2.60 = £13,000) + (4,000 x £2.75 = £11,000)

\*\* (4,000 x £2.75 = £11,000) + (6,500 x £2.80 = £18,200)

## b. AVCO Method

| Inventory Record Card for Material FT34 | | | | | | | | |
|---|---|---|---|---|---|---|---|---|
| Date | Receipts | | | Issues | | | Balance | |
| | Kg | Cost/Unit | Cost | Kg | Cost/Unit | Cost | Kg | Cost |
| 1/5 | | | | | | | 15,000 | £39,000 |
| 5/5 | 8,000 | £2.75 | £22,000 | | | | 23,000 | £61,000 |
| 12/5 | | | | 10,000 | £2.65217* | £26,522 | 13,000 | £34,478 |
| 18/5 | 6,500 | £2.80 | £18,200 | | | | 19,500 | £52,678 |
| 22/5 | | | | 9,000 | £2.70144** | £24,313 | 10,500 | £28,365 |

\* (£61,000 / 23,000) = £2.65217

\*\* (£52,678 / 19,500) = £2.70144

 **Example 3.5**

Let's look at a slightly more complex example.

The stock record card, shown below, for Chemical FD6 has only been fully completed up until 26 June.

a) Enter the following two transactions in the inventory record card (showing the cost per litre in pence to 2 decimal places):

- **27 June: received 200,000 litres at a total cost of £184,000**
- **28 June: issued 180,000 litres with a total cost of £162,000**

# Chapter 3: Inventory

b) Identify the stock issue method being used for costing issues of Chemical FD6.

c) Complete ALL entries in the stock record card for the remaining two transactions in the month and for the closing balance at the end of November.

**Answer**

We start by updating the Inventory Record Card for the two transactions:

**Inventory record card for Chemical FD6**

| Date | Receipts | | | Issues | | | Balance | |
|---|---|---|---|---|---|---|---|---|
| | Quantity | Cost per litre | Total cost | Quantity | Cost per litre | Total cost | Quantity | Total cost |
| | litres | p | £ | litres | p | £ | litres | £ |
| Balance 26 June | | | | | | | 220,000 | 198,000 |
| 27 June | **200,000** | | **184,000** | | | | **420,000** | **382,000** |
| 28 June | | | | **180,000** | | **162,000** | | |
| 29 June | 100,000 | | 94,000 | | | | | |
| 30 June | | | | 260,000 | | | | |

Now we can calculate the unit costs of these issues, and also update the Balance columns of the table:

**Inventory record card for Chemical FD6**

| Date | Receipts | | | Issues | | | Balance | |
|---|---|---|---|---|---|---|---|---|
| | Quantity | Cost per litre | Total cost | Quantity | Cost per litre | Total cost | Quantity | Total cost |
| | litres | p | £ | litres | p | £ | litres | £ |
| Balance 26 June | | | | | | | 220,000 | 198,000 |
| 27 June | 200,000 | **92.00** | 184,000 | | | | 420,000 | 382,000 |
| 28 June | | | | 180,000 | **90.00** | 162,000 | **240,000** | **220,000** |
| 29 June | 100,000 | **94.00** | 94,000 | | | | **340,000** | **314,000** |
| 30 June | | | | 260,000 | | | | |

Before we can update the Inventory Record card for the final issue of the Chemical on 30th June, we need to determine which of the three valuation methods is being used.

If we look at the opening balance, we can see that there were 220,000 litres at a total cost of £198,000, which is 90p per litre. There was a subsequent receipt of another 200,000 litres which now cost 92p per litre. Yet the issue on 28th June was costed at 90p per litre (£162,000/180,000 litres). This would suggest that the issue on 28th June was made from the original inventory which was valued at 90p per litre. In other words, this inventory has been valued using the First In First Out (FIFO) model.

Now we can complete the Inventory Record Card using the FIFO basis of valuation.

**Inventory record card for Chemical FD6**

| Date | Receipts | | | Issues | | | Balance | |
|---|---|---|---|---|---|---|---|---|
| | Quantity | Cost per litre | Total cost | Quantity | Cost per litre | Total cost | Quantity | Total cost |
| | litres | p | £ | litres | p | £ | litres | £ |
| Balance 26 June | | | | | | | 220,000 | 198,000 |
| 27 June | 200,000 | 92.00 | 184,000 | | | | 420,000 | 382,000 |
| 28 June | | | | 180,000 | 90.00 | 162,000 | 240,000 | 220,000 |
| 29 June | 100,000 | 94.00 | 94,000 | | | | 340,000 | 314,000 |
| 30 June | | | | 260,000 | **91.85** | **238,800** | **80,000** | **75,200** |

The last issue of 260,000 litres is made up of three parts:

- The remaining 40,000 litres from the opening balance of 220,000 litres (remember 180,000 litres of this have already been issued).
- The 200,000 litres which were received on 27th June.
- 20,000 litres of the 100,000 litres which were received on 29th June.

These are valued at:

40,000 x 90p =        £  36,000
200,000 litres x 92p = £ 184,000
20,000 litres x 94p =  £  18,800
                      £ 238,800

The closing inventory is 80,000 litres, which are treated as being from the 29 June receipt, and therefore valued at 94p per litre. 80,000 litres x 94p = £75,200.

It may seem a little strange to see items costing 91.85 pence. It is of course impossible to purchase anything for a fraction of a penny, but because we are working with averages it is quite possible to work with costs expressed in such a way.

# Chapter 3: Inventory

 Activity 3.1

Use the FIFO method to complete the inventory record card below for mushrooms.

**Inventory record card for mushrooms**

| Date | Receipts | | | Issues | | | Balance | |
|---|---|---|---|---|---|---|---|---|
| | Quantity | Cost per tonne | Total cost | Quantity | Cost per tonne | Total cost | Quantity | Total cost |
| | tonnes | £ | £ | tonnes | £ | £ | tonnes | £ |
| Balance as at: 1 June | | | | | | | 72 | 10,512 |
| 2 June | 70 | 150.00 | 10,500 | | | | 142 | 21,012 |
| 3 June | | | | 90 | | | | |
| 4 June | 50 | 152.00 | | | | | | |
| 5 June | | | | 70 | | | | |

 Activity 3.2

You are told that the opening inventory of a single raw material in the stores is 28,000 units at £2.00 per unit. During the period a receipt of 6,000 units at £2.20 per unit is received. This is followed by an issue of 8,500 units.

Identify the valuation method described in the statements below. Indicate which is which by selecting the relevant column of the table below.

| Statement | FIFO | AVCO |
|---|---|---|
| The closing inventory is valued at £51,900. | | |
| The closing inventory is valued at £52,200. | | |

# Chapter 3: Inventory

## Activity 3.3

Identify whether the following statements are true or false by selecting the relevant column of the table below.

| Statement | True | False |
|---|---|---|
| If using AVCO it is necessary to recalculate the weighted average cost every time there is a new receipt of goods. | | |
| FIFO values all issues at the most recent price. | | |
| LIFO can be used for internal use, but not for the valuation of inventory in the financial statements. | | |

## Activity 3.4

A business has the following movements in a certain type of inventory into and out of its stores for the month of April.

| Date | Receipts | | Issues | |
|---|---|---|---|---|
| | Units | Cost | Units | Cost |
| 1st April | 800 | £4,800 | | |
| 5th April | 400 | £2,500 | | |
| 14th April | 600 | £3,840 | | |
| 18th April | | | 1,000 | |
| 26th April | 200 | £1,300 | | |

Complete the table below for the issue costs and the closing inventory value. Show all answers as whole numbers.

| Method | Cost of issues on 18th April | Value of inventory on 26th April |
|---|---|---|
| FIFO | | |
| AVCO | | |

# Chapter 3: Inventory

## Accounting Entries for Materials

Bookkeeping for the movement of materials throughout the organisation follows the same principles of double entry bookkeeping that you are already familiar with - each 'movement' of materials must be recorded as a debit and a credit entry.

Let's look again at the diagram we saw previously:

*Goods received from suppliers are placed in stores for safe-keeping*

*Materials are issued to the factory as required*

When goods are purchased from a supplier, the double entry is:

**Debit**     Inventory

**Credit**    Purchase Ledger Control Account (or cash if a cash purchase)

When goods are issued from the Stores to Production:

**Debit**     Production / Work-in-progress

**Credit**    Inventory

If goods are returned from the Stores Department to the supplier (e.g. because they are faulty) the double entry will be:

**Debit**     Purchase Ledger Control Account

**Credit**    Inventory

Similarly, if goods are returned from the Production Department to the Stores Department (maybe if too many items were issued or they are faulty) the double entry will be:

**Debit**     Inventory

**Credit**    Production / Work-in-progress

 **Example 3.6**

Soundbites Ltd manufactures and sells microphones. The company uses the Average Cost (AVCO) method of inventory valuation.

The inventory movement of materials used in April for the manufacture of one particular product, the MCP900, is shown below. The inventory record card has not been completed, nor have any bookkeeping entries been made.

(a) Complete the inventory record card shown below (to 3 dp).

| Date | Receipts Quantity | Receipts Cost per unit | Receipts Total cost | Issues Quantity | Issues Cost per unit | Issues Total cost | Balance Quantity | Balance Total cost |
|---|---|---|---|---|---|---|---|---|
| | units | £ | £ | units | £ | £ | units | £ |
| Balance as at: 1 April | | | | | | | 3,000 | 60,000 |
| 8 April | 1,800 | 20.20 | | | | | | |
| 13 April | | | | 1,400 | | | | |
| 24 April | 900 | 20.32 | | | | | | |
| 28 April | | | | 2,150 | | | | |

**Answer**

| Date | Receipts Quantity | Receipts Cost per unit | Receipts Total cost | Issues Quantity | Issues Cost per unit | Issues Total cost | Balance Quantity | Balance Total cost |
|---|---|---|---|---|---|---|---|---|
| | units | £ | £ | Units | £ | £ | units | £ |
| Balance as at: 1 April | | | | | | | 3,000 | 60,000 |
| 8 April | 1,800 | 20.20 | **36,360** | | | | **4,800** | **96,360** |
| 13 April | | | | 1,400 | £96,360 / 4,800 =£20.075 | 28,105 | 3,400 | 68,255 |
| 24 April | 900 | 20.32 | **18,288** | | | | **4,300** | **86,543** |
| 28 April | | | | 2,150 | £86,543 / 4,300 = £20.126 | 43271.50 | 2,150 | 43,271.50 |

The cost codes used by Soundbites Ltd are as follows:

| Cost Centre | Code |
|---|---|
| Inventory | 4000 |
| Production | 6000 |
| Purchase Ledger Control Account | 7102 |

(b) Prepare the bookkeeping entries in the table below using the relevant cost codes.

| Date | Cost Code | Debit (£) | Credit (£) |
|---|---|---|---|
| 8 April | | | |
| 8 April | | | |
| 13 April | | | |
| 13 April | | | |
| 24 April | | | |
| 24 April | | | |
| 28 April | | | |
| 28 April | | | |

**Answer**

| Date | Cost Code | Debit (£) | Credit (£) |
|---|---|---|---|
| 8 April | 4000 | 36,360 | |
| 8 April | 7102 | | 36,360 |
| 13 April | 6000 | 28,105 | |
| 13 April | 4000 | | 28,105 |
| 24 April | 4000 | 18,288 | |
| 24 April | 7102 | | 18,288 |
| 28 April | 6000 | 43,271.50 | |
| 28 April | 4000 | | 43,271.50 |

 **Activity 3.5**

Gumboil Ltd manufactures and sells computer games for a popular game console. The company uses the Last In First Out (LIFO) method of inventory valuation.

The inventory movement of the packaging materials used May for the manufacture of one particular game, Robotricks, is shown below. The inventory record card has not been completed, nor have any bookkeeping entries been made.

# Chapter 3: Inventory

a) Complete the inventory record card shown below (to 2 dp).

| Date | Receipts | | | Issues | | | Balance | |
|---|---|---|---|---|---|---|---|---|
| | Quantity | Cost per unit | Total cost | Quantity | Cost per unit | Total cost | Quantity | Total cost |
| | units | £ | £ | Units | £ | £ | units | £ |
| Balance as at: 1 May | | | | | | | 2,100 | 1,050 |
| 5 May | 2,000 | 0.55 | | | | | | |
| 18 May | | | | 2,500 | | | | |
| 24 May | 200 | 0.50 | | | | | | |
| 28 May | | | | 300 | | | | |

The receipt of units on 24th May represented 200 units which were returned from production, as they had been over-issued in error.

The cost codes used by Gumboil Ltd are as follows:

| Cost Centre | Code |
|---|---|
| Inventory | 3500 |
| Production | 4150 |
| Purchase Ledger Control Account | 8618 |

b) Prepare the bookkeeping entries in the table below using the relevant cost codes.

| Date | Cost Code | Debit (£) | Credit (£) |
|---|---|---|---|
| 5 May | | | |
| 5 May | | | |
| 18 May | | | |
| 18 May | | | |
| 24 May | | | |
| 24 May | | | |
| 28 May | | | |
| 28 May | | | |

# Chapter 3: Inventory

## Further Rules for Inventory Valuation

As we have seen, businesses are entitled to value inventory using whichever inventory valuation method they wish. However, they must apply the method consistently, rather than switching from one method to another on a regular basis.

IAS 2, however, does not permit the use of Last In First Out as an inventory valuation model for financial statements. Therefore, if the management wishes to use LIFO for management accounting purposes (which they are perfectly entitled to do), they must then adjust their valuation to either a FIFO or AVCO basis before inclusion in the final accounts.

IAS 2 also requires that inventory is valued at **the lower of cost and net realisable value**. Cost is determined using the appropriate valuation method (i.e. FIFO or AVCO), whilst the net realisable value is the amount which realistically could be expected to be obtained by selling the inventory, less any additional costs which would be incurred in selling them (such as completion costs or the costs of marketing or transportation). Different items, or groups of similar items, of inventory must be valued independently.

IAS 2 also guides the valuation of work-in-progress (i.e. part-finished) goods and finished goods. All direct costs (materials, labour and expenses) must be included, as must any production overheads incurred (but not distribution or administrative expenses). This is the reason that IAS 2 does not permit the use of marginal costing - marginal costing only includes the variable (marginal) costs in the cost of the product, whilst all fixed overheads are treated as period costs. Marginal and Absorption Costing will be dealt with in detail in later chapters.

 **Example 3.7**

The Mannequin Furniture Company makes wooden high chairs for small children. It started trading on 1st January 20X8 and during its first year of trading it sold 400 units. At the end of the year, on 31st December 20X8, there were 80 finished units in inventory and a further 40 units which were exactly half finished in terms of the direct materials, direct labour and production overheads.

The costs incurred by the company during 20X8 were:

| | |
|---|---|
| Direct Materials | £ 5,980 |
| Direct Labour | £ 9,020 |
| Production Overheads | £ 3,000 |
| Administrative Overheads | £ 4,980 |
| Distribution Expenses | £ 2,890 |
| Total Cost for 20X8 | £25,870 |

At 31st December it is estimated that each of the finished high chairs in inventory would sell for £85, except for ten units which were damaged and would only sell for £20.

© Accountext

# Chapter 3: Inventory

At 31st December 20X8, the company also holds raw materials in inventory as follows:

|  | Cost | Net Realisable Value |
|---|---|---|
| Oak | £960 | £2,000 |
| Teak | £840 | £1,800 |
| Fixings | £290 | £ 150 |

(a) Calculate the value of raw materials at 31st December 20X8.

(b) Calculate the value of finished goods at 31st December 20X8.

(c) Calculate the value of work-in-progress at 31st December 20X8.

**Answer**

(a) <u>Value of Raw Materials</u>

| Oak | £ 960 (cost) |
|---|---|
| Teak | £ 840 (cost) |
| Fixings | £ 150 (net realisable value) |
|  | **£1,950** |

(b) <u>Value of Finished Goods</u>

Administrative overheads and distribution expenses are not included in the cost of inventory. The cost is therefore: (£5,980 + £9,020 + £3,000) = £18,000.

This has produced 400 units which have been sold, and 80 units which are in finished goods as they are unsold. There are 40 further units which are 50% complete, so this is the equivalent of 20 finished units. The total production is therefore 500 units.

The cost per unit is therefore £18,000 / 500 = £36

The value of finished goods is therefore:

| High chairs in top condition | 70 x £36 = | £2,520 |
|---|---|---|
| High chairs (damaged) | 10 x £20 = | £ 200 |
|  |  | **£2,720** |

(c) <u>Value of Work-in-Progress</u>

There are forty part-completed (50%) units in work-in-progress - this is the equivalent of twenty fully completed units. IAS 2 states that the value of these units must include all direct costs and production overheads.

So, the value of the work-in-progress is 20 x £36 = **£720**

# Chapter 3: Inventory

 **Activity 3.6**

Burdell Ltd makes table lamps. It started trading on 1st May 20X6, and during its first year of trading, it sold 5,000 lamps. At the end of the year, on 30th April 20X7, there were 250 finished units in inventory and a further 150 units which were exactly one third finished in terms of the direct materials, direct labour and production overheads.

The costs incurred by the company during the year were:

| | |
|---|---|
| Direct Materials | £ 28,900 |
| Direct Labour | £ 41,250 |
| Production Overheads | £ 30,550 |
| Administrative Overheads | £ 10,740 |
| Distribution Expenses | £ 8,208 |
| **Total Cost for 20X7** | **£119,648** |

At 30th April, it is estimated that each of the finished lamps in inventory would sell for £55, except for twenty units which were damaged and would have to be scrapped for no resale value.

At 30th April 20X7 the company also holds raw materials in inventory as follows:

| | Cost | Net Realisable Value |
|---|---|---|
| Metal | £3,200 | £5,680 |
| Electronics | £1,975 | £1,565 |
| Fabric | £ 950 | £ 400 |

a) Calculate the value of raw materials at 30th April 20X7.

b) Calculate the value of finished goods at 30th April 20X7.

c) Calculate the value of work-in-progress at 30th April 20X7.

# Chapter 3: Inventory

 **Activity 3.7**

Parnell Ltd makes concrete garden light stands. In the previous quarter, they manufactured 2,000 finished units, of which 20 remained in inventory at the end of the period. A further 200 units were work-in-progress and only partially complete at the period end date.

Of the 200 partially completed units:

    Material was 75% complete

    Labour was 40% complete

    Overheads were 55% complete

a) Complete the table below to calculate the cost per equivalent unit.

|  | Completed Units | WIP equivalent units | Total equivalent units | Total cost | Cost per equivalent unit |
|---|---|---|---|---|---|
| Material | 2,000 |  |  | £75,250.00 |  |
| Labour | 2,000 |  |  | £99,840.00 |  |
| Overheads | 2,000 |  |  | £28,485.00 |  |

b) What was the total value of finished goods in inventory? £ 

c) What was the total value of work-in-progress (WIP)? £ 

## Planning the Purchases of Materials

For most businesses, the expenditure on materials forms a significant element of their overall expenditure in any year. Remember that 'materials' includes both raw materials (for a manufacturing business) and goods for resale (for a wholesale or retail business).

It is important, therefore, for businesses to have robust policies and procedures to ensure that purchases of materials are made as efficiently and economically as possible. Failure to purchase materials in this way can be extremely costly for a business for the following reasons.

**Over-purchasing of materials** - if a business orders too much it will face a number of costs and risks:

> **Storage and Handling Costs** - this includes rent and rates, insurance and security costs. Businesses which hold large inventories of materials must find somewhere to store them prior to issue or sale - usually in some form of warehouse. This inevitably increases costs for the organisation

# Chapter 3: Inventory

**Risk of Obsolescence** - this occurs when the inventory which is being held goes out-of-date, unseasonal, out of fashion or technologically out of date. Remember that under IAS 2 inventory must be valued at the **lower of cost and net realisable value**. If the net resale value of the inventory falls because it is obsolescent, the business may have to record it in the accounts at this lower amount, meaning there will be an increased expense in the statement of profit or loss to reflect the fall in value.

**Inefficient use of cash** - purchases of materials must, of course, be paid for by the business, either in cash or after a period of credit. Having large amounts of cash 'tied up' in slow-moving inventories is damaging to the business's liquidity. For example, the business may have a large bill to pay but are unable to do so because they do not have sufficient funds in the bank even though they have large amounts of (as yet unused or unsold) inventories.

**Failure to take advantage of falling prices** - a business will be disadvantaged if they buy large amounts of materials today and prices then subsequently fall in the future.

**Under-purchasing of materials** - a business which only orders very small quantities each time, and runs low levels of inventories, will avoid the problems listed above. However, there are other disadvantages they may encounter.

**Risk of 'Stock-Out'** - where a business only keeps very low levels of inventory of materials, there is a constant danger of running out of a particular material or product. In the retail environment, this can lead to a dissatisfied customer who starts to shop elsewhere. In manufacturing, the whole production process can be brought to a standstill if the business runs out of a particular type of material.

**Supplier Unreliability** - the more frequently a business places orders the more likely it is they will encounter issues around supplier reliability or lead times. The **lead time** is the time it takes from placing an order with the supplier to actually receiving the goods. If goods are ordered from overseas, the lead time will usually be longer than if the goods are ordered from a local supplier.

**Loss of discounts** - discounts and improved credit terms are often available to organisations which purchase above specified quantities or values from their suppliers. Purchasing relatively small quantities may reduce the availability of these special offers.

**Failure to take advantage of rising prices** - if prices are rising, it may be beneficial to purchase a larger quantity today rather than delaying purchases to the future.

The problem facing businesses is therefore one of balancing the quantities of materials ordered in each purchase to ensure that it is holding sufficient inventories at all times to cover the risk of stock-outs (taking into account the lead times involved in purchasing replenishment inventory) whilst not holding excessive inventory which leads to increased costs.

There are a number of techniques which can help organisations maintain the optimum levels of inventory.

# Chapter 3: Inventory

## Methods of Determining Inventory Requirements

Before being able to determine the best quantities to order an organisation must first identify the best level of inventories to hold. This will be determined by a number of factors, including available storage space, demand and price.

Some small organisations will simply rely on **estimation and knowledge of the business**. A sole trader operating a small cafe will know roughly how many bacon sandwiches he is likely to sell each day, and so will try to ensure he has enough bacon and bread rolls each day to meet that demand. However, he will not want to hold surplus stock as it would become unsaleable within a day or two. There is little danger of a stock-out, but in the event of an unexpected surge in demand (e.g. ten builders from a local building site turn up unexpectedly and each order a large sandwich), the lead time for both materials is very short (both items are easily available from a local supermarket).

Estimation is only effective in relatively small organisations where there is a limited range of materials. When the organisation is bigger or more complex, a more sophisticated approach is needed.

The **Two Bin** system is a straightforward method of ensuring an organisation never runs out of materials. It works by using two storage devices for every material (although the term 'bin' is used it could be boxes, barrels or any other type of storage).

 **Example 3.8**

Tommy Toubin owns a small engineering factory. He uses a wide variety of screws, nuts, bolts and similar fixings in his work. These are kept in a small storage shed at the back of his workshop. Each different type of fixing is kept in a drawer in a storage chest. Two drawers are used for each type of fixing, as in the picture below:

| 18mm Screws | 18mm Screws |
|---|---|
| Box A | Box B |

The Two Bin system works by ensuring that one box is full (e.g. Box A), and then using this inventory as required. However, Box B is then filled before Box A runs out of screws. When Box A is empty, Tommy starts using screws from Box B. He then replenishes Box A, so that when Box B is empty he can start taking screws from Box A, and so on.

This system works well but can be expensive, as it requires increased storage space and may mean that excess inventory is being carried by the business.

## Chapter 3: Inventory

### The 'Levels' Method

The levels method is a technique used to calculate the optimal volume of materials to be purchased, when materials are to be purchased in the same quantity each time.

To be able to implement this method the business will first need to identify the following information:

- **The Maximum Inventory Level** – this is the maximum volume of materials which can be held in stock at any point in time. This is usually determined by the amount of storage space which is available for that material.
- **The Inventory Buffer Level** – this is the level below which the business would not want the inventory level to fall. The buffer level is determined by the management of the business, taking into account factors including how long the lead time for the material is, the rate at which the materials are issued to production and the likely damage caused by any possible stock-out.
- **The Lead Time** – how long it takes a supplier to deliver any order of materials to the business.
- **The Re-order Level** – the level of inventory at which the business should place its next order.
- **The Re-order Quantity** – how much the business should order each time.

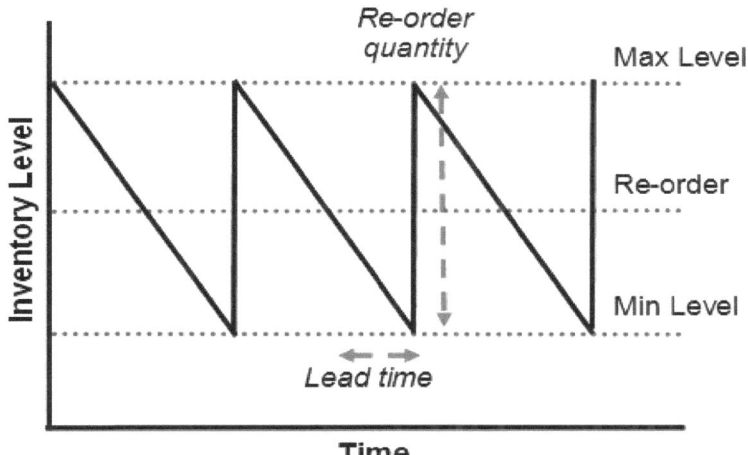

In the graph above, the solid line represents the quantity of material in inventory at any point in time. It falls as inventory is used, and rises when new inventory is received. The maximum inventory level is shown by the top dotted line – the volume of inventory cannot be allowed to be higher than this as the business does not have storage facilities for them.

The buffer inventory level (minimum level) is shown by the bottom dotted line – although the inventory <u>could</u> fall below this level the business has decided that it does not want this to happen. The buffer inventory provides a form of safety net for the business – if, for example, delivery of an order was delayed due to bad weather, the business would still have enough inventory to prevent a stock-out (at least for a period of time).

Therefore, the inventory level at any point in time should be between these two levels. When an order of materials is received, the inventory level should be replenished to the maximum level. Then as materials are used, the inventory level will fall until eventually a new order has to be placed. Ideally, this new order will be received just as the actual inventory level has fallen to the buffer level – this way the business will see its inventory be replenished back to the maximum level at just the point where otherwise it would have fallen below the buffer level.

Where there is a lead time, this must be taken into account when calculating the levels. The purchasing department should be able to identify the lead time through communication with suppliers and the contractual terms applied to any agreements.

There is an assumption in this diagram that inventory is used evenly over time by the business – and therefore the solid line is a straight diagonal in the graph. In reality, this may not always be the case; inventory may be used unevenly over time. Therefore, it may be necessary to use **average figures,** as well as **maximum and minimums**.

These can apply to quantities and also lead times, and enable the business to establish the optimal levels using the following formulae:

**Formula 1**

> **Inventory Buffer Level =**
> **Re-order Level – (Average Usage x Average Lead Time)**

The '**average use x average lead time**' calculates the average amount of material that will be used during the time it takes for the new order to be delivered. Therefore, if this is subtracted from the re-order level it will show how much should be in inventory by the time the order has been received – in other words the buffer level.

**Formula 2**

> **Re-order Level =**
> **(Average Usage x Average Lead Time) + Inventory Buffer**

This is effectively the same as formula 1 but has been re-arranged to enable the re-order level to be calculated.

**Formula 3**

> **Re-order Quantity=**
> **Maximum Inventory Level – Inventory Buffer**

The re-order quantity is the amount of material ordered each time. It should be enough to restore the inventory from the buffer level back to the maximum level.

 **Example 3.9**

Woolsies Ltd makes a range of knitwear. They purchase wool from a single supplier based in India. The average lead time is 12 days.

Woolsies Ltd has a warehouse in which they keep all inventories of material. One material used is 4ply yarn, which is bought in boxes, each containing 20 spools. The maximum inventory for this yarn is 500 spools.

Woolsies use 10 spools of this yarn per day on average, and a minimum inventory level of six days of use has been established.

Calculate the optimum re-order level (in spools) and quantity to be ordered (in boxes) for this yarn.

**Answer**

a) Re-order level = (Average Usage x Average Lead Time) + Inventory Buffer

Re-order level = (10 x 12) + 60

Re-order level = 180 spools

The business should place an order as soon as the inventory reaches 180 spools.

b) Re-order quantity = Maximum Inventory Level – Inventory Buffer

Re-order quantity = (500 – 60)

Re-order quantity = 440 spools

440 spools = 22 boxes

Explanation: Let us imagine the business has 500 spools in inventory – the maximum level. It will use (on average) 10 spools a day. So, the inventory level will fall by an average of 10 spools each day.

When the inventory level has fallen to 180 spools (which should be after 500 – 180 = 320 / 10 = 32 days), an order should be placed for 22 boxes (440 spools).

This will not be received for another twelve days (the lead time) by which time a further (10 x 12) = 120 spools will have been used. Therefore, the inventory level will have fallen to (180 – 120) = 60 spools – which is, of course, the buffer level.

When the order is delivered, the inventory level will be restored from 60 spools to 500 spools (the maximum level).

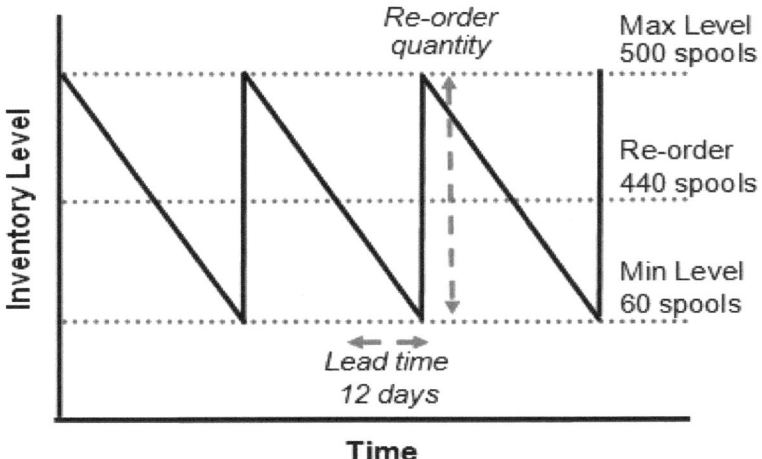

 **Activity 3.8**

Milby College has a reprographics department which meets all its printing and photocopying needs. It has a maximum storage capacity of 2,400 reams of A4 paper (one ream is 500 sheets).

Usage of paper varies on a daily basis, but it has been calculated that on average the department uses 40 reams a day. The supplier of paper is based locally and the lead time is just two days between the college placing the order and the paper being delivered. However, the college's internal purchasing procedure is somewhat bureaucratic, and so it takes on average a further four days between the reprographics department advising the purchasing department of the need for an order to be placed and the order actually being placed with the supplier.

The minimum level of paper to be held in the reprographics department has been determined to be a buffer of 200 reams.

Calculate the optimum re-order level (in reams) and quantity to be ordered (in reams) for A4 paper.

# Chapter 3: Inventory

## The Economic Order Quantity (EOQ)

Another method which is used to manage inventories is the Economic Order Quantity (EOQ). This is a formula which is used to identify the most economic ('least expensive') quantity of inventory to be ordered, bearing in mind that any organisation has two different types of cost associated with materials – beyond the actual cost of the materials themselves.

These two types of costs are:

### Ordering Costs

These are costs associated with placing an order with a supplier. These are largely administrative costs – a purchasing officer may need to source a suitable supplier, read through a catalogue to identify products and prices, complete forms and make telephone calls or send emails. Sales orders must be processed and recorded, and then the orders must be checked when delivered. Finally, when the purchase invoice is received from the supplier, this must be recorded and payment must be made.

These activities all incur costs for the organisation. The more orders that are placed by an organisation, the more costs are incurred.

### Holding Costs

As we have previously identified, an organisation which holds inventory will incur costs as a result. These are related to storage, insurance and handling costs, as well as the cost of inventory having to be written off due to obsolescence and costs associated with having funds tied up in inventory.

The total cost for an organisation is therefore:

$$\text{Total Cost} = \text{Ordering Costs} + \text{Holding Costs}$$

An organisation is faced with a choice – if they place fewer but larger orders, the ordering costs will fall but the holding costs will rise. Alternatively, if more smaller orders are placed, the ordering costs will rise but the storage costs will fall.

The Economic Order Quantity calculates the combination of order size and number of orders to minimise the total cost.

The Economic Order Quantity is calculated as:

$$\sqrt{\frac{2 \times Co \times D}{Ch}}$$

Where:

**Co** = the **Cost** of placing one **Order**

**D** = the annual **Demand** for the material

**Ch** = the **Cost** of **Holding** one unit of the material in inventory for one year

# Chapter 3: Inventory

The √ symbol is the square root; it can be found on most calculators. The square root is the number which, when multiplied by itself, gives the original number.

Therefore, the square root of 9 is 3 (because 3 x 3 = 9).

**NOTE:** You will be expected to know this formula for your exam. Using the acronym 2 **Co**D and **Ch**ips could be a useful way to help you remember this formula.

 **Example 3.10**

The cost of holding one kilogram of material GG88 has been calculated at £4.

The cost of placing an order for material GG88 is £50, and the annual demand for the material is 45,000kg.

Material GG88 can only be purchased in quantities of 100kg. Calculate the economic order quantity for this material, and how many orders should be placed each year.

**Answer**

The formula is $\sqrt{\dfrac{2 \times Co \times D}{Ch}}$

In this example Co is £50, D is 45,000kg and Ch is £4.

Substituting these figures into the formula;

$$EOQ = \sqrt{\dfrac{2 \times 50 \times 45{,}000}{4}}$$

Therefore, the Economic Order Quantity is 1,060.66 kg.

However, as the material can only be purchased in quantities of 100 kg the organisation would purchase either 1,000 kg or 1,100 kg at a time.

Assuming the organisation purchases 1,100 kg at a time, it will need to purchase 45,000 kg during the year to meet the demand – this means placing (45,000 / 1,100) = 41 orders during the year.

 **Activity 3.9**

A company uses 90,000 litres of a particular chemical a year. They have calculated that it costs £25 to place an order and that the cost of holding one litre of the chemical for one year is £2.

Calculate the economic order quantity for this chemical.

How many orders a year the company should place?

## Other Factors to Take into Account

We have considered some statistical methods to help organisations manage their materials more effectively. However, it is important to recognise that these methods are simply tools to aid management and that they should not be seen as the only 'correct' method of managing inventory.

Other factors to be considered are:

- **Demand for the material** – as we have seen, materials and products often suffer from obsolescence, either due to natural deterioration or fashion and trends. Where this is the case, it may be necessary to re-calculate order levels and quantities
- **Seasonal Variations** – where there is marked seasonal variation in demand for a particular material, it will be necessary to tailor purchases to reflect this. For example, an ice cream shop will need to make larger and more frequent purchases during the summer months rather than in the winter.
- **Discounts and carriage charges** – if there are significant discounts to be received by placing larger orders (or significant carriage charges for smaller orders) these can influence the purchasing decision.

Whatever policies and procedures are adopted by an organisation to control inventory, it is essential that all staff understand and adhere to them. Failure to do so can have significant consequences for the organisation, and lead to unnecessary expenditure and wastage.

Many organisations operate a **preferred supplier** list, which means that only suppliers which have been vetted and approved by the organisation should be used. Purchasing goods from non-approved suppliers may mean the organisation does not take advantage of preferential agreed terms, or purchases materials of an inferior standard.

We have already looked at different models of calculating the **re-order quantity** (i.e. the amount of materials to purchase) and the **re-order level** (the point in time at which to place the order). If these are not complied with there is a danger of **overstocking** (i.e. allowing inventory levels to rise) or **stock-outs** (where the inventory of a particular material runs out). Both of these can be extremely costly and inefficient.

# Chapter 3: Inventory

 **Activity 3.10**

Spangles Ltd had an opening balance of raw material BG56 on 1st May as shown below. During May it made four transactions, but unfortunately, the stock record card has not been fully completed. Spangles Ltd uses the Average Cost (AVCO) method of stock valuation.

a) Complete the stock record card on the next page. Show cost per litre to 3dp.

| Date | Receipts | | | Issues | | | Balance | |
| --- | --- | --- | --- | --- | --- | --- | --- | --- |
| | Quantity (litres) | Cost per Litre | Total Cost £ | Quantity (litres) | Cost per Litre | Total Cost | Quantity (litres) | Total Cost £ |
| | | £ | | | £ | £ | | |
| 1 May | | | | | | | 10,000 | 24,500 |
| 5 May | 8,000 | 2.50 | | | | | | |
| 12 May | | | | 5,000 | | | | |
| 19 May | | 2.58 | 23,220 | | | | | |
| 28 May | | | | 8,400 | | | | |

Below is an extract from Spangles Ltd's inventory control policy.

*"BG56 should be ordered in quantities of at least 8,000 litres when the inventory balance falls below 12,000 litres."*.

Indicate where the following is true.

b) The policy of ordering BG56 in quantities of at least 8,000 litres has been complied with:

| | ✓ |
| --- | --- |
| On the 5th May but not on the 19th May | |
| On the 19th May but not on the 5th May | |
| On both the 5th May and the 19th May | |
| On neither the 5th May nor the 19th May | |

## Chapter 3: Inventory

c) The policy of ordering when the inventory balance falls below 12,000 litres has been complied with:

|  | ✓ |
|---|---|
| On the 5th May but not on the 19th May |  |
| On the 19th May but not on the 5th May |  |
| On both the 5th May and the 19th May |  |
| On neither the 5th May nor the 19th May |  |

The following information is available for component KK88 used in the production process by Spangles Ltd.

Annual demand = 40,000 units
Average holding cost for one unit for twelve months = £1.40
Fixed ordering cost = £560

d) Assuming component KK88 can only be ordered in batches of 100 units, which of these is the most economic order quantity for Spangles Ltd?

|  | ✓ |
|---|---|
| 200 units |  |
| 5,600 units |  |
| 5,657 units |  |
| 5,700 units |  |
| 32,000,000 units |  |

### Activity 3.11

a) Which IAS deals with Inventory? [ ]

b) Ballardy made the following purchases of plastic GB56 during August. There were 2,000 kg in stock on 1st August, which were valued at £6,000.

| Date Purchased | Quantity (kg) | Cost per kg (£) | Total Cost (£) |
|---|---|---|---|
| August 4th | 10,000 | 3.10 | 31,000 |
| August 17th | 4,000 | 3.15 | 12,600 |
| August 24th | 12,000 | 3.20 | 38,400 |

# Chapter 3: Inventory

On 20th August, 13,500 kg of plastic GB56 were issued to production. Calculate the cost of issues and also the value of the balance of remaining inventory on August 31st using:

- First In First Out (FIFO)
- Weighted Average Cost (AVCO)

Round your answers to the nearest whole £.

|  | Cost £ |
|---|---|
| FIFO Cost of Issues |  |
| AVCO Cost of Issues |  |
| FIFO Balance - kg |  |
| AVCO Balance - kg |  |
| FIFO – Balance (£) |  |
| AVCO – Balance (£) |  |

c) In times of rising prices, which of the following inventory valuation methods would you expect to result in the **highest** profit for the period?

|  | ✓ |
|---|---|
| First In First Out (FIFO) |  |
| Last In First Out (LIFO) |  |
| Average Cost (AVCO) |  |

d) The following information is available for component 65FT, a plastic screw used in the production process by Grafts Ltd.

> Annual demand = 400,000 screws
> 
> Average holding cost for one screw in inventory for twelve months = £0.02
> 
> Fixed ordering cost = £12

Assuming screws can only be ordered in multiples of 1,000 at a time, calculate how many screws should be purchased at a time, and approximately how many orders should be placed a year.

| Economic Order Quantity |  |
|---|---|
| Approximate Number of Orders per Year |  |

# Chapter 3: Inventory

e) Identify **four** advantages and **four** disadvantages to a business of holding high levels of inventory

| Four Advantages |
|---|
|  |
|  |
|  |
|  |

| Four Disadvantages |
|---|
|  |
|  |
|  |
|  |

## Assessment 3

You are now required to log in to your ROGO account to complete your online assessment before progressing on to the next chapter.

This page is left intentionally blank.

# Chapter 4: Calculating Direct Labour Costs

**At the end of this chapter, you should be able to:**

- Calculate direct labour costs per unit of production or service
- Calculate overtime premiums and bonuses
- Complete timesheets and pay calculations (including overtime and bonuses)
- Prepare cost accounting journal entries for direct and indirect labour

## Chapter 4: Calculating Direct Labour Costs

### Introduction

For most organisations, labour costs form a significant proportion of the total costs of the business. Labour costs cover all costs associated with employing staff, including pay and associated employer costs such as national insurance and pension contributions. We will start this unit by recapping the knowledge gained in AAT Level 2.

### Direct and Indirect Labour

Let's start by reminding ourselves of the difference between **direct labour** and **indirect labour.**

**Direct Labour** – the costs of any labour which can be directly attributed to the production of units of output.

*Direct labour - factory workers manufacturing Ford Model A cars in the early 20th Century.*

**Indirect Labour** - any labour costs for staff who are not directly involved in the production process, this includes management, supervisory staff and support staff (e.g. in administration, HR or finance).

*Indirect Labour - quality assurance is an example of a role not **directly** involved in the manufacture of a product or provision of a service.*

### Different Methods of Paying for Labour

There are many different ways of rewarding staff (both direct labour and indirect labour) for the work they do for an organisation.

# Chapter 4: Calculating Direct Labour Costs

You need to understand the following methods:
- Time Rate
- Overtime
- Piecework
- Guaranteed Minimum Payments
- Bonus Payments

We will look at each of these in turn.

## Time Rate

This is perhaps the most common way of paying direct labour employees. The employee is rewarded by a set rate per hour worked. Hence the total amount earned by an employee will be determined by the number of hours he or she is at work (and therefore does not take into account their **productivity** - how efficiently they perform whilst they are at work). The time rate is sometimes also called the **day rate**.

 **Example 4.1**

Alice is a production worker for Tyebarn Ltd and is hourly paid at a rate of £12.00 per hour. In the week commencing 14th August 20X6, Alice works 38 hours.

**Calculate Alice's pay for the week commencing 14th August 20X6.**

Alice will receive total (gross) pay: (38 x £12) = **£456** for that week's work.

## Overtime

Most employees are contracted to work a maximum number of hours for which they will receive their normal, or standard, hourly rate of pay. However, some weeks they may be asked to work additional hours over their contracted number, for example, if there is an urgent order to fulfil or to help cover other staff absences.

It is customary for employers to pay a **premium** for this overtime; that is, the employee receives their normal rate of pay plus an additional amount for each extra hour worked. This overtime premium is usually calculated as a percentage of their normal hourly rate. The most common overtime premiums are:

- **Time and a Third** - the employee receives an additional premium of one third of their normal hourly rate per hour of overtime.
- **Time and a Half** - the employee receives an additional premium of one half of their normal hourly rate per hour of overtime.
- **Double Time** - the employee receives an additional premium of the same amount as their normal hourly rate per hour of overtime.

The overtime premium is viewed as an overhead to the business and recorded separately for costing purposes.

 **Example 4.2**

Alice (from the previous example) is contracted to work a 38 hour week. However, in the week commencing 21st August 20X6, Alice actually works 46 hours to help fulfil an urgent order. Alice is paid for overtime hours on a 'time and a third' basis.

**Calculate Alice's pay for the week commencing 21st August 20X6.**

This can be recorded in two ways.

**Recording overtime premium:**

| | | |
|---|---|---|
| Basic pay | 46 hours x £12.00 = | £552.00 |
| Overtime premium | 8 hours x £4.00 = | £32.00 |
| Total cost of Alice's gross pay | £552 + £32 = | **£584.00** |

**Recording with cost of overtime payment:**

| | | |
|---|---|---|
| Basic (contracted) hours | 38 hours x £12.00 = | £456.00 |
| Cost of overtime payment | 8 hours x £16.00 = | £128.00 |
| Total cost of Alice's gross pay | | **£584.00** |

You will see that whichever method is chosen, the final pay for the week will be the same.

When a customer buys a standard product, they would expect to pay a standard price for that product. If the business has had to work overtime to fulfil an order, that could not be passed onto the customer. Therefore, this is a cost to the business and recorded as an indirect cost/overhead.

However, should a customer request a special order that could only be fulfilled by working overtime then then overtime premium could be passed onto the customer and could be charged as a direct cost.

It is not uncommon for employees to earn overtime premiums at different rates in the same week; for example, overtime hours worked Monday-Friday may be paid at 'time and a half', whilst any overtime hours worked on a weekend or bank holidays may be paid at 'double time'.

**Piecework**

An alternative approach to paying employees based on the length of time they are at work is to reward them for the number of units produced, or for each task carried out, at an agreed rate.

This method can also be calculated on a **'standard hour produced'** basis, whereby there is an agreed level of output to be produced per hour (**'the standard'**), and the employee's actual output is converted into standard hours produced to calculate their pay.

# Chapter 4: Calculating Direct Labour Costs

 **Example 4.3**

Beatrice is a marker for an examining body. The standard length of time it takes to mark one exam is agreed to be twenty minutes, and Beatrice is paid £20 per standard hour produced.

In October 20X5 Beatrice marks 72 exam papers.

**Calculate:**

    a. The standard hours produced by Beatrice in October 20X5.

    b. How much Beatrice will be paid in October 20X5.

**Answer**

a. Standard time to mark one paper = 20 minutes, so in one hour the standard is three exam papers. Beatrice marked 72 exam papers, which is **72/3 = 24 standard hours produced**.

b. Beatrice is paid £20 per standard hour produced, so in October 20X5 she will be paid **24 x £20 = £480**.

 **Activity 4.1**

Parker Ltd pays its workers £12.00 per hour for a standard 40 hour week. Any hours worked in excess of this are paid at a rate of time and a third.

Calculate the gross wages of the following employees:

**Note:** If no overtime is paid you should enter 0 into the overtime column

| Employee | Hours Worked | Basic Wage | Overtime Premium | Gross Wage |
|---|---|---|---|---|
| | | £ | £ | £ |
| A Toal | 46 | | | |
| B Fewster | 39 | | | |
| C Tindall | 36 | | | |
| D Hall | 42 | | | |

### Guaranteed Minimum Payments

In addition to paying a piecework rate, a business may also have a guaranteed minimum payment scheme in place. This would mean that an employee would receive **either** pay at the piecework rate or the minimum guaranteed payment amount (whichever is higher).

The guaranteed minimum payment would generally tend to be lower, encouraging employee productivity.

# Chapter 4: Calculating Direct Labour Costs

 **Example 4.4**

Hereson Records presses and labels vinyl records. Employees are paid £0.25 for every unit produced. They also guarantee a minimum payment of £311.85 a week for each 35 hour week.

An employee has produced the following output:

| Total units produced | Piecework Rate £ | Guaranteed Minimum Payment £ |
|---|---|---|
| 1,990 | 497.50 | 311.85 |

The employee would be paid £497.50 as this is the higher amount.

## Bonus Payments

A bonus payments system is based on a basic time rate (i.e. hourly rate), with a bonus being paid if production by the employee reaches a certain level for the time period.

 **Example 4.5**

Colin is paid an hourly rate of £15 for 40 contracted hours per week. If he makes more than an average of 5 units per hour over the week, he is paid a bonus of £30 for the week. In the week commencing 28th August, Colin works for 40 hours and produces 209 units.

Calculate Colin's total pay for the week commencing 28th August.

**Answer**

Colin's bonus payment only occurs if he makes more than 5 x 40 = 200 units over the week. During this week, he makes 209 units, and so is entitled to receive the bonus.

His total pay is therefore:

|  |  |
|---|---|
| 40 hours x £15 | = £600 |
| Bonus | = £30 |
| Total | = £630 |

Bonus payments may be offered to staff on condition that they achieve a pre-determined level of output, productivity or profitability:

**Output** - *the number of units produced*

**Productivity** - *relates to how quickly units are produced*

**Profitability** - *a measure of the financial success of the organisation over a period of time*

Bonuses can be calculated on an individual basis (i.e. per worker), or for a whole team, department or organisation - with the bonus being shared amongst eligible staff. Bonus schemes are often used as a way to motivate staff to work harder or faster - but an issue can arise if staff become so focussed on achieving their bonus, they perhaps start to ignore quality issues. In this situation output increases but the quality of the finished goods may fall below an acceptable level which may mean later problems for the organisation as they have to deal with returns of faulty goods, product recalls or falling reputation.

 **Example 4.6**

Alec and Barry both receive £10 per hour and work a 40 hour shift. If, in total, they produce more than 12 units per hour in a week they each split a £100 bonus. During the previous week, Alec produced 235 units and Barry produced 258 units.

Calculate the total pay for Alec and Barry for the week.

**Answer**

Alec and Barry produced 493 units between them. In 40 hours worked they needed to produce (40 x 12) = at least 480 units to earn the bonus.

**Their total pay is therefore:**

Alec:   40 x £10 = £400 + £50 bonus = £450

Barry:  40 x £10 = £400 + £50 bonus = £450

 *An Important Note about Bonuses:*

You should note that under the terms of this bonus scheme, Alec receives a bonus even though he did not produce output at the required level (he only produced 235 units against a target of 240 units). Alec and Barry both received the same bonus even though Barry produced almost 10% more output than Alec.

Does this seem fair? How would you feel if you were Barry? Or Alec? Can you think of a more effective bonus system than this?

**Other Labour Payment Methods**

There are many other payment methods for direct labour, but they are usually a variation of one of the five main methods described above. For example, receiving a basic wage or a guaranteed minimum payment with an addition of a piecework system or bonuses.

Indirect labour is usually paid by a **salary**, where the employee receives an agreed amount of pay for the year, split into twelve equal monthly payments (or possibly 52 equal weekly payments). Salaried employees do not benefit from working longer hours (as under time rate systems), nor from working harder (as with a piecework system). However, some salaried employees may also be eligible to receive bonus payments.

 ## Activity 4.2

An employee is paid £15 per hour and is expected to produce 100 units per hour.

Any production in excess of this is paid a bonus of £0.40 per unit.

Identify whether the following statements are true or false by selecting the relevant column of the table below.

| Statement | True | False |
|---|---|---|
| If during a 40 hour week, the employee produces 4,600 units a bonus of £1,840 will apply. | | |
| An employee who works 35 hours and produces 3,450 units will not be entitled to a bonus. | | |
| An employee who works 42 hours and produces 4,475 units will be due a total payment of £740 | | |

 ## Activity 4.3

Griffin Ltd is looking at paying its employees using either the time rate with a bonus or the piecework method. The time rate used is £12.00 per hour and each employee is expected to produce 250 units per hour. Anything over this is paid a bonus of £0.60 per unit. The piecework payment rate is £0.06 per unit.

Complete the following table for the two methods, showing the gross wage for the time rate with bonus and the piecework wage.

**Note:** If no bonus is paid, you should enter 0 as the bonus for that employee in the table.

| Hours worked | Unit Output | Basic Wage | Bonus Pay | Gross Wage | Piecework Wage |
|---|---|---|---|---|---|
| | | £ | £ | £ | £ |
| 36 | 9,200 | | | | |
| 40 | 9,950 | | | | |
| 38 | 9,780 | | | | |
| 42 | 10,860 | | | | |

# Chapter 4: Calculating Direct Labour Costs

 **Activity 4.4**

Supercheese Ltd operates a small factory in Middlefield, making cheese products. They pay their employees using a mixture of payment methods as identified below.

**Machine operators** are paid on a time rate, with the hourly rate depending on their role, experience and length of service with the company. All hourly paid staff work a contracted 39 hour week, and overtime is payable at time and a third for the first ten hours of overtime in a week. Any overtime worked in excess of ten hours is then paid at time and a half.

**Packaging operators** are paid on a piece rate, being paid 5 pence for every item packaged. A full time packaging operator works up to 40 hours a week and is expected to package 240 items an hour. Under trade union rules a packaging operator must not work more than 40 hours a week so no overtime is available. If a full time employee packages more than 10,000 items in a week they receive a bonus of £50.

**Supervisors** are paid a monthly salary. A bonus of 5% of their monthly salary is payable each month if they achieve certain targets related to health and safety and productivity.

**Administration staff** are all salaried and paid monthly – they are contracted to work 37 hours a week and no overtime is payable if they work longer than this.

The following data is available for the week/month ended 31st January 20X7.

| Name | Position | Hours worked | Hourly Rate / Annual Salary | Items Packaged | Entitled to Bonus? |
|---|---|---|---|---|---|
| Alan Adams | Machine Operator | 46 | £15.00 per hour | n/a | n/a |
| Barney Brown | Machine Operator | 51 | £12.50 per hour | n/a | n/a |
| Cheetan Chauna | Packaging Operator | 40 | n/a | 11,200 | n/a |
| Daisy Dawson | Packaging Operator | 40 | n/a | 9,950 | n/a |
| Edgar Ellis | Machine Operator | 48 | £12.50 per hour | n/a | n/a |
| Faisal Fakir | Administration | 42 | £18,900 | n/a | n/a |
| Gary Gibson | Packaging Operator | 37 | n/a | 10,140 | n/a |
| Hamid Haseef | Supervisor | 45 | £28,400 | n/a | Yes |
| Ivory Ilonga | Supervisor | 44 | £26,900 | n/a | No |
| Jimmy Jones | Machine Operator | 44 | £10.00 per hour | n/a | n/a |
| Karen Keith | Packaging Operator | 30 | n/a | 9,900 | n/a |
| Larry Long | Administration | 37 | £18,500 | n/a | n/a |

Calculate the amount to be paid to each employee and complete the table below.

| Name | Amount £ | Workings |
|---|---|---|
| Alan Adams | | |
| Barney Brown | | |
| Cheetan Chauna | | |
| Daisy Dawson | | |
| Edgar Ellis | | |
| Faisal Fakir | | |
| Gary Gibson | | |
| Hamid Haseef | | |
| Ivory Ilonga | | |
| Jimmy Jones | | |
| Karen Keith | | |
| Larry Long | | |

## Comparison of the Different Systems

We have seen there are many different ways an organisation can pay its staff. Each method has its advantages and disadvantages. Whatever method is implemented, it should have the following attributes:

- The amount paid to each employee should be a fair reflection of their skills and effort
- It should be easy to understand by employees
- It should be easy and economic to administer
- Payments should be made regularly and shortly after the period to which it relates – most weekly paid staff are paid on a Friday and most salaried staff are paid on (or shortly before) the last day of the month in question
- It should be flexible, to allow management to reward outstanding effort or to reflect changes in operating methods.

# Chapter 4: Calculating Direct Labour Costs

The key advantages and disadvantages of each method are outlined below:

| Time Rate: Advantages | Time Rate: Disadvantages |
|---|---|
| • Easy to understand and calculate<br>• No requirement to establish piecework rates<br>• A regular wage for employees – not affected by variations in production<br>• Cash flow planning is easier<br>• Can be used for all direct labour employees<br>• Quality of finished product not affected by rushed work | • Both efficient and inefficient employees receive the same pay<br>• No incentive for employees to work harder<br>• Slower working does not affect basic wage but may lead to overtime<br>• May require more supervisors to ensure that output is maintained |

| Piece Rate: Advantages | Piece Rate: Disadvantages |
|---|---|
| • Payment of wages is directly linked to output<br>• More efficient workers earn more than those who are less efficient<br>• Work is done quicker and less time is wasted | • Not suitable for all direct labour employees<br>• Pay is reduced if production problems out of the control of employees<br>• Quality of finished products may be low<br>• Control systems are needed to check the output of each worker<br>• More complex calculations<br>• Difficulty agreeing to piecework rates |

| Bonus: Advantages | Bonus: Disadvantages |
|---|---|
| • Wages are linked to output, but a minimum wage is guaranteed<br>• Work done quicker, with less wasted time<br>• More efficient workers can earn more<br>• A bonus system can be applied to the whole workforce, or just sections<br>• Staff more settled | • Bonus may be lost through events out of workers' control<br>• Quality of the finished product may be low<br>• More inspectors and controls may be needed<br>• Calculations may be more complex<br>• Difficulties in agreeing to bonus rates<br>• Group rates may cause conflict |

# Chapter 4: Calculating Direct Labour Costs

## Idle Time and Overtime Premiums

Idle time occurs when the production process is halted for some reason. This could be machine breakdown, maintenance, stock out etc. Hourly paid workers will still expect to be paid during periods of idle time. Similarly, piece-rate paid employees will also expect to be compensated during idle time, as they are unable to produce output during this time through no fault of their own. This is normally done by paying an hourly rate for periods of idle time.

Payments made during periods of idle time are usually treated as an **indirect labour cost**, even though they are payments made to employees who would normally be classified as direct labour. Remember that a direct cost is one which can be attributed to the cost of a particular unit of output – because there is no production during idle time, the costs cannot be directly attributed to a unit of output and so must be treated as indirect (overhead) costs.

Similarly, many organisations treat overtime premiums as an indirect cost. It is only the **premium** which is treated in this way – the normal hourly cost is always treated as a direct cost. If this is not done (i.e. the whole cost of overtime hours is treated as a direct cost) then some products will become more expensive than other, identical units produced during normal working time.

 **Example 4.7**

Posey Ltd pays its hourly paid staff at £15 per hour for a normal 40 hour week, with any hours worked above this paid at time and a half. All overtime premiums and idle time are to be charged to indirect costs. The following data applies to the week ended 31st March 20X2.

Angus worked 45 hours, Bob worked 41 hours and Clive worked 42 hours. During the week Clive's machine was being repaired for three hours and Clive is to be paid at his normal hourly rate for this time (in addition to the hours above).

Calculate the amount to be charged to direct labour costs and the amount to be charged to indirect labour costs.

**Answer**

|       | Direct Cost        | Indirect Cost                              |
|-------|--------------------|--------------------------------------------|
| Angus | 45 x £15 = £675    | 5 x £7.50 = £37.50                         |
| Bob   | 41 x £15 = £615    | 1 x £7.50 = £7.50                          |
| Clive | 39 x £15 = £585    | 2 x £7.50 = £15.00<br>3 x £15.00 = £45.00  |

*The overtime premiums are treated as indirect costs. The three hours of idle time paid to Clive are also treated as indirect labour.*

# Chapter 4: Calculating Direct Labour Costs

## Sources of Information for Labour

Organisations must ensure that they have systems in place to accurately record the hours worked by staff in each time period, and the work completed by them in that time. There are a variety of different methods of capturing this data.

- **Timesheets** are perhaps the most common method. Employees record the hours they have worked, and the data contained in the timesheet is used to calculate the wage for the employee, including overtime and any bonuses. The data contained in timesheets can be entered manually by the employee or may be collected by 'clocking in' systems whereby the employee registers their attendance at, and departure from, work. This can be done in a variety of ways, including a manual card system or, computerised systems such as scanned swipe cards or biometric recognition.
- **Piecework Tickets** – these are completed by employees who are paid on a piece rate system, and show the number of units completed.
- **Job Cards** – in some professions such as accountancy or motor mechanics it is necessary to record the number of hours worked on each individual job, to enable the customer or client to be charged the appropriate amount for the work done.

 **Example 4.8**

Joe Down is an employee at Fluffy Ltd. He is paid a £15 per hour basic rate for working a basic seven hour shift Monday to Friday. Any overtime worked from Monday to Friday is paid at time and a third. However, any hours worked on a Saturday or Sunday are paid at double time.

a) Complete the timesheet below for the week ended 15th August.

| Employee Name – Joe Down | | | | Cost Centre - Assembly | | |
|---|---|---|---|---|---|---|
| | Hours spent on production | Hours spent on indirect work | Notes | Basic Pay £ | Overtime Premium £ | Total Pay £ |
| Monday | 6 | 1 | Machine Breakdown | 105 | | 105 |
| Tuesday | 7 | 0 | | 105 | | 105 |
| Wednesday | 9 | 0 | | 135 | 10 | 145 |
| Thursday | 4 | 3 | Training Course | 105 | | 105 |
| Friday | 8 | 0 | | 120 | 5 | 125 |
| Saturday | 3 | 0 | | 45 | 45 | 90 |
| Sunday | 2 | 0 | | 30 | 30 | 60 |
| **Total** | **39** | **4** | | **645** | **90** | **735** |

# Chapter 4: Calculating Direct Labour Costs

b) How much should be charged to direct costs and how much to indirect costs?

Direct Labour costs = 39 hours x £15 = £585

Indirect Labour costs

| | | |
|---|---|---|
| 1 x hour (machine breakdown) | = | £15 |
| 3 x hours (training) | = | £45 |
| Overtime premium | = | £90 |
| Total Indirect cost | | £150 |

*We can reconcile this to check that Total Pay (£735) = Direct Labour Cost (£585) + Indirect Labour Cost (£150).*

## Accounting for Labour Costs

A **wages control account** is often used to 'link' the costing system to the payroll system.

Through the wages control account, the following charges are made:

**Direct Labour Costs** are charged to **Production** (or **Work-In-Progress**)

**Indirect Labour Costs** are charged to **Production Overheads** (or **Operating Overheads**)

**Administration Labour Costs** are charged to **Non-Production Overheads** (or **Non-Operating Overheads**)

The bookkeeping entries therefore are:

For direct labour:

**Debit** **Production**
**Credit** **Wages Control Account**

For indirect labour to production overheads:

**Debit** **Production Overheads**
**Credit** **Wages Control Account**

For indirect labour to non-production overheads:

**Debit** **Non-production Overheads**
**Credit** **Wages Control Account**

# Chapter 4: Calculating Direct Labour Costs

 **Example 4.9**

Soundbites Ltd manufactures and sells microphones. The payroll for the week ended 24th April has been produced as follows:

| | |
|---|---:|
| Net wages paid to employees in week | £ 8,400 |
| Income Tax and NICs payable to HMRC | £ 1,900 |
| Pension contributions owing to pension company | £ 650 |
| | **£10,950** |

This has been analysed as follows:

| | |
|---|---:|
| Direct labour costs | £ 7,340 |
| Indirect labour costs | £ 1,640 |
| Administration labour costs | £ 1,970 |
| | **£10,950** |

The cost codes used by Soundbites Ltd are as follows:

| Cost Centre | Code |
|---|---|
| Wages Control | 1100 |
| Production | 6000 |
| Production Overheads | 6500 |
| Non-Production Overheads | 6800 |

**Answers**

a) Prepare the wages control account at 24th April.

| Wages Control Account | | | |
|---|---:|---|---:|
| | £ | | £ |
| Bank | 8,400 | Production | 7,340 |
| HMRC | 1,900 | Production Overheads | 1,640 |
| Pension Contributions | 650 | Non-Production Overheads | 1,970 |
| | | | |
| | **10,950** | | **10,950** |

b) Prepare the bookkeeping entries in the table below using the relevant cost codes, showing how the total cost of payment is split between the different cost centres of the organisation.

| Date | Cost Code | Debit (£) | Credit (£) |
|---|---|---|---|
| 24 April | 6000 | 7,340 | |
| 24 April | 1100 | | 7,340 |
| 24 April | 6500 | 1,640 | |
| 24 April | 1100 | | 1,640 |
| 24 April | 6800 | 1,970 | |
| 24 April | 1100 | | 1,970 |

## Activity 4.5

You work for Gremlin Ltd. The payroll for factory employees for the week ending 30 April has been completed. The following payments are to be made:

| | £ |
|---|---|
| Net wages/salaries to pay to employees | 10,000 |
| Income tax and national insurance contributions (NIC) to pay to HMRC | 2,000 |
| Pension contributions to pay to F4L pension scheme | 1,000 |
| **Gross payroll costs** | **13,000** |

The payroll for the week is analysed as:

| | £ |
|---|---|
| Direct labour costs | 7,000 |
| Indirect labour costs | 4,000 |
| Factory administration labour costs | 2,000 |
| **Gross payroll costs** | **13,000** |

The following cost account codes are used to record production labour costs:

| Code | Description |
|---|---|
| 8200 | Production direct labour |
| 8400 | Production overheads |
| 8600 | Production administration |
| 9100 | Wages control |

a) Complete the wages control account entries in the account shown below:

| Wages control account | | | |
|---|---|---|---|
| **Debit** | £ | **Credit** | £ |
| Bank (net wages/salaries) | | Direct Labour | |
| HMRC (income tax and NIC) | | Production Overhead | |
| Pension contributions | | Non-Production Overhead | |
| | | | |

b) Complete the table below to show how the gross payroll cost for the week is charged to the various cost accounts of the business:

| Date | Code | Debit | Credit |
|---|---|---|---|
| 30 April | | | |
| 30 April | | | |
| 30 April | | | |
| 30 April | | | |
| 30 April | | | |
| 30 April | | | |

 **Activity 4.6**

Oarsome Ltd manufactures and sells oars for rowing boats. The payroll for the week ended 31st July has been produced as follows:

| | |
|---|---|
| Net wages paid to employees in week | £ 9,130 |
| Income Tax and NICs payable to HMRC | £ 2,075 |
| Pension contributions owing to pension company | £    854 |
| | **£12,059** |

This has been analysed as follows:

| | |
|---|---|
| Direct labour costs | £ 8,690 |
| Indirect labour costs | £ 2,017 |
| Administration labour costs | £ 1,352 |
| | **£12,059** |

The cost codes used by Oarsome Ltd are as follows:

| Cost Centre | Code |
|---|---|
| Wages Control | 1850 |
| Production | 8880 |
| Production Overheads | 8920 |
| Non-Production Overheads | 8960 |

a) Prepare the wages control account at 31st July.

| Wages Control Account | | | |
|---|---|---|---|
| | £ | | £ |
| | | | |
| | | | |
| | | | |
| | | | |
| | | | |

b) Prepare the bookkeeping entries in the table below using the relevant cost codes, showing how the total cost of payment is split between the different cost centres of the organisation.

| Date | Cost Code | Debit (£) | Credit (£) |
|---|---|---|---|
| | | | |
| | | | |
| | | | |
| | | | |
| | | | |
| | | | |

### Activity 4.7

a) Benny Rich is an employee at Joffey Ltd. He is paid a £14 per hour basic rate for working a basic eight hour shift Monday to Friday. Any overtime worked from Monday to Friday is paid at time and a half. However, any hours worked on a Saturday or Sunday are paid at double time.

# Chapter 4: Calculating Direct Labour Costs

Complete the timesheet below for the week ended 24th April.

| Employee Name – Benny Rich | | | | Cost Centre - Machining | | |
|---|---|---|---|---|---|---|
| | Hours spent on production | Hours spent on indirect work | Notes | Basic Pay £ | Overtime Premium £ | Total Pay £ |
| Monday | 8 | 0 | | | | |
| Tuesday | 8 | 0 | | | | |
| Wednesday | 6 | 2 | Compulsory Staff Meeting | | | |
| Thursday | 9 | 0 | | | | |
| Friday | 7 | 1 | Fire Evacuation | | | |
| Saturday | 4 | 0 | | | | |
| Sunday | 4 | 0 | | | | |
| **Total** | **46** | **3** | | | | |

How much should be charged to direct costs and how much to indirect costs?

| Direct Costs | |
|---|---|
| Indirect Costs | |

b) Below are extracts from the payroll information of Miltonby Manufacturing Ltd for last week

| Date | Labour Costs |
|---|---|
| November 15th | **Manufacturing.** Production employees pay: 900 hours at £9.50 per hour |
| November 16th | **Packing.** Production employees basic pay £3,450 + £1,245 overtime |
| November 17th | **Stores.** Employees pay £956 + 8% bonus |
| November 18th | **Administration.** Staff salaries £6,450 + 2.5% bonus |

Complete the cost journal entries to record the four payroll payments made last week using the following information for the 'code' section of the table.

- 9001 Direct manufacture costs
- 9002 Direct packing costs
- 9301 Manufacturing overheads
- 9302 Non manufacturing overheads
- 9800 Wages control account.

| Date | Code | Dr £ | Cr £ |
|---|---|---|---|
| Nov 15th | | | |
| Nov 15th | | | |
| Nov 16th | | | |
| Nov 16th | | | |
| Nov 17th | | | |
| Nov 17th | | | |
| Nov 18th | | | |
| Nov 18th | | | |

 **Assessment 4**

You are now required to log in to your ROGO account to complete your online assessment before progressing on to the next chapter.

# Chapter 5: Absorption Costing

**At the end of this chapter, you should be able to:**

- Use allocation and absorption techniques to share overheads between departments

- Reapportion overheads from service departments to production departments, including where reciprocal services take place

- Calculate the Budgeted Overhead Absorption Rate (BOAR)

- Calculate the amount of overhead to be absorbed into a product using the most appropriate basis, including per unit, per labour hour and machine hour

- Use actual figures to calculate the under- or over-absorption of fixed overheads

- Complete cost accounting journal entries for overheads

# Chapter 5: Absorption Costing

## Introduction

Overhead expenditure is a significant element of cost for most organisations – and indeed modern businesses tend to form a larger proportion of total costs than ever before.

Overhead expenditure includes all indirect costs – that is all costs incurred by the business which are not directly associated with the cost of an individual product.

In absorption costing the total overheads must somehow be included in the cost of each specific product. Where there is only one product made by an organisation, this is relatively straightforward; we simply divide the total overheads by the total number of units made.

 **Example 5.1**

Easyone Ltd makes a single product, the Ludell. The direct costs associated with this product are:

| | |
|---|---|
| Direct Materials | £ 8.00 |
| Direct Labour | £ 6.00 |
| Total Direct Cost | £14.00 |

In the next period, Easyone Ltd expects to incur fixed overheads of £50,000 and to produce 40,000 units.

The overhead to be absorbed into each unit is therefore calculated as £50,000 / 40,000 = £1.25 per unit.

The cost per unit is therefore £14.00 + £1.25 = **£15.25**

The issue of deciding how much overhead should be absorbed becomes more complicated when the business manufactures more than one product. Each product is likely to take a different time to produce, and therefore to 'absorb' overheads at different rates. A product which takes ten minutes on the production line could reasonably be expected to 'absorb' twice as much of the overheads as a product which only takes five minutes to make. Therefore we need to find a way to absorb the overheads on a time basis, rather than simply according to the number of units made.

There is also the issue of how to deal with non-production overheads. These are indirect costs which are not related to the production of goods or provision of services, such as administration costs. These are still expenses which must be met by the business and which will reduce the organisation's profits, and therefore (under absorption costing) must be included in the fully absorbed cost of each product.

The objective is to identify a **fair** way of sharing the overhead costs between the different products which are made by the organisation. This is achieved by a technique of **allocation, apportionment and absorption.**

# Chapter 5: Absorption Costing

## Allocation and Apportionment

You should be familiar with the concept of **responsibility centres** – either cost centres, profit centres or investment centres. These are departments of a business to which costs (and possibly revenues) can be 'charged'.

Responsibility centres will vary from business to business, depending on their size and structure. However, it can be useful to differentiate between **production centres** and **support centres**.

A **production centre** is involved in the manufacture of goods or the provision of services to customers. In a manufacturing environment, production centres often include:

- Milling, turning or fabrication – these are specific engineering processes
- Mixing – for example the mixing of chemicals
- Assembly – of finished goods from components
- Painting – of components or finished goods

A **support centre (or service centre)** does not directly manufacture products or provide services to customers but instead supports the production centres. Typical examples include:
- Maintenance
- Catering
- Human Resources
- Administration
- Finance

Each of these centres will incur costs to the organisation. Only the production centres will incur direct costs (eg materials and labour), but all will incur overheads.

Some overheads will be incurred by only one responsibility centre. Where this is the case, these overheads can be **allocated** directly to the relevant centre. Typical examples include:

- **Supervisors' salaries** – where the supervisor works only in one centre
- Rental costs of leased buildings which are only used by one centre
- Cost of indirect materials (e.g. stationery) which have been issued to a particular centre.

However, many overheads cannot be directly allocated to a specific centre in this way, because they are 'shared' between two or more centres. In this situation, the overhead cannot be allocated to one centre, and must therefore be **apportioned** between the different centres to which it relates on a **fair basis**.

 **Example 5.2**

Petra is a supervisor for Teaswell Ltd. She supervises the work of three production departments – cutting, milling and painting. She also recently purchased a new set of stepladders for use solely in the cutting department, and arranged a job advertisement to be placed in the local newspaper for a vacancy in the painting department.

# Chapter 5: Absorption Costing

The cost of the stepladders can be allocated to the 'cutting' department and the cost of the advertisement could be allocated to the painting department. However, Petra's salary will need to be apportioned between the three different centres.

This could be done in a number of ways; the easiest is perhaps to simply divide it by three and charge each department with a third of the cost. However, this may not be the fairest. The apportionment could therefore be carried out on based on the respective number of hours per week that Petra works in each department, or perhaps the respective number of staff employed in each department. There is no 'right' and 'wrong' answer; instead, the fairest method should be adopted.

**Apportionment**, therefore, means sharing out overhead costs between different responsibility centres on a fair basis. This will be different between different organisations, but common apportionment bases are shown on the following page:

| Overhead | Common Basis of Apportionment |
| --- | --- |
| Rent | Floor space (or volume) of centres |
| Rates | Floor space (or volume) of centres |
| Heating and Lighting | Floor space (or volume) of centres |
| Power | Floor space (or volume) of centres |
| Insurance (Buildings) | Floor space (or volume) of centres |
| Insurance (Machinery) | Carrying value of machinery in each centre |
| Depreciation of Machinery | Machine usage (hours) or value of machinery |
| Supervisor Costs | Number of staff in each centre, or time spent |
| Canteen | Number of staff in each centre |
| Stores Department | Number of requisitions / issues by each centre |

Remember that overheads should be **allocated** directly to a responsibility centre wherever possible; apportionment should only be carried out where this is not possible.

Overheads are **pro-rated** between the relevant centres on whatever basis is chosen. This simply means that they are shared between the centres based on the ratio of the proportion of the total overhead incurred by each centre.

 **Example 5.3**

Paddles Ltd has two production centres (assembly and finishing) and two service centres (canteen and administration). All four centres are based in the same building, which is rented by Paddles Ltd. The cost of renting this building is £30,000 per year.

It has been agreed that the most appropriate basis for apportioning this overhead of rent is on floor area. The building has been measured, and the following data collected:

Area of assembly department    2,400 square feet
Area of finishing department    1,600 square feet
Area of canteen    400 square feet
Area of administration    600 square feet
**Total**    **5,000 square feet**

To pro-rata the overhead expense according to floor area, the following calculations are carried out:

| Centre | Overhead / | Total x | Department = | Apportioned Overhead |
|---|---|---|---|---|
| Assembly | £30,000 / | 5,000 x | 2,400 | £14,400 |
| Finishing | £30,000 / | 5,000 x | 1,600 | £9,600 |
| Canteen | £30,000 / | 5,000 x | 400 | £2,400 |
| Administration | £30,000 / | 5,000 x | 600 | £3,600 |
| **Total** | | | **5,000** | **£30,000** |

You will see that using either calculation will give the same result.

This means that the assembly department will be 'charged' £14,400 as its share of the total rent cost of £30,000, with £9,600 charged to the finishing department and so on.

 **Example 5.4**

Ruskey Ltd has identified the following overheads, which are to be allocated or apportioned between the company's two production centres (milling and turning) and two service support centres (administration and maintenance):

Heat and Light    £30,000
Power    £24,000
Insurance – buildings    £ 6,000
Insurance – machinery    £ 2,800
Staff canteen    £15,000
Supervisor's salary    £20,000

The following data has been identified:

**The supervisor works solely in the milling department.**

# Chapter 5: Absorption Costing

|  | Milling | Turning | Maintenance | Administration |
|---|---|---|---|---|
| Floor Area m² | 40 | 50 | 10 | 20 |
| Value of machinery | £240,000 | £380,000 | £60,000 | £20,000 |
| Number of staff | 20 | 16 | 6 | 8 |

Complete the following table to show how overheads are allocated and apportioned between the four centres.

|  | Basis Used | Total | Milling | Turning | Maintenance | Admin |
|---|---|---|---|---|---|---|
| Heat & Light | Floor Area | £30,000 | £10,000 | £12,500 | £2,500 | £5,000 |
| Power | Floor Area | £24,000 | £8,000 | £10,000 | £2,000 | £4,000 |
| Insurance Buildings | Floor Area | £6,000 | £2,000 | £2,500 | £500 | £1,000 |
| Insurance Machinery | Value | £2,800 | £960 | £1,520 | £240 | £80 |
| Canteen | No of Staff | £15,000 | £6,000 | £4,800 | £1,800 | £2,400 |
| Supervisor Salary | Allocated | £20,000 | £20,000 |  |  |  |

*The supervisor's salary is allocated to the Milling department, as this cost is incurred only by that one centre. The other overheads are shared between ('apportioned') all the centres, as they all are responsible for some of the total costs.*

Heat & Light is calculated as follows:

Milling = £30,000/120 x 40
Turning = £30,000/120 x 50
Admin = £30,000/120 x 20
Maintenance = £30,000/120 x 10

*The other overheads are apportioned in a similar way, using whichever basis of apportionment is most appropriate.*

# Chapter 5: Absorption Costing

 **Activity 5.1**

Polypipes Ltd has identified the following overheads, which are to be allocated or apportioned between the company's two production centres (assembly and painting) and two service support centres (administration and stores):

| | |
|---|---|
| Heat and Light | £60,000 |
| Power | £48,000 |
| Insurance – buildings | £10,000 |
| Insurance – machinery | £ 6,500 |
| Depreciation – machinery | £12,000 |
| Staff canteen | £15,000 |
| Supervisor's salary | £32,000 |

The following data has been identified:

The supervisor works 60% in the assembly department and 40% in the painting department.

| | Assembly | Painting | Admin | Stores |
|---|---|---|---|---|
| **Floor Area m²** | 50 | 60 | 25 | 15 |
| Value of machinery | £400,000 | £220,000 | £100,000 | £80,000 |
| Number of staff | 12 | 18 | 4 | 2 |

Complete the following table to show how overheads are allocated and apportioned between the four centres.

| | Basis Used | Total | Assembly | Painting | Admin | Stores |
|---|---|---|---|---|---|---|
| Heat & Light | | | | | | |
| Power | | | | | | |
| Insurance Buildings | | | | | | |
| Insurance Machinery | | | | | | |
| Depreciation Machinery | | | | | | |
| Canteen | | | | | | |
| Supervisor Salary | | | | | | |

# Chapter 5: Absorption Costing

## Reapportioning Overheads from Support Centres to Production Centres

So far we have looked at how to allocate and apportion overheads to responsibility centres. The next stage in the process is to reapportion any overheads which are currently being charged to service centres to the production centres. The aim is that all the overheads will therefore be apportioned to the production centres only – with no overheads being left in the service centres.

This is done in a very similar way to the original apportionments of the overheads.

 **Example 5.5**

In Example 5.4, the overheads for Ruskey Ltd were allocated and apportioned as shown below:

|  | Basis Used | Total | Milling | Turning | Maintenance | Admin |
|---|---|---|---|---|---|---|
| Heat & Light | Floor Area | £30,000 | £10,000 | £12,500 | £2,500 | £5,000 |
| Power | Floor Area | £24,000 | £8,000 | £10,000 | £2,000 | £4,000 |
| Insurance Buildings | Floor Area | £6,000 | £2,000 | £2,500 | £500 | £1,000 |
| Insurance Machinery | Value | £2,800 | £960 | £1,520 | £240 | £80 |
| Canteen | No of Staff | £15,000 | £6,000 | £4,800 | £1,800 | £2,400 |
| Supervisor Salary | Allocate | £20,000 | £20,000 |  |  |  |

# Chapter 5: Absorption Costing

We start by totalling each of the department's overheads:

|  | Basis Used | Total | Milling | Turning | Maintenance | Admin |
|---|---|---|---|---|---|---|
| Heat & Light | Floor Area | £30,000 | £10,000 | £12,500 | £2,500 | £5,000 |
| Power | Floor Area | £24,000 | £8,000 | £10,000 | £2,000 | £4,000 |
| Insurance Buildings | Floor Area | £6,000 | £2,000 | £2,500 | £500 | £1,000 |
| Insurance Machinery | Value | £2,800 | £960 | £1,520 | £240 | £80 |
| Canteen | No of Staff | £15,000 | £6,000 | £4,800 | £1,800 | £2,400 |
| Supervisor Salary | Allocate | £20,000 | £20,000 | | | |
| | **TOTALS** | **£97,800** | **£46,960** | **£31,320** | **£7,040** | **£12,480** |

It is good practice at this point to **cross-cast** your totals – make sure that the totals of each column are equal to the overall total figure. In this case, £46,960 + £31,320 + £12,480 + £7,040 = £97,800.

### Direct Reapportionment

We now need to reapportion the overheads currently charged to administration (£12,480) and maintenance (£7,040) to the two production centres (milling and turning). To do this we need some further information about how the two service centres actually support the production centres.

Suppose we are given the information that 60% of the administration department's time is spent supporting the milling department and 40% is spent supporting the turning department. However, only 20% of the maintenance department's activity supports the milling department, whilst 80% supports turning.

The overheads would therefore be reapportioned as follows:

## Chapter 5: Absorption Costing

| | Basis Used | Total | Milling | Turning | Maintenance | Admin |
|---|---|---|---|---|---|---|
| Heat & Light | Floor Area | £30,000 | £10,000 | £12,500 | £2,500 | £5,000 |
| Power | Floor Area | £24,000 | £8,000 | £10,000 | £2,000 | £4,000 |
| Insurance Buildings | Floor Area | £6,000 | £2,000 | £2,500 | £500 | £1,000 |
| Insurance Machinery | Value | £2,800 | £960 | £1,520 | £240 | £80 |
| Canteen | No of Staff | £15,000 | £6,000 | £4,800 | £1,800 | £2,400 |
| Supervisor Salary | Allocate | £20,000 | £20,000 | | | |
| | TOTALS | £97,800 | £46,960 | £31,320 | £7,040 | £12,480 |
| **Reapportion** | | | | | | |
| **Admin** | 60%:40% | | £7,488 | £4,992 | | -£12,480 |
| **Maintenance** | 20%:80% | | £1,408 | £5,632 | -£7,040 | |
| | TOTALS | £97,800 | £55,856 | £41,944 | - | - |

Now all the overheads have been removed from the service departments and have been reapportioned to the production centres. It is advisable to cross-cast again: £55,856 + £41,944 = £97,800.

*Workings:*

*Admin*

*Milling: £12,480 x 60% = £7,488*

*Turning: £12,480 x 40% = £4,992*

*Maintenance*

*Milling: £7,040 x 20% = £1,408*

*Turning: £7,040 x 80% = £5,632*

 **Activity 5.2**

Flighty Ltd is a small commercial airline. It has budgeted for the following overheads for its two profit and three cost centres for Quarter 1 of the next financial year:

|  | £000 | £000 |
|---|---|---|
| Depreciation of aircraft |  | 36,400 |
| Aviation fuel and other variable costs |  | 42,200 |
| Pilots and aircrew salaries: |  |  |
|     Scheduled services | 5,250 |  |
|     Charter flights | 4,709 |  |
| Total pilots and aircrew salaries |  | 9,959 |
| Rent and rates and other premises costs |  | 12,600 |
| Indirect labour costs: |  |  |
|     Aircraft maintenance and repairs | 9,600 |  |
|     Fuel and parts store | 3,200 |  |
|     General administration | 7,800 |  |
| Total indirect labour cost |  | 20,600 |

The following information is also available:

| Profit/cost centre | Net book value of aircraft (£000) | Planned number of miles flown | Floor space (square metres) | Number of employees |
|---|---|---|---|---|
| Scheduled services | 1,080,000 | 215,600 |  | 105 |
| Charter flights | 720,000 | 176,400 |  | 96 |
| Aircraft maintenance and repairs |  |  | 190,000 | 260 |
| Fuel and parts store |  |  | 114,000 | 146 |
| General administration |  |  | 76,000 | 220 |
| Total | 1,800,000 | 392,000 | 380,000 | 827 |

Primary allocations or apportionments are made on the most appropriate basis. The support cost centres are then reapportioned to the two flight profit centres using the direct method.

- The Aircraft maintenance and repairs cost centre spends 60% of its time maintaining the aircraft in the scheduled services profit centre and the remainder in the charter flights profit centre.
- 55% of the issues from the Fuel and parts store cost centre are made to the scheduled services profit centre and the remainder to the charter flights profit centre.
- The scheduled services profit centre and the charter flights profit centre both incur general administration costs equally.
- The three support cost centres are not involved in reciprocal servicing.

Use the following table to allocate or apportion the overheads between the profit/cost centres, using the most appropriate basis.

| | Basis of apportionment | Scheduled services £000 | Charter flights £000 | Aircraft maintenance and repairs £000 | Fuel and parts store £000 | General admin. £000 | Totals £000 |
|---|---|---|---|---|---|---|---|
| Depreciation of aircraft | | | | | | | |
| Aviation fuel and other variable costs | | | | | | | |
| Pilots and aircrew salaries | | | | | | | |
| Rent and rates and other premises costs | | | | | | | |
| Indirect labour | | | | | | | |
| Totals | | | | | | | |
| Reapportion Aircraft maintenance and repairs | | | | | | | |
| Reapportion Fuel and parts store | | | | | | | |
| Reapportion General admin. | | | | | | | |
| Total overheads to profit centres | | | | | | | |

# Chapter 5: Absorption Costing

## Step-Down Reapportionment

In the previous example, it has been assumed that there is no reciprocal servicing between the two service departments – that is, the administration centre spends no time supporting the maintenance department, and the maintenance department does not support the administration department. Of course, in reality, this is unlikely. The administration department will have to support the work of the maintenance department – perhaps placing orders, chasing up deliveries, paying invoices, doing printing – whilst the maintenance department may support the administration centre by repairing and maintaining equipment such as photocopiers or computers.

Imagine a business with four service centres: Human Resources (HR), IT Support, a canteen and a stores department.

**Reciprocal Service Departments**

The HR department will support the other three service departments, by recruiting staff, dealing with disciplinary or performance issues, organising appraisals and so on.

**Reciprocal Service Departments**

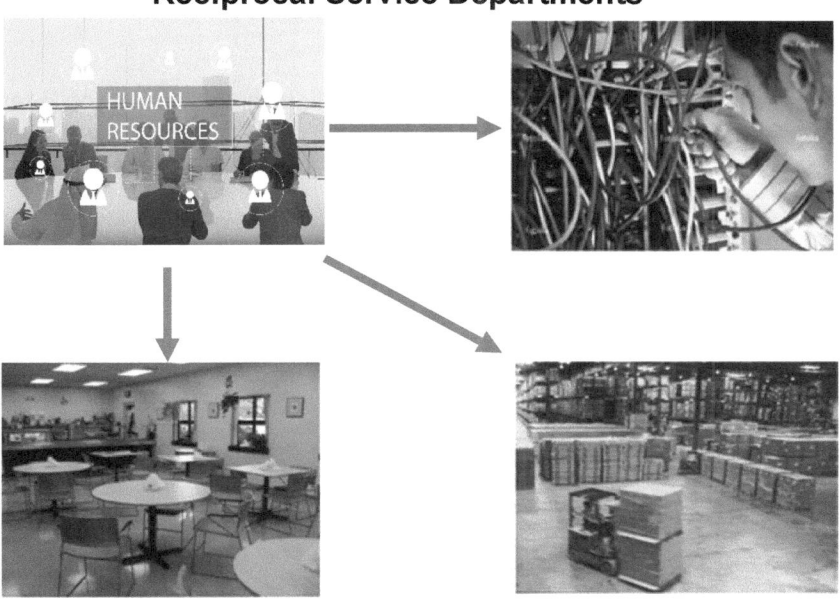

## Chapter 5: Absorption Costing

However, the IT department will also support all the other service departments, by fixing computers, installing software etc. The canteen will provide services to the staff of the other departments, by feeding them all. The stores department will order and keep materials such as stationery for the HR department, cabling and software for the IT department, and food and consumables for the canteen.

In effect, each service centre supports each of the other centres:

**Reciprocal Service Departments**

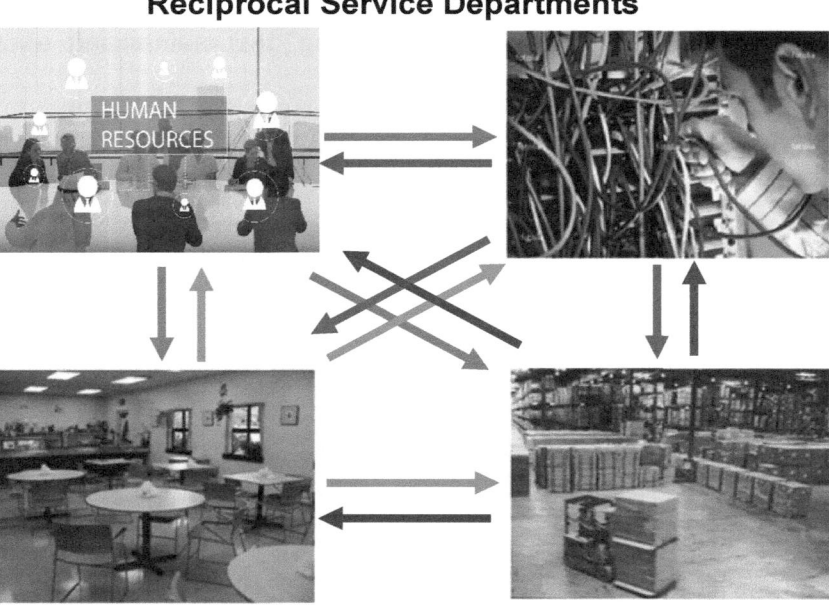

When service centres offer reciprocal servicing in this way, the overheads need to be reapportioned using the **step-down method.** This is very similar to the **direct method** considered earlier but allows the overheads to be reapportioned in a fairer way, taking into account the patterns of use of each department.

 **Example 5.6**

In the earlier Example 5.5 (Ruskey Ltd) we established the totals of overheads for each department as below:

# Chapter 5: Absorption Costing

|  | Basis Used | Total | Milling | Turning | Maintenance | Admin |
|---|---|---|---|---|---|---|
| Heat & Light | Floor Area | £30,000 | £10,000 | £12,500 | £2,500 | £5,000 |
| Power | Floor Area | £24,000 | £8,000 | £10,000 | £2,000 | £4,000 |
| Insurance Buildings | Floor Area | £6,000 | £2,000 | £2,500 | £500 | £1,000 |
| Insurance Machinery | Value | £2,800 | £960 | £1,520 | £240 | £80 |
| Canteen | No of Staff | £15,000 | £6,000 | £4,800 | £1,800 | £2,400 |
| Supervisor Salary | Allocate | £20,000 | £20,000 |  |  |  |
|  | TOTALS | £97,800 | £46,960 | £31,320 | £7,040 | £12,480 |

Now, however, we are given the following information:

The Administration Department's time is spent servicing Milling (50%), Turning (40%) and Maintenance (10%)

The Maintenance Department's time is spent servicing Milling (20%), Turning (80%)

The difference here is that the admin department also supports the maintenance department. We therefore use the step-down method.

|  | Basis | Total | Milling | Turning | Maintenance | Admin |
|---|---|---|---|---|---|---|
| Heat & Light | Floor Area | £30,000 | £10,000 | £12,500 | £2,500 | £5,000 |
| Power | Floor Area | £24,000 | £8,000 | £10,000 | £2,000 | £4,000 |
| Insurance Buildings | Floor Area | £6,000 | £2,000 | £2,500 | £500 | £1,000 |
| Insurance Machinery | Value | £2,800 | £960 | £1,520 | £240 | £80 |
| Canteen | No of Staff | £15,000 | £6,000 | £4,800 | £1,800 | £2,400 |
| Supervisor Salary | Allocate | £20,000 | £20,000 |  |  |  |
|  | TOTALS | £97,800 | £46,960 | £31,320 | £7,040 | £12,480 |
| Reapportion |  |  |  |  |  |  |
| Admin | 50:40:10 |  | £6,240 | £4,992 | £1,248 | -£12,480 |
|  |  |  | £53,200 | £36,312 | £8,288 | - |

You will see that the overheads in the maintenance department have now increased by £1,248 to £8,288.

We now need to reapportion the maintenance department's overheads across the production departments in the ratio of 20:80.

|  | Basis | Total | Milling | Turning | Maintenance | Admin |
|---|---|---|---|---|---|---|
| Heat & Light | Floor Area | £30,000 | £10,000 | £12,500 | £2,500 | £5,000 |
| Power | Floor Area | £24,000 | £8,000 | £10,000 | £2,000 | £4,000 |
| Insurance Buildings | Floor Area | £6,000 | £2,000 | £2,500 | £500 | £1,000 |
| Insurance Machinery | Value | £2,800 | £960 | £1,520 | £240 | £80 |
| Canteen | No of Staff | £15,000 | £6,000 | £4,800 | £1,800 | £2,400 |
| Supervisor Salary | Allocate | £20,000 | £20,000 |  |  |  |
|  | TOTALS | £97,800 | £46,960 | £31,320 | £7,040 | £12,480 |
| **Reapportion** |  |  |  |  |  |  |
| Admin | 50:40:10 |  | £6,240 | £4,992 | £1,248 | -£12,480 |
|  |  | £97,800 | £53,200 | £36,312 | £8,288 | - |
| Maintenance | 20:80 |  | £1,658 | £6,630 | -£8,288 |  |
|  |  | £97,800 | £54,858 | £42,942 | - |  |

The required objective of reapportioning all of the overheads to just the production department has been achieved. This is a slightly longer process than the direct methods but should lead to a fairer distribution of the overheads between the service departments.

## Activity 5.3

Burnley Ltd makes a range of pie fillings which are sold in cans. It has two production departments involved in producing its range of products, the Ingredients Mixing Department and the Canning Department. It also has two service departments – Stores and Factory Maintenance.

The budgeted overhead costs relating to these departments for the next quarter (to 30th September) are shown in the following table, together with their behaviour and details of how some of these costs are apportioned to departments.

## Chapter 5: Absorption Costing

| Budgeted overhead cost | Cost behaviour | £ | Comments |
|---|---|---|---|
| Rent and rates | Fixed | 320,000 | |
| Insurance | Fixed | 18,000 | Apportion on same basis as rent and rates. |
| Light, heat and power | Semi-variable | 90,000 | Apportion fixed element of £30,000 equally between all four departments. Apportion variable element according to floor area. |
| Supervision | Fixed | 80,000 | Apportion to the two production departments pro rata to direct labour costs. |
| Stores wages | Fixed | 68,000 | |
| Factory maintenance wages | Fixed | 96,000 | |
| Depreciation of fixed assets | Fixed | 56,000 | Apportion according to net book value of fixed assets. |
| Other overhead costs | Dependant on specific cost | 64,000 | Apportion 30% to Ingredients mixing, 40% to Canning, and the balance equally between Stores and Factory maintenance. |

**Additional data:**

| Department | Floor area (square metres) | Net book value of fixed assets (£) | Number of stores requisitions | Direct labour costs (£) |
|---|---|---|---|---|
| Ingredients mixing | 220,000 | 200,000 | 33,600 | 47,600 |
| Canning | 100,000 | 150,000 | 22,400 | 71,400 |
| Stores | 40,000 | 50,000 | | |
| Factory maintenance | 40,000 | 100,000 | | |

**Notes:**
- The Factory maintenance department services the other three departments equally.
- The Stores department services the Ingredients mixing and Canning departments only, and in proportion to the number of stores requisitions.
- There is no reciprocal servicing between the service departments.

Allocate or apportion the budgeted overhead costs between the four departments, using the **most appropriate basis**. Then apportion the two service departments' costs to the two production departments using the additional data. (Round to the nearest £ throughout).

## Chapter 5: Absorption Costing

| Overhead | Basis of allocation | Ingredients mixing | Canning | Stores | Factory maintenance | Total |
|---|---|---|---|---|---|---|
| | | £ | £ | £ | £ | £ |
| Rent and rates | | | | | | |
| Insurance | | | | | | |
| Light, heat and power fixed cost | | | | | | |
| Light, heat and power variable cost | | | | | | |
| Supervision | | | | | | |
| Stores wages | | | | | | |
| Factory maintenance wages | | | | | | |
| Depreciation of fixed assets | | | | | | |
| Other overhead costs | | | | | | |
| | | | | | | |
| Totals | | | | | | |
| Reapportion Factory maintenance | | | | | | |
| Reapportion Stores | | | | | | |
| Total production department overheads | | | | | | |

### Calculating the Budgeted Overhead Absorption Rate

Now we have calculated the total production overheads, the final stage of this process is to calculate the **overhead absorption rate** per hour. This is also known as the **overhead recovery rate** because it suggests that each time a unit is produced, some of the fixed overheads incurred by the business have been 'recovered'. This rate can then be used to calculate the amount of overheads to be absorbed into each product, based on the length of time each different product or service takes. The longer the production time is for a product, the more overhead it will absorb.

# Chapter 5: Absorption Costing

In manufacturing, there are two common bases for calculating the overhead recovery rate:
- The direct labour hour rate
- The machine hour rate.

## The Direct Labour Hour Rate

To calculate on this basis, the total budgeted overheads for a responsibility centre are divided by the total budgeted number of labour hours to be used in that centre during the period.

## The Machine Hour Rate

This is calculated by dividing the total budgeted overheads for a responsibility centre by the total budgeted number of machine hours to be used in that centre during the period. One machine hour is measured as one machine in the department running for one hour – so if a cost centre had twenty machines running for eight hours, this would be calculated as 160 machine hours.

In non-manufacturing organisations, a suitable measure will need to be identified for the specific business. For example, in a tram or bus company, overheads may be absorbed on the basis of passenger miles, whilst in a hospital they may be absorbed on the basis of patient bed days. In an exam, the required basis for apportionment would be made clear to you.

You will note that absorption rates are always calculated on **budgeted** figures – both the **budgeted fixed overheads** and also **budgeted hours** (or other measures). This is because the overhead absorption rate which is calculated is then used to determine how much overhead should be included in the full cost of each product. This must be done in advance because the cost is often used to determine the selling price of each product. It would not be possible to delay identifying the overheads until after the period has ended, as the business would not be able to cost them, and would therefore not be able to establish a selling price or make any sales.

## Determining Which Basis to Use

We saw previously there are two bases for calculating the overhead absorption rate – the **direct labour hour basis** and the **machine hour basis**. The organisation may choose whichever basis it wishes; however, as a general rule you should use the direct labour hour basis when the responsibility centre is labour intensive (i.e. uses a proportionately higher number of labour hours than machine hours), and the machine hour basis when the centre is relatively machine intensive.

 **Example 5.7**

Redrose Ltd has three production cost centres – milling, turning and assembly. The budgeted overhead costs for June, and budgeted hours, for these three centres have been calculated as follows:

# Chapter 5: Absorption Costing

|  | Budgeted overheads | Budgeted Labour Hours | Budgeted Machine Hours |
|---|---|---|---|
| Milling | £240,093 | 1,020 | 3,108 |
| Turning | £175,750 | 660 | 1,850 |
| Assembly | £65,046 | 1,480 | 460 |

You are required to calculate the overhead absorption rate for each cost centre.

**Answer**

**Milling**

Budgeted Overhead Absorption Rate = £240,093 / 3,108 = **£77.25** per machine hour

**Turning**

Budgeted Overhead Absorption Rate = £175,750 / 1,850 = **£95.00** per machine hour

**Assembly**

Budgeted Overhead Absorption Rate = £65,046 / 1,480 = **£43.95** per direct labour hour

Note that the milling and turning departments are both machine intensive (using more machine hours than labour hours) whereas the assembly department is more labour intensive. This determines which of the overhead absorption bases to use.

 **Activity 5.4**

Ryder Ltd has estimated its overheads and activity levels for the next month.

|  | Assembly Dept | Painting Dept |
|---|---|---|
| Budgeted overheads (£) | 205,600 | 452,500 |
| Budgeted direct labour hours | 25,700 | 18,100 |
| Budgeted machine hours | 16,448 | 22,625 |

What would be the budgeted overhead absorption rate for each department if:

a) Both rates were set based on direct labour hours?

b) Both rates were set based on machine hours?

|  | Direct Labour Hour | Machine Hour |
|---|---|---|
| **Assembly Department** |  |  |
| **Painting Department** |  |  |

## Chapter 5: Absorption Costing

### Absorbing Overheads into Product Costs

Once we have established the overhead absorption rates for each production responsibility centre, we can then use these to calculate the amount of overhead to be absorbed into each product.

This is done by identifying the number of machine hours or direct labour hours each product spends in each department and then multiplying the number of hours by the applicable overhead absorption rate in each centre.

 **Example 5.8**

In Example 5.7 we established the overhead absorption rates for the three production centres as follows:

**Milling**

Budgeted Overhead Absorption Rate = £240,093 / 3,108 = **£77.25** per machine hour

**Turning**

Budgeted Overhead Absorption Rate = £175,750 / 1,850 = **£95.00** per machine hour

**Assembly**

Budgeted Overhead Absorption Rate = £65,046 / 1,480 = **£43.95** per direct labour hour

We are now told that Redrose Ltd manufactures four different products, with production times as follows:

| Product | Time in Milling | Time in Turning | Time in Assembly |
|---|---|---|---|
| A111 | 2 hours | 3 hours | 2 hours |
| B222 | 1 hour | 3 hours | 1 hour |
| C333 | 2 hours | 4 hours | 3 hours |
| D444 | 3 hours | 5 hours | 4 hours |

The direct costs of each product have also been identified:

|  | A111 | B222 | C333 | D444 |
|---|---|---|---|---|
| Direct Materials | £205 | £340 | £750 | £695 |
| Direct Labour | £80 | £145 | £335 | £410 |
| **Total Direct Costs** | **£285** | **£485** | **£1,085** | **£1,105** |

Calculate the fully absorbed cost of each product.

### Product A111

| Direct Materials | £205.00 |
|---|---|
| Direct Labour | £80.00 |
| Fixed Overheads | £527.40 |
| **Total Cost** | **£812.40** |

*Working for fixed overheads:*

| Milling | 2 hours x £77.25 | = | £154.50 |
| Turning | 3 hours x £95.00 | = | £285.00 |
| Assembly | 2 hours x £43.95 | = | £ 87.90 |
| | | | £527.40 |

### Product B222

| Direct Materials | £340.00 |
|---|---|
| Direct Labour | £145.00 |
| Fixed Overheads | £406.20 |
| **Total Cost** | **£891.20** |

*Working for fixed overheads:*

| Milling | 1 hour x £77.25 | = | £ 77.25 |
| Turning | 3 hours x £95.00 | = | £285.00 |
| Assembly | 1 hour x £43.95 | = | £ 43.95 |
| | | | £406.20 |

### Product C333

| Direct Materials | £750.00 |
|---|---|
| Direct Labour | £335.00 |
| Fixed Overheads | £666.35 |
| **Total Cost** | **£1,751.35** |

*Working for fixed overheads:*

| Milling | 2 hours x £77.25 | = | £154.50 |
| Turning | 4 hours x £95.00 | = | £380.00 |
| Assembly | 3 hours x £43.95 | = | £131.85 |
| | | | £666.35 |

**Product D444**

| Direct Materials | £695.00 |
|---|---|
| Direct Labour | £410.00 |
| Fixed Overheads | £882.55 |
| **Total Cost** | **£1,987.55** |

*Working for fixed overheads:*

| Milling | 3 hours x £77.25 | = | £231.75 |
|---|---|---|---|
| Turning | 5 hours x £95.00 | = | £475.00 |
| Assembly | 4 hours x £43.95 | = | £175.80 |
| | | | £882.55 |

Each of the product costs in the previous example are **fully absorbed costs** – that is they include not just the cost of direct materials and labour, but also a share of the organisation's fixed overheads which have been allocated and apportioned on a fair basis. The organisation can then use these full costs to calculate the required selling price to make the profit required for each product.

 **Example 5.9**

In Example 5.8, we calculated the full product costs as follows:

| Product | Full Absorption Cost |
|---|---|
| A111 | £812.40 |
| B222 | £891.20 |
| C333 | £1,751.35 |
| D444 | £1,987.55 |

The management of Redrose Ltd has directed that a mark-up of 80% should be applied to the full absorption cost of each product to calculate the selling price.

Calculate the selling price of each product (to 2 decimal places).

| Product | Full Absorption Cost | Mark-Up (80%) | Selling Price |
|---|---|---|---|
| A111 | £812.40 | £649.92 | **£1,462.32** |
| B222 | £891.20 | £712.96 | **£1,604.16** |
| C333 | £1,751.35 | £1,401.08 | **£3,152.43** |
| D444 | £1,987.55 | £1,590.04 | **£3,577.59** |

# Chapter 5: Absorption Costing

 **Activity 5.5**

Carrom Ltd's budgeted overheads and activity levels for the next quarter are:

|  | Machining | Assembly |
|---|---|---|
| Budgeted Overheads (£) | £512,000 | £406,000 |
| Budgeted Direct Labour Hours | 8,000 | 101,500 |
| Budgeted Machine Hours | 64,000 | 25,375 |

Using the most appropriate absorption rate;

The Budgeted Overhead Absorption Rate for Machining is £ [ ] per [ ]

The Budgeted Overhead Absorption Rate for Assembly is £ [ ] per [ ]

## Under and Over Absorption

Once the absorption rates have been determined, the overheads are absorbed into products as demonstrated above. Remember that the overhead absorption rates are based on **budgeted**, or estimated, figures.

**Budgeted O/H Absorption Rate = Budgeted O/H**
                                 **Budgeted Activity**

Of course, in reality, it is highly probable that one or both of these estimates will prove to be incorrect. When this happens, the total amount of fixed overheads absorbed through production will not equal the actual expenditure on fixed overheads for the period. There will be either:

**Under-Absorption of Fixed Overheads** – occurs when not enough fixed overheads are absorbed during the production process to cover the actual fixed overheads incurred during the period.

Or

**Over-Absorption of Fixed Overheads** – occurs when too much is absorbed during the production process, so that more is absorbed than is actually spent.

# Chapter 5: Absorption Costing

 **Example 5.10**

Rajkot Ltd makes two products, the Alpa and the Mara. At the start of this quarter, they forecast the following:

|  | Alpa | Mara |
|---|---|---|
| Budgeted Production (units) | 10,000 | 25,000 |
| Standard Hours per Unit Machining | 2 | 3 |
| Standard Hours per Unit Assembly | 3 | 4 |

The budgeted fixed overheads for the Machining department were £380,000 and for the Assembly department they were £780,000.

At the end of the period the total hours worked in the Machining department was 105,000 and in the Assembly department was 118,000. The actual number of units produced was 12,000 of Alpa and 22,000 of Mara. The actual fixed overhead for the period was £1,200,000.

Calculate the under or over absorption of fixed overheads in the quarter.

**Answer**

**Step One**

To tackle this question we first need to calculate the fixed overheads absorbed during the period – and to do this we will need to know how many hours were budgeted to be worked in each department.

Budgeted Hours Worked in Machining = (10,000 x 2) + (25,000 x 3) = **95,000 hours**

Budgeted Hours Worked in Assembly = (10,000 x 3) + (25,000 x 4) = **130,000 hours**

**Step Two**

The Budgeted Overhead Absorption Rate for each department can now be calculated:

BOAR (Machining) = £380,000 / 95,000 = **£4 per hour**

BOAR (Assembly) = £780,000 / 130,000 = **£6 per hour**

**Step Three**

The Overhead Absorbed per unit is therefore:

Alpa = (2 x £4) + (3 x £6) = **£26**

Mara = (3 x £4) + (4 x £6) = **£36**

## Step Four

The total overhead absorbed during the quarter is calculated by multiplying the **actual** number of units produced by the overhead absorbed per unit:

Alpa = 12,000 units x £26 = £312,000

Mara = 22,000 units x £36 = £792,000

**£1,104,000**

## Step Five

The under- or over-absorption can be calculated by comparing the overhead absorbed with the actual overhead incurred.

Amount absorbed = £1,104,000

Actual expenditure = £1,200,000

**£ 96,000**

Because more has been spent than was absorbed, there has been an **under-absorption** of fixed overheads.

This may seem complicated at first but follow each step carefully. Be careful to identify the difference correctly as either an under- or an over-absorption.

 **Activity 5.6**

Jolson Ltd has identified the following data for January 20X6.

- Budgeted overhead absorption rate = £8.80 per machine hour
- Actual machine hours in January = 8,210 hours
- Actual overheads incurred in January = £65,800

Calculate the under or over absorption of fixed overheads in January 20X6.

| £ | *under absorbed / over absorbed.* |
|---|---|

As we have seen, under- or over-absorptions are caused by differences between the original budget and the actual figures for both expenditure and activity. An **over-recovery** suggests that the Budgeted Overhead Recovery Rate was set too high, whereas an **under-recovery** suggests that the BOAR was too low. However, you must remember that this only becomes apparent **after** the end of the period. It is not necessarily that there was an avoidable error in the calculation of the BOAR. However, if there are repeated discrepancies over subsequent periods it may indicate that the budgeting process is weak, and the estimates and standards should be reviewed.

# Chapter 5: Absorption Costing

## Accounting Entries for Overheads

A **Production Overheads Control Account** is used to transfer production overheads (the amount of overheads absorbed during the production process) to the production cost centres.

Any under or over absorption of fixed overheads must also be dealt with at the end of the period. This is done by debiting the production overheads control account and crediting the statement of profit and loss with any <u>over absorbed</u> overheads, or crediting the production overheads account and debiting the statement of profit and loss with any <u>under absorption</u>.

The entries for the overheads that are absorbed are:

**Dr** Production

**Cr** Production Overheads Control Account

Actual overheads that are incurred are then paid out of the bank:

**Dr** Production Overhead Control Account

**Cr** Bank

The over or under absorption is the balancing amount on the account and will be posted to the Statement of Profit or Loss.

Where over absorption has occurred, the entries would be:

**Dr** Production Overheads Control Account

**Cr** Statement of Profit or Loss

With any over absorption of overheads – this will reduce the total cost of production and so increase profit.

Where under absorption has occurred, the entries would be:

**Dr** Statement of Profit or Loss

**Cr** Production Overheads Control Account

With any under absorption of overheads – this will increase the total cost of production and so reduce profit.

Here are the entries summarised in the Production Overheads Control Account.

| Production Overheads Control Account ||
|---|---|
| Bank | Production |
| Statement of Profit or Loss (over absorbed) | Statement of Profit or Loss (under absorbed) |

The concept of adjusting profits at the period end may be difficult to grasp at first; what happens is that in the costing system, the production cost is based on the **absorbed** overheads as production happens during the period. In the financial accounting ledgers, of course, the **actual** expenditure is recorded. Hence the profit calculated in the costing system

## Chapter 5: Absorption Costing

will differ from the profit reported in the financial ledgers. The adjustment to profit is, therefore, necessary to bring the profit in the costing system into line with the actual financial profit.

 **Example 5.11**

Foyles Ltd manufactures and sells decorative candles. The candles pass through two production stages – forming and finishing. Details of overheads for the two departments for the month ended 31st July are as follows:

**Forming Department**

Overhead absorption rate is £4.00 per labour hour

Labour hours worked were 1,200

Actual cost of production overhead was £5,200

**Finishing Department**

Overhead absorption rate is £8.00 per machine hour

Machine hours worked were 1,500

Actual cost of production overhead was £11,000

The following cost accounting codes are relevant:

| Code | Cost Centre |
| --- | --- |
| 2010 | Production |
| 2800 | Production Overheads – Forming |
| 2900 | Production Overheads – Finishing |
| 7500 | Statement of Profit or Loss |

You are required to prepare the two production overhead accounts and to record the journal entries for the overheads and the under- or over-recovery of fixed overheads.

**Answer**

a) Prepare the production overhead accounts:

| Production Overheads - Forming | | | |
| --- | --- | --- | --- |
| Bank (overheads incurred) | £5,200 | Production (overheads absorbed) | £4,800 |
| | | Statement of P&L (under absorption) | £400 |
| | **£5,200** | | **£5,200** |
| | | | |

## Chapter 5: Absorption Costing

| Production Overheads - Finishing | | | |
|---|---|---|---|
| Bank (overheads incurred) | £11,000 | Production (overheads absorbed) | £12,000 |
| Statement of P& L (over absorption) | £1,000 | | |
| | £12,000 | | £12,000 |
| | | | |

b) Prepare the journals

| Date | Cost Centre Code | Debit | Credit |
|---|---|---|---|
| 31st July | 2010 | £4,800 | |
| 31st July | 2800 | | £4,800 |
| 31st July | 2010 | £12,000 | |
| 31st July | 2900 | | £12,000 |
| 31st July | 7500 | £400 | |
| 31st July | 2800 | | £400 |
| 31st July | 2900 | £1,000 | |
| 31st July | 7500 | | £1,000 |

 **Activity 5.7**

Parrot Ltd has the following departments involved in producing plastic toolboxes:

- Plastics Moulding
- Labelling
- Stores
- Equipment Maintenance

The budgeted overheads relating to these departments for the next quarter are shown below, together with their behaviour and how they are apportioned to departments.

# Chapter 5: Absorption Costing

| Budgeted cost | Cost behaviour | £ | Comments |
|---|---|---|---|
| Heat and lighting | Semi-variable | 60,000 | Apportion fixed element of £24,000 equally between all four departments. Apportion variable element according to floor area. |
| Power for machinery | Variable | 28,000 | Apportion 70% to Plastics Moulding, and 30% to Labelling. |
| Supervision | Fixed | 120,000 | Apportion to the two production departments pro rata to direct labour costs. |
| Stores wages | Fixed | 72,000 | |
| Equipment Maintenance salaries | Fixed | 188,200 | |
| Depreciation of fixed assets | Fixed | 84,000 | Apportion according to net book value of fixed assets. |
| Other overhead costs | Dependant on specific cost | 128,000 | Apportion 60% to Plastics Moulding, 20% to Labelling, and 10% each to Stores and Equipment Maintenance. |

The following information is also available:

| Department | Square metres occupied | Net book value of fixed assets (£) | Number of material requisitions | Direct labour costs (£) |
|---|---|---|---|---|
| Plastics Moulding | 320,000 | 160,000 | 162,750 | 100,000 |
| Labelling | 180,000 | 80,000 | 56,000 | 140,000 |
| Stores | 80,000 | 30,000 | | |
| Equipment Maintenance | 20,000 | 10,000 | | |

Use the following table to allocate or apportion the overheads between the production departments, using the most appropriate basis. Round to the nearest £ throughout.

**Note:**
The Equipment Maintenance department's total costs should be apportioned equally to the other three departments. Then the total of the Stores department's costs should be apportioned according to the number of material requisitions.

## Chapter 5: Absorption Costing

| Overhead | Basis of allocation | Plastics Moulding | Labelling | Stores | Equipment Maintenance | Total |
|---|---|---|---|---|---|---|
| | | £ | £ | £ | £ | £ |
| Heat and lighting fixed cost | | | | | | |
| Heat and lighting variable cost | | | | | | |
| Power for machinery | | | | | | |
| Supervision | | | | | | |
| Stores wages | | | | | | |
| Equipment Maintenance salaries | | | | | | |
| Depreciation of fixed assets | | | | | | |
| Other overhead costs | | | | | | |
| | | | | | | |
| Total of primary apportionments | | | | | | |
| Reapportion Equipment Maintenance | | | | | | |
| Reapportion Stores | | | | | | |
| Total production department overheads | | | | | | |

**Data**

The Plastics Moulding department recovers its overheads on the basis of the budgeted machine hours. The Labelling department, however, recovers its overheads on the basis of the budgeted direct labour hours.

The following information relates to these two departments for July:

| | Plastics Moulding department | Labelling department |
|---|---|---|
| Budgeted machine hours | 8,404 | 6,500 |
| Budgeted direct labour hours | 10,005 | 16,250 |

# Chapter 5: Absorption Costing

Using the above information and your calculations from above, calculate the budgeted overhead recovery (absorption) rate for:

a) The Plastics Moulding department: _____

b) The Labelling department: _____

Actual fixed overheads incurred in the period were:

        Plastics Moulding    £444,500

        Labelling             £289,800

Actual hours worked in the period were:

|  | Plastics Moulding department | Labelling department |
| --- | --- | --- |
| Actual machine hours | 8,612 | 6,490 |
| Actual direct labour hours | 4,994 | 16,620 |

c) Calculate the under or over absorption of fixed overheads for each department.

| **Plastics Moulding:** | £ | *over / under* absorbed |
| --- | --- | --- |
| **Labelling:** | £ | *over / under* absorbed |

 **Assessment 5**

You are now required to log in to your ROGO account to complete your online assessment before progressing on to the next chapter.

# Chapter 6: Marginal Costing

**At the end of this chapter, you should be able to:**

- Explain the differences between absorption costing and marginal costing.

- Describe why the treatment of fixed costs as period costs leads to different profits under marginal costing to absorption costing when there is a change in inventory levels.

- Perform key marginal costing calculations including contribution (total and per unit), break-even point, margin of safety, target profit volumes and contribution/sales(C/S) ratio.

# Chapter 6: Marginal Costing

## Introduction

This chapter will explain further the principles of marginal costing, as well as explore the reasons why its development was necessary in modern business and how it can be used to improve short term decision making by management.

## The Need for Marginal Costing

'Traditional' manufacturing businesses developed full absorption costing (covered in Chapter 5) as a way of identifying how much a particular unit of output costs. Because the fully absorbed cost includes a share of the fixed overheads of a business, it provides a starting point for the business to establish selling prices for its products which should ensure that the business remains profitable.

However, it could be argued that this over-simplifies the situation, and removes some of the flexibility which management needs to make effective decisions. Furthermore, it could also be argued that the treatment of fixed overheads as a **product cost**, rather than as a **period cost**, is inherently wrong.

The fundamental objective of most business organisations is to **maximise profits**. Therefore, all the activities of the business should be geared towards that objective – and effective management will do everything possible to make this happen. Absorption costing can be considered to overstate the true cost of each product, leading to management overpricing or perhaps turning down potential sales.

## Contribution

**Contribution** is a particularly important concept in costing. It sometimes causes difficulties for students, so make sure you follow this section carefully.

Contribution is the difference between the selling price of a product and the variable cost of it. The variable cost of a product is usually the cost of direct materials and the cost of direct labour needed to produce it. However, there may also be other variable direct expenses which need to be included. The variable cost of a product is also called the **marginal cost** - it is the cost of making one more unit of output.

 **Example 6.1**

Highlights Ltd make hair products. They have calculated the direct cost (marginal cost) of one of their products, a shampoo, as £1.40 per litre.

Under absorption costing, this product is also charged with 95 pence per litre of fixed overheads, making the cost per litre £2.35. The relevant managers would not be prepared to accept any offer from potential customers to purchase the shampoo at a price below £2.35 per litre, as this is the fully absorbed cost of one litre. To do so would therefore mean that the sale had been made at a loss.

# Chapter 6: Marginal Costing

However, an alternative approach would identify the relevant cost as being the marginal cost of £1.40. Therefore, any revenue earned above £1.40 is the **contribution per litre**, which (so long as all the fixed costs of the business have been met during the period) will increase the profit of the business.

For example, an offer from a customer to purchase 10,000 litres of shampoo at a discounted price of £1.90 would be rejected under absorption costing, but under marginal costing would be accepted as each litre sold would generate a contribution of (£1.90 - £1.40) = 50p per litre.

Total profits would therefore increase by 10,000 x 50p = **£5,000**

 **Example 6.2**

Eureka Ltd manufactures a single product, the Baffle. The costs associated with making each Baffle are as follows:

| Direct Materials | £8.45 |
|---|---|
| Direct Labour | £3.50 |
| Direct Expense (fee for use of image on the packaging) | £0.20 |
| **Total variable cost** | **£12.15** |

Each Baffle sells for £24.99. The **contribution per unit** is therefore £24.99 - £12.15 = **£12.84**

The **contribution** therefore represents the amount of money which the business earns towards meeting the fixed overheads it incurs. Only once these fixed overheads have been fully covered will the business be able to start making a profit.

Once the fixed costs have been covered the remaining contribution represents the profit the business has made.

 **Activity 6.1**

Calculate the **contribution per unit** for each of the following:

| Selling Price | Variable Cost | Contribution per Unit |
|---|---|---|
| £35.00 | £14.00 | |
| £480.00 | £225.00 | |
| £9.99 | £6.75 | |
| £249.49 | £109.80 | |

# Chapter 6: Marginal Costing

As we have seen, contribution is calculated as the difference between the **selling price** of a unit and the **marginal (variable) cost** of producing it. The marginal cost is an important concept – it is the cost of producing one more unit of output. It is therefore the same as the variable cost – this is because all of the fixed costs for a period have been incurred whether or not the additional unit is made. Remember that fixed costs do not change when the level of activity changes, so producing one extra unit will have no impact whatsoever on the fixed costs of the business. The only increase in cost will be the extra variable costs (direct materials, direct labour and direct expenses) incurred by making the extra unit.

Contribution can be calculated on either a **total** basis or on a **per unit** basis. Total Contribution is the contribution per unit multiplied by the number of units sold, whilst Contribution per Unit can be calculated by dividing the total contribution by the number of units sold. Both are extremely useful measures in marginal costing.

Once the direct costs of the product have been calculated and deducted from the selling price, the remainder is the **contribution per unit.**

### Activity 6.2

Calculate the **total contribution** and the **profit (or loss) for the period** for each of the following:

| Contribution per unit | Total Fixed Overheads | Number of Units sold | Total Contribution | Profit (or loss) for period |
|---|---|---|---|---|
| £12.00 | £90,000 | 9,800 | | |
| £25.00 | £220,000 | 12,600 | | |
| £28.50 | £304,200 | 9,900 | | |
| £2.20 | £65,000 | 36,500 | | |

## Chapter 6: Marginal Costing

### Break-Even Analysis

One important use of marginal costing is in break-even analysis. The break-even point for any product is the number of units which need to be sold to ensure that all the relevant fixed costs will have been covered – at this point, the business will not be making a profit, but will also not be making a loss.

We can think of this graphically:

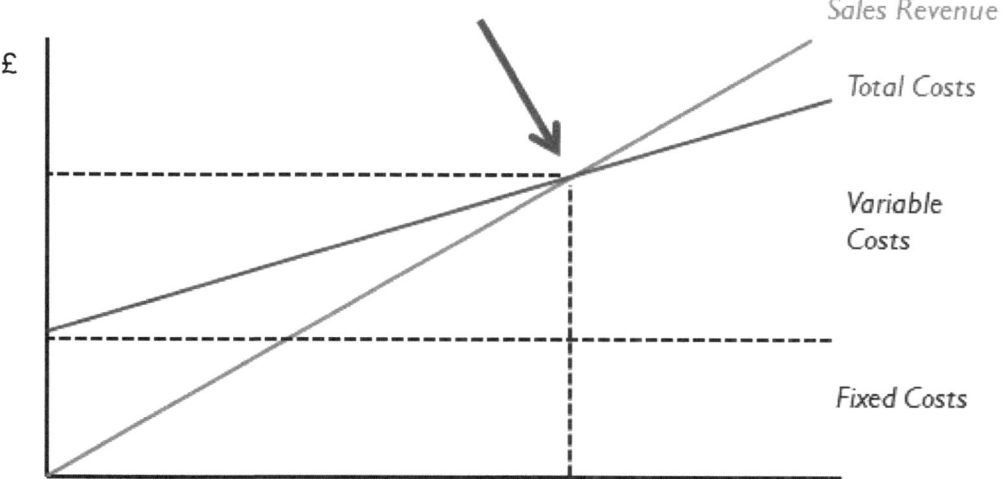

The Sales Revenue line and the Total Costs line intersect at the break-even point, indicated with the arrow. At any level of output to the left of this, the business is making a loss; once output goes beyond this level (i.e. further to the right on the graph) the business is making a profit.

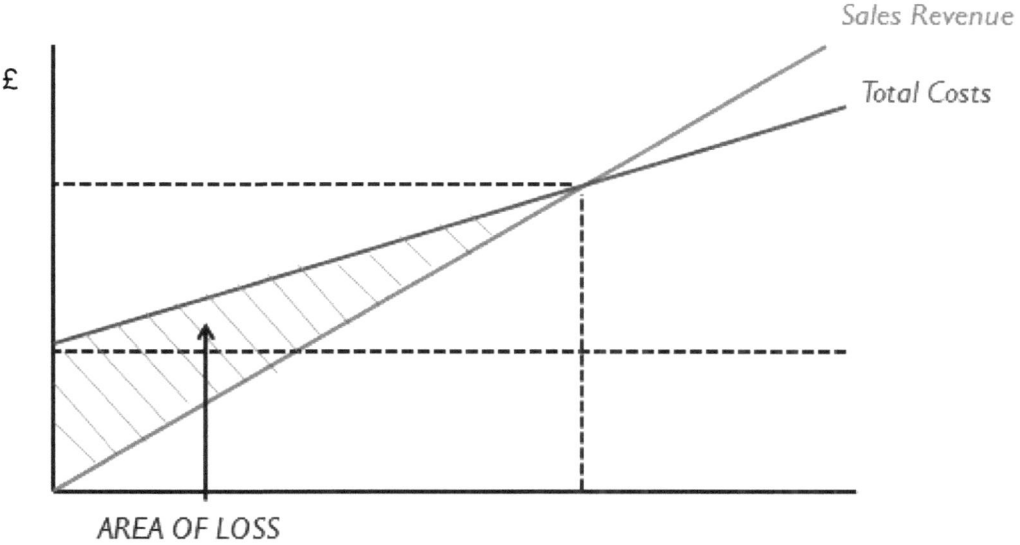

AREA OF LOSS

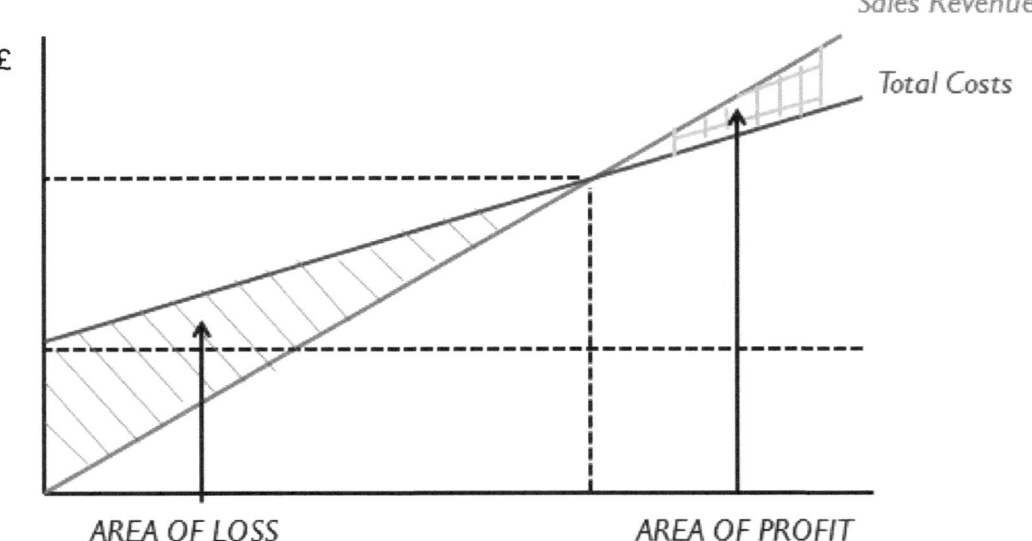

This is an important concept for businesses – particularly for new businesses or for existing businesses looking to launch a new product. It allows management to have a good idea of how many units the business needs to sell before it starts to make a profit – which will help to establish how viable the new venture is.

The break-even point in units is calculated as follows:

**Fixed Overheads**
**Contribution per Unit**

Remember that contribution per unit is the difference between the selling price and variable cost per unit, and represents how much the sale of one unit will 'contribute' towards meeting the fixed costs for the period. Therefore, by dividing the fixed overheads for the period by the contribution per unit, we can see how many units will need to be sold to cover the fixed costs for the period.

Where the break-even point is calculated in this way, a whole number may not always be derived. In this situation, the number must always be rounded up to the next whole number, rather than rounding down. This is because if the figure is rounded down, the fixed overheads will not quite be covered. If the figure is rounded up, all the fixed overheads will be covered, and the business will in fact make a profit (albeit a very small one!)

 **Example 6.3**

Logan Ltd are considering three possible new products to add to their range of board games. Each would necessitate the purchase of a new machine which would increase the fixed overheads of the business. The company can only introduce one of the new games.

# Chapter 6: Marginal Costing

Relevant information is:

|  | Game A | Game B | Game C |
|---|---|---|---|
| Increase in fixed overheads | £80,000 | £60,000 | £75,000 |
| Selling Price | £30 | £25 | £20 |
| Variable Costs | £18 | £10 | £6 |

Calculate the break-even point for each of the three games.

**Answer**

Firstly, calculate the contribution per unit.

|  | Game A | Game B | Game C |
|---|---|---|---|
| Increase in fixed overheads | £80,000 | £60,000 | £75,000 |
| Selling Price | £30 | £25 | £20 |
| Variable Costs | £18 | £10 | £6 |
| **Contribution per Unit** | **£12** | **£15** | **£14** |

**Now we can calculate the break-even point for each game:**

Game A

$$\frac{\text{Fixed Overheads}}{\text{Contribution per Unit}} = \frac{£80,000}{£12} = \textbf{6,667 units}$$

Game B

$$\frac{\text{Fixed Overheads}}{\text{Contribution per Unit}} = \frac{£60,000}{£15} = \textbf{4,000 units}$$

Game C

$$\frac{\text{Fixed Overheads}}{\text{Contribution per Unit}} = \frac{£75,000}{£14} = \textbf{5,358 units}$$

*Notice that for Game A and Game C, the break-even point is rounded up to the nearest unit as a unit cannot be sold before it is complete. Therefore, the breakeven point is not reached unit that partial unit is completed.*

The business would use this information alongside other information to help inform any decision taken about which product to launch. On first inspection, Product B appears to be the least risky of the options – it requires the fewest units to be sold before it starts to make a profit. However, if market research indicates that Product A is only likely to sell 6,000 units and Product B will sell only 3,800 units, then both of these are likely to make a loss as the fixed overheads will not be covered. Product C, on the other hand, is forecast to sell 8,000 units, and so in this case, only Product C is likely to be profitable.

# Activity 6.3

a) Which of these is the correct formula to calculate the contribution per unit?

|  | ✓ |
|---|---|
| Selling Price – Total Cost |  |
| Total Cost – Variable Cost |  |
| Selling Price – Fixed Cost |  |
| Selling Price – Variable Cost |  |
| Selling Price + Variable Cost |  |

b) Freggly Ltd is considering launching a new product. They have identified the following forecasts:

| Selling price per unit | £32 |
| Variable cost per unit | £15 |
| Fixed costs | £424,000 |

Calculate:

i. The contribution per unit.

ii. The break-even point.

If the selling price per unit was reduced from £32 to £30 per unit, and fixed costs increased by 5%, calculate:

iii. The contribution per unit.

iv. The revised break-even point.

## Activity 6.4

Calculate the **break-even point** in units for each of the following products. Round your answers up to the nearest whole number.

| Selling Price | Variable Cost | Total Fixed Overheads | Break-Even Point |
|---|---|---|---|
| £80.00 | £36.00 | £124,000 | |
| £235.00 | £108.50 | £220,800 | |
| £1,040.99 | £657.85 | £85,600 | |
| £399.99 | £198.54 | £654,350 | |

## Activity 6.5

Victor Ltd are considering three possible new products to add to their range of children's bicycles. Each would necessitate the purchase of a new machine which would increase the fixed overheads of the business. The company can only introduce one of the new bicycles.

Relevant information is:

| | Flyer | Ace | Whizzer |
|---|---|---|---|
| Increase in fixed overheads | £320,000 | £150,000 | £540,000 |
| Selling Price | £230 | £200 | £450 |
| Variable Costs | £95 | £120 | £240 |

Calculate the break-even point for each of the three bicycles.

| | Flyer | Ace | Whizzer |
|---|---|---|---|
| Break-even point (units) | | | |

The break-even point can be expressed in terms of units, and also as an amount of revenue. The break-even point in revenue is simply the break-even point in units multiplied by the selling price per unit.

 **Example 6.4**

In Example 6.3, Logan Ltd were considering three possible new products to add to their range of board games. We calculated the break-even point for each game as follows:

|  | Game A | Game B | Game C |
| --- | --- | --- | --- |
| Increase in fixed overheads | £80,000 | £60,000 | £75,000 |
| Selling Price | £30 | £25 | £20 |
| Variable Costs | £18 | £10 | £6 |
| Contribution per Unit | £12 | £15 | £14 |
| **Break-even point (Units)** | **6,667** | **4,000** | **5,358** |

Calculate the break-even point in revenue.

**Answer**

Game A

    Break-even point (units) x Selling Price = 6,667 x £30    **= £200,010**

Game B

    Break-even point (units) x Selling Price = 4,000 x £25    **= £100,000**

Game C

    Break-even point (units) x Selling Price = 5,358 x £20    **= £107,160**

Note that we can check the accuracy of the calculation of the break-even point by producing a short profit/loss statement at that level of sales.

For example, for Game A:

    Profit/Loss Statement for Game A at 6,667 units

| | |
| --- | --- |
| Sales Revenue | £200,010 |
| Variable Costs | £120,006 |
| Total Contribution | £ 80,004 |
| Less Fixed Costs | £ 80,000 |
| Profit | £ 4 |

*The £4 profit is created due to rounding the break-even point up to the nearest whole number; had we rounded it down to 6,666 units a small loss (of £8) would have been generated.*

## Chapter 6: Marginal Costing

### Margin of Safety

No business wants to break-even; doing so means that they will not make a profit. So, whilst knowing what the break-even point is can be useful for businesses, most established businesses are more interested in measuring **how far above** the break-even point they are operating. The further above the break-even volume, the more profitable they are and the less likely they are to slip into a loss-making position.

The margin of safety (in units) is calculated as:

> **Budgeted Sales (Units) – Break-even Sales (Units)**

 **Example 6.5**

Fergus Ltd is considering launching a new product, the FG56. Forecast data is as follows:

| | |
|---|---|
| Forecast sales | 28,000 units |
| Forecast selling price | £70.00 |
| Forecast direct costs | £28.00 |
| Forecast fixed overheads | £780,000 |

Calculate the break-even point and budgeted margin of safety (in units).

**Answer**

Break-even point = £780,000 / (£70 - £28) = **18,572 units**

Margin of safety = 28,000 – 18,572 = **9,428 units**

This means that Fergus Ltd could see its sales fall from the budgeted level of 28,000 to 18,572 units before it stopped making a profit. The larger the margin of safety, the 'safer' the product is.

So far, we have looked at measuring the margin of safety only in **absolute terms** – that is, in terms of the number of units. It can also be expressed in terms of revenue by multiplying the margin of safety (in units) by the selling price.

## Example 6.6

In the previous example, Fergus Ltd was considering launching a new product, the FG56. Forecast data was as follows:

| Forecast sales | 28,000 units |
|---|---|
| Forecast selling price | £70.00 |
| Forecast direct costs | £28.00 |
| Forecast fixed overheads | £780,000 |

The margin of safety (in units) was calculated as:

Margin of safety = 28,000 – 18,572 = **9,428 units**

In revenue terms, this is 9,428 x £70 = **£659,960**

One problem with calculating the margin of safety in units or revenue is that either measure does not really give an indication of the size of the business, and how this can affect the margin of safety.

Larger businesses will have a larger forecast sales volume, and therefore the margin of safety will 'seem' narrower than it does for a smaller business.

## Example 6.7

Sainsco Ltd is a large national supermarket chain, whilst John Drewery owns a small local supermarket.

Sainsco Ltd sells 20,000,000 units a week, while John sells 200,000 units. Both have a margin of safety of 150,000 units.

John will feel very secure with this margin of safety – he only sells 200,000 units a week so it would take a proportionately high fall in sales for him to hit his break-even point. However, Sainsco Ltd would be very concerned. It would be a relatively small decrease in sales for the break-even point to be reached.

It is often useful therefore to express the margin of safety in terms of a percentage of the budgeted sales level, rather than in absolute terms of either units or revenue.

The formula for this is:

$$\frac{\text{Budgeted Sales} - \text{Break-Even Sales}}{\text{Budgeted Sales}} \times 100$$

# Chapter 6: Marginal Costing

You should see that the top line of this formula (Budgeted Sales – Break-Even Sales) is actually the formula for the margin of safety in units – and so the formula can be re-written as:

$$\frac{\underline{\text{Margin of Safety}}}{\text{Budgeted Sales}} \times 100$$

 **Example 6.8**

Using the information in Example 6.7, calculate the margin of safety as a percentage for both Sainsco Ltd and John Drewery.

**Answer**

Sainsco Ltd

150,000 / 20,000,000 = 0.0075 x 100 = 0.75%

John Drewery

150,000 / 200,000 = 0.75 x 100 = 75%

In other words, whilst John would need his sales to fall by 75% before his break-even point is reached, Sainsco Ltd would only need a fall of less than 1%!

## An Elephant and an Ant – helping to explain the margin of safety

Imagine an ant is walking along a cliff top. Although it is walking quite close to the edge, it is still quite safe a few feet, or even a few inches, from the edge.

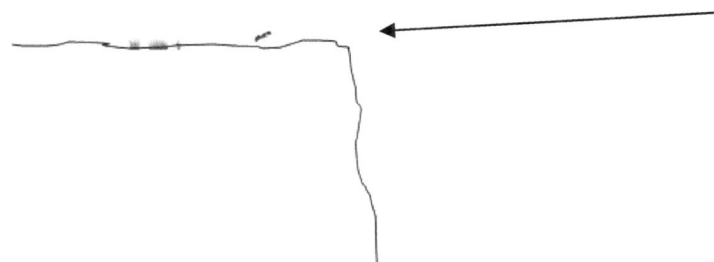

Now imagine an elephant walking along the same clifftop. The elephant, because it is much, much bigger than the ant, must keep a larger distance between it and the edge of the cliff - otherwise, it risks toppling over the edge.

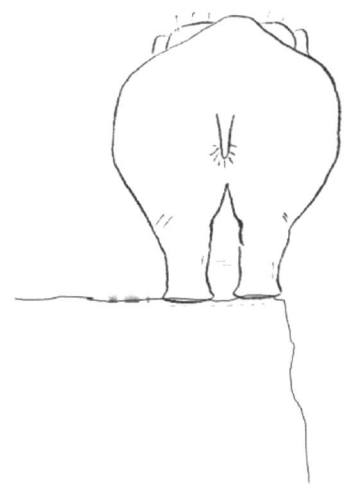

So although both animals are only a couple of inches away from the edge, the potential consequences of moving just a little bit nearer the edge are far greater for the bigger animal. And so is the case with margin of safety. Expressing the margin of safety as a percentage of the current sales gives a much clearer indication of the likelihood of slipping into a loss-making situation than simply expressing it as a number of units.

The margin of safety is affected by two factors – the current level of production and the break-even point. In turn, the break-even point is affected by both the contribution per unit and the fixed overheads. Changes in any of these will therefore affect on the margin of safety.

 **Example 6.9**

Arial Ltd makes a single product, the Kipling. In April 20X6 the direct costs of one unit were £15, and the selling price was £27. Fixed overheads were £144,000 and actual sales were 15,000 units.

a) Calculate the break-even point and the margin of safety (in units) for April.

b) In May 20X6 it is predicted that there may be a number of changes. These are:

   i. A pay increase of 5% to the workforce
   ii. An increase in the selling price from £27 to £29
   iii. A reduction in sales from 15,000 units to 12,500 units
   iv. An increase in fixed overheads from £144,000 to £160,000

For each of these, identify the effect on the break-even point and the margin of safety. You can assume that each possible change happens in isolation from any of the other changes, and you do not need to re-calculate each figure – simply state whether it will increase or decrease.

**Answer**

a) Break-even point = £144,000 / £12 = **12,000 units**

Margin of safety = 15,000 units – 12,000 units = **3,000 units**

b) The effect on the break-even point and margin of safety.

   i. A pay increase will increase direct costs, and so reduce contribution per unit. This will increase the break-even point (more units will need to be sold to cover the fixed overheads) and so reduce the margin of safety.
   ii. An increase in the selling price will increase the contribution per unit, reducing the break-even point (fewer units will need to be sold to cover the fixed overheads) and so increase the margin of safety
   iii. The reduction in sales volume will not affect the break-even point; however, it will reduce the margin of safety
   iv. An increase in fixed overheads will increase the break-even point (as more units will need to be sold to cover the increase in cost) and therefore reduce the margin of safety.

# Chapter 6: Marginal Costing

 **Activity 6.6**

Fleur Ltd makes a single product, the Mubble. In June 20X8 the direct variable costs of one unit were £26, and the selling price was £51. Fixed overheads were £210,000 and actual sales were 11,300 units.

a) Calculate the break-even point for June.

b) Calculate the margin of safety in units for June.

c) Calculate the margin of safety (%) for June to 2 d.p.

d) Identify three factors which would increase the margin of safety for Fleur Ltd.

## Target Profit

As we have seen, businesses do not want to break-even – they want to make a profit. We can use similar techniques to calculate the number of units that must be sold in order to earn a **target level of profit.**

The formula is:

$$\frac{\underline{\textbf{Fixed Overheads + Target Profit}}}{\textbf{Contribution per Unit}}$$

You will note that this is exactly the same formula as is used to calculate the break-even point but with the additional element of the required (or target) profit. This is because contribution per unit continues to add profit once the fixed overheads have been fully covered.

# Chapter 6: Marginal Costing

 **Example 6.10**

Floorbug Ltd makes remote-controlled vacuum cleaners. The selling price per unit is £300, and the direct variable costs are £125 per unit. The company's fixed overheads have been calculated as £390,000, and the company wishes to make a profit of £410,000 in the next period.

How many units must be sold to:

a) Break-even

b) Make the target profit of £410,000

**Answer**

a) The break-even point is £390,000 / (£300 - £125) = **2,229 units**

b) The sales required to make the target profit of £410,000 is:

(£390,000 + £410,000) / (£300 - £125) = £800,000 / £175 = **4,572 units**

 **Activity 6.7**

Brookes Ltd has the following budgeted costs per unit for one of its products, the Jagstack.

|  |  | £ |
|---|---|---|
| **Variable Costs** | Materials | 6.00 |
|  | Labour | 8.00 |
|  | Overheads | 2.20 |
|  |  | 16.20 |
| **Fixed Costs** |  |  |
|  | Overheads | 13.80 |
| **Total Cost** |  | 30.00 |

The Jagstack has a budgeted selling price of £64.00 and the budgeted production this month is 12,000 units.

a. Calculate the Budgeted Fixed Overheads for this product £ ☐

b. Calculate the Break-Even Volume for this product ☐ units.

# Chapter 6: Marginal Costing

Using your answers from part b above, and assuming Brookes Ltd sells 11,000 units:

c. Calculate the Margin of Safety (Units) [ ] units.

d. Calculate the Margin of Safety (%) [ ] %

e. Due to civil unrest in the country of origin of one of the key components, Brookes Ltd faces an unavoidable 5% rise in the cost of raw materials. Assuming all other costs and revenue per unit stayed the same, which of the following statements is correct?

| | ✓ |
|---|---|
| The breakeven point will decrease and the margin of safety will increase | |
| The breakeven point will stay the same and the margin of safety will decrease | |
| The breakeven point will stay the same and the margin of safety will increase | |
| The breakeven point will increase and the margin of safety will decrease | |

f. The manager of the factory which produces the Jagstack wants to earn a profit in the next month of £80,000. Using your answers to parts a-d only (i.e. assuming there is no increase in materials costs), what is the required level of sales to earn a target profit of £80,000?

The required level of sales is [ ] units.

## Contribution / Sales Ratio

Another way of utilising the same information is to consider the **ratio** between the contribution per unit and the selling price per unit. Earlier we considered a tin of baked beans which had a selling price of £1. If the direct variable costs of this tin of beans are 45p, the contribution per unit must be 55p.

The Contribution : Sales Ratio (or CS Ratio) is measured as:

$$\frac{\underline{\textbf{Contribution per Unit}}}{\textbf{Selling Price per Unit}}$$

The same calculation can be made using the total contribution and total sales revenue:

$$\frac{\underline{\textbf{Total Contribution}}}{\textbf{Sales Revenue}}$$

# Chapter 6: Marginal Costing

 Example 6.11

Boggs Ltd makes one product, the Delphin. The selling price of one Delphin is £240, and direct variable costs are £134 per unit. Calculate the Contribution : Sales Ratio.

**Answer**

CS Ratio = (£240 - £134) / £240 x 100 = **44.17%** (to 2 dp)

This effectively means that for every £1 of sales, a little over 44p contribution is earned.

We can use the CS Ratio to help with calculations of the break-even point or target profit volume.

$$\text{Break-Even Point (in £ Revenue)} = \frac{\text{Fixed Costs}}{\text{CS Ratio}}$$

and

$$\text{Target Profit Volume (in £ Revenue)} = \frac{\text{Fixed Costs + Target Profit}}{\text{CS Ratio}}$$

You should note that both of these calculations give answers expressed as revenue (i.e. in £s). To calculate the volume (in units) you should therefore divide the answer by the selling price.

 Example 6.12

Argyll Ltd makes a single product, the Yapple. The fixed overheads in 20X1 are forecast to be £400,000 and the CS ratio is 40%. The company wishes to make a profit in 20X1 of £280,000. The selling price of one unit of Yapple is £50.

Calculate the break-even point and the required volume of sales (both in units) to achieve the target profit in 20X1.

Break-even point

    £400,000 / 0.40 = **£1,000,000**

    £1,000,000 / £50 = **20,000 units**

Target Profit volume

    £680,000 / 0.40 = **£1,700,000**

    £1,700,000 / £50 = **34,000 units**

# Chapter 6: Marginal Costing

 **Activity 6.8**

Bartholomew Ltd makes different varieties of pasta. Data for two types of pasta, spaghetti and fusilli, are given below.

| Product | Spaghetti | Fusilli |
|---|---|---|
| Packets made and sold | 1,200,000 | 1,800,000 |
| Machine hours required | 6,000 | 9,000 |
| Sales revenue (£) | 720,000 | 900,000 |
| Direct materials (£) | 84,000 | 108,000 |
| Direct labour (£) | 72,000 | 126,000 |
| Variable overheads (£) | 24,000 | 54,000 |
| Fixed overheads attributable to both types of pasta (£) | 652,000 ||

Complete the table below (in pence) to show the budgeted contribution per packet for both types of pasta, and the company's budgeted profit or loss for the year from these two products (in £).

|  | Spaghetti | Fusilli |  |
|---|---|---|---|
|  | pence | pence |  |
| Selling price per packet |  |  |  |
| Less: variable costs per packet |  |  |  |
| Direct materials |  |  |  |
| Direct labour |  |  |  |
| Variable overheads |  |  |  |
| Contribution per packet |  |  |  |
|  | No. of packets | No. of packets |  |
| Sales volume (packets) |  |  |  |
|  |  |  |  |
|  | £ | £ | Total (£) |
| Total contribution |  |  |  |
| Less: fixed costs |  |  |  |
| Budgeted profit or loss |  |  |  |

Penne pasta sells for 80p per packet. It has a marginal cost of production of 30p per packet. Fixed costs attributable to this type of pasta total £312,500.

a) Calculate the sales revenue of penne pasta Bartholomew Ltd has to achieve to break-even.

| £ |
|---|

# Chapter 6: Marginal Costing

b) Calculate the sales revenue of penne pasta Bartholomew Ltd needs to achieve to make a profit of £200,000.

£ ☐

c) If Bartholomew Ltd were to sell £875,000 worth of penne pasta, what would be the margin of safety (in units) and margin of safety (%)?

☐ units        ☐ %

## Absorption Costing and Marginal Costing

The reason why contribution is such an important concept is because it focuses on the **marginal costs** of production - what it will cost the business to produce one more unit of output and how each extra unit will contribute towards meeting the fixed overheads or towards increasing the profit.

This has led to two different approaches to costing. Neither is 'correct' nor 'incorrect' - they are just two different ways of looking at the same costs.

### Absorption Costing

You should already be familiar with the concept of absorption costing. The cost of each unit of output is calculated as follows:

|      | **Direct Materials**        | X |
|------|-----------------------------|---|
| plus | **Direct Labour**           | X |
| plus | **Direct Expenses**         | X |
|      | **PRIME COST**              | X |
| plus | **Fixed Overhead**          | X |
|      | **TOTAL Absorption COST**   | X |

A share of the fixed overheads of the business is incorporated into the cost of each unit produced.

### Marginal Costing

Under marginal costing, only the variable costs are treated as product costs.

Therefore, assuming all direct costs are variable, the cost of each unit of output is calculated as follows:

|      | **Direct Materials**     | X |
|------|--------------------------|---|
| plus | **Direct Labour**        | X |
| plus | **Direct Expenses**      | X |
|      | **TOTAL Marginal COST**  | X |

# Chapter 6: Marginal Costing

No share of the fixed overhead is included within the cost of the product; instead, all fixed overheads are treated as a period cost. This means the total fixed overheads are deducted from the total contribution to determine the profit for the period.

So long as the business makes and sells the same number of units in a given period, the profit under both methods will be identical.

 **Example 6.13**

Gumball Ltd make and sell one type of product, the Yaffle. The direct cost of one unit of Yaffle is £40, and during January 20X4 the business makes and sells 12,000 units at £60 each. The fixed overheads for January 20X4 are £150,000.

Calculate the profit for January using:

a) Absorption Costing

b) Marginal Costing

**Answer**

a) Absorption Costing

The absorbed fixed overhead is (£150,000/12,000 units) = £12.50 per unit

| | | |
|---|---|---|
| Total Sales | (12,000 x £60) | £720,000 |
| Direct Costs | (12,000 x £40) | £480,000 |
| Fixed Overheads | (12,000 x £12.50) | £150,000 |
| **Profit** | | **£ 90,000** |

b) Marginal Costing

| | | |
|---|---|---|
| Total Sales | (12,000 x £60) | £720,000 |
| Direct Costs | (12,000 x £40) | £480,000 |
| Contribution | | £240,000 |
| Fixed Overheads for period | | £150,000 |
| **Profit** | | **£ 90,000** |

However, if the business either makes more units than it sells or makes fewer units than it sells, the profit for the period will be different under both methods.

# Chapter 6: Marginal Costing

 **Example 6.14 (with closing inventory)**

Continuing from Example 6.13, Gumball Ltd makes and sells one type of product, the Yaffle. The direct cost of one unit of Yaffle is £40, and during February 20X4 the business makes 12,000 units. It sells 11,000 units at £60 each. The fixed overheads for February 20X4 are £150,000.

Calculate the profit for February using:

a) Absorption Costing

b) Marginal Costing

**Answer**

a) Absorption Costing

The absorbed fixed overhead is (£150,000/12,000 units) = £12.50 per unit

|  |  |  |  |
|---|---|---|---|
| | Total Sales (11,000 x £60) | | £660,000 |
| | Direct Costs (12,000 x £40) | £480,000 | |
| | Fixed Overheads (12,000 x £12.50) | £150,000 | |
| | Total cost of production | £630,000 | |
| Less | Closing inventory (1,000 x £52.50) | £ 52,500 | |
| | Cost of Sales | | £577,500 |
| | **Profit** | | **£ 82,500** |

b) Marginal Costing

|  |  |  |  |
|---|---|---|---|
| | Total Sales (11,000 x £60) | | £660,000 |
| | Direct (variable) Costs (12,000 x £40) | £480,000 | |
| Less | Closing inventory (1,000 x £40) | £ 40,000 | |
| | Cost of Sales | | £440,000 |
| | Contribution | | £220,000 |
| | Fixed Overheads for period | | £150,000 |
| | **Profit** | | **£ 70,000** |

We can see there is a difference between the profit for the period which is calculated using absorption costing (£82,500) and the profit for the period calculated using marginal costing (£70,000). This can be explained as follows:

Under absorption costing, the fixed overhead of £150,000 is shared between the 12,000 units made in the month. However, only 11,000 units were sold, whereas 12,000 units were made. Because in absorption costing the cost of the product includes a share of the fixed overheads, the 1,000 extra units which were made but unsold are valued at £52.50 each (direct cost of £40 + £12.50 absorbed fixed overheads).

These 1,000 units are not sold in the period, and so are carried forward into the following period at an inventory value of (1,000 x £52.50) = £52,500. This means some fixed costs are carried forward in the value of closing inventory under absorption costing.

In marginal costing, however, the full cost of the fixed overheads for the period is charged against that period's profits. The unsold items which are carried forward to the following period are only valued at their **marginal** cost – i.e. 1,000 x £40 = £40,000.

Therefore £12,500 more of the fixed overheads are written off in full and charged against February's profits under marginal costing.

## Example 6.15 (with opening and closing inventory)

Continuing from Examples 6.13 and 6.14, Gumball Ltd makes and sells one type of product, the Yaffle. The direct cost of one unit of Yaffle is £40, and during March 20X4 the business makes 12,000 units. It sells 12,500 units at £60 each. The fixed overheads for March 20X4 are £150,000.

Calculate the profit for March using:

a) Absorption Costing

b) Marginal Costing

**Answer**

a) Absorption Costing

The absorbed fixed overhead is (£150,000/12,000 units) = £12.50 per unit

|  |  |  |  |
|---|---|---|---|
|  | Total Sales (12,500 x £60) |  | £750,000 |
|  | Opening Inventory (1,000 x £52.50) | £ 52,500 |  |
|  | Direct Costs (12,000 x £40) | £480,000 |  |
|  | Fixed Overheads (12,000 x £12.50) | £150,000 |  |
| Less | Closing Inventory (500 x £52.50) | £ 26,250 |  |
|  | Cost of Sales |  | £656,250 |
|  | **Profit** |  | **£ 93,750** |

b) Marginal Costing

|  |  |  |
|---|---|---|
| Total Sales (12,500 x £60) |  | £750,000 |
| Opening Inventory (1,000 x £40) | £ 40,000 |  |
| Direct Costs (12,000 x £40) | £480,000 |  |
| Less Closing Inventory (500 x £40) | £ 20,000 |  |
| Cost of Sales |  | £500,000 |
| Contribution |  | £250,000 |
| Fixed Overheads for period |  | £150,000 |
| **Profit** |  | **£100,000** |

You should note that if we looked at the whole life of a business, the total profits under both methods would be identical. This is because the opening inventory for a new business, and the closing inventory for a business which ceases trading, will both be nil. Therefore, the total profits under absorption costing and marginal costing would be the same - but it's the actual timing of the profits would be different over the life of the business.

 **Activity 6.9**

Foulsyke Ltd makes and sells 20,000 garden gnomes each week and its costs are as follows:

| Direct Materials | £18,000 |
|---|---|
| Direct Labour | £15,000 |
| Production overheads | £ 8,000 |

£1,800 of the production overheads are variable in nature; the remainder is fixed.

All direct costs are variable. The selling price of each gnome is £6.00.

a) Calculate the marginal cost of producing each gnome. ☐

b) Calculate the contribution per gnome. ☐

# Chapter 6: Marginal Costing

c) Complete the marginal costing statement on the next page to show the total contribution and the total profit each week.

|  | £ |
|---|---|
| Sales |  |
| *Less Variable Costs* |  |
|     Direct Materials |  |
|     Direct Labour |  |
|     Variable Production Overheads |  |
| Total Contribution |  |
| *Less Fixed Costs* |  |
|     Fixed Production Overheads |  |
| **Profit for the Week** |  |

d) Calculate the absorption cost of producing each gnome.

e) Complete the absorption costing statement below to show the total profit each week.

|  | £ |
|---|---|
| Sales |  |
| *Less Costs* |  |
|     Direct Materials |  |
|     Direct Labour |  |
|     Production Overheads |  |
| **Profit for the Week** |  |

## Example 6.16

WP Ltd makes large components for use in the engineering industry. In April their fixed costs totalled £350,000. The selling price for each component is £25,000 and the direct costs total £8,000 per unit. In April the company has orders for 35 components and plans to manufacture this number.

Calculate the profit made by WP Ltd using:

a) Absorption Costing

b) Marginal Costing

**Answer**

a) Absorption costing:

*Overheads are absorbed at (£350,000 / 35) = £10,000 per unit*

| | | |
|---|---|---|
| Total Revenue | (35 x £25,000) | £875,000 |
| Direct Costs | (35 x £ 8,000) | £280,000 |
| Overheads Abs | (35 x £10,000) | £350,000 |
| **Profit** | | **£245,000** |

b) Marginal Costing:

| | | |
|---|---|---|
| Total Revenue | (35 x £25,000) | £875,000 |
| Marginal Costs | (35 x £ 8,000) | £280,000 |
| Total Contribution | | £595,000 |
| Fixed Overheads | | £350,000 |
| **Profit** | | **£245,000** |

Where the amount produced each period is the same as the amount sold (i.e. there is no increase or decrease in closing inventories) the profit calculated under absorption costing and marginal costing will be the same. However, this is not the case where there are differences in the amount produced and the amount sold.

## Activity 6.10

SD Ltd makes 60,000 ceramic mugs each month and its costs are as follows:

| | |
|---|---|
| Direct Materials | £45,000 |
| Direct Labour | £20,000 |
| Production overheads | £30,000 |

£5,000 of the production overheads are variable in nature; the remainder is fixed.

All direct costs are variable. The selling price of each mug is £5.50.

In November only 45,000 mugs were sold; the remaining mugs were placed in inventory.

a) Calculate the marginal cost of producing each mug.

b) Calculate the contribution per mug.

# Chapter 6: Marginal Costing

c) Complete the marginal costing statement below to show the total contribution and the total profit for November.

|  | £ |
|---|---|
| Sales |  |
| *Less Variable Costs* |  |
|    Direct Materials |  |
|    Direct Labour |  |
|    Variable Production Overheads |  |
| Total Contribution |  |
| *Less Fixed Costs* |  |
|    Fixed Production Overheads |  |
| **Profit for the Month** |  |

d) Calculate the absorption cost of producing each mug.

e) Complete the absorption costing statement below to show the total profit for November.

|  | £ |
|---|---|
| Sales |  |
| *Less Costs* |  |
|    Direct Materials |  |
|    Direct Labour |  |
|    Production Overheads |  |
| **Profit for the Month** |  |

# Chapter 6: Marginal Costing

 **Example 6.17**

Continuing from Example 6.3, in May the fixed costs of WP Ltd again totalled £350,000. The selling price for each component is £25,000 and the direct costs total £8,000 per unit. In May, the company has orders for 32 components, but still plans to manufacture 35, putting the extra 3 units into inventory.

Calculate the profit made by WP Ltd using:

a) Absorption Costing

b) Marginal Costing

**Answer**

a) Absorption costing:

*Overheads are absorbed at (£350,000 / 35) = £10,000 per unit*

| | | | |
|---|---|---|---|
| Total Revenue | (32 x £25,000) | | £800,000 |
| Direct Costs | (35 x £ 8,000) | £280,000 | |
| Overheads Abs | (35 x £10,000) | £350,000 | |
| | | £630,000 | |
| Less Closing inventory | (3 x £18,000) | £ 54,000 | |
| Cost of sales | | | £576,000 |
| **Profit** | | | **£224,000** |

b) Marginal Costing:

| | | | |
|---|---|---|---|
| Total Revenue | (32 x £25,000) | | £800,000 |
| Marginal Costs | (35 x £ 8,000) | £280,000 | |
| Less Closing inventory | (3 x £ 8,000) | £ 24,000 | |
| Cost of Sales | | | £256,000 |
| Total Contribution | | | £544,000 |
| Fixed Overheads | | | £350,000 |
| **Profit** | | | **£194,000** |

In this example, a lower profit (equating to 3 x £10,000) of £30,000 is calculated under marginal costing. This is because the three additional units which were manufactured but not yet sold have been carried forward to the future period (as opening inventory) at their marginal cost of £8,000 each instead of the fully absorbed cost of £18,000 each. An alternative way of looking at this is to recognise that the fixed overheads have been treated as a **period cost** under marginal costing – therefore all £350,000 has been recognised in this period, whereas under absorption costing only £320,000 has been recognised, with £30,000 being carried forward into the future period.

 **Example 6.18**

Steve Reo Ltd commenced trading on 1st May 20X3. It manufactures a single product, a PA system used by DJs and other entertainers.

The following information about the business's first year of trading has been collated:

| | |
|---|---|
| Selling price per machine | £495 |
| Direct materials | £145 per machine |
| Direct labour | £80 per machine |

Fixed production overheads for the year were £1,400,000.

During the year to 30th April 20X3, 20,000 machines were made and 18,800 were sold.

Using the templates provided, calculate the profit for the year using both the absorption costing and marginal costing methods.

**Answer**

| Absorption Costing | |
|---|---|
| | £ |
| Sales Revenue | 9,306,000 |
| | |
| Opening Inventory | 0 |
| Production Costs | |
| - Direct Materials | 2,900,000 |
| - Direct Labour | 1,600,000 |
| - Fixed Production Overheads | 1,400,000 |
| Less Closing Inventory | (354,000) |
| Cost of Goods Sold | 5,546,000 |
| **Profit** | 3,760,000 |

# Chapter 6: Marginal Costing

| Marginal Costing | |
|---|---|
| | £ |
| Sales Revenue | 9,306,000 |
| | |
| Opening Inventory | 0 |
| Variable Costs | |
|    - Direct Materials | 2,900,000 |
|    - Direct Labour | 1,600,000 |
| Less Closing Inventory | (270,000) |
| Cost of Goods Sold | 4,230,000 |
| **Contribution** | 5,076,000 |
| Less Fixed Production Overheads | (1,400,000) |
| **Profit** | 3,676,000 |

**Explanation**

There is a difference in the profit figures of £84,000. This is caused because under absorption costing the value of the closing inventory is calculated including a proportion of the fixed overheads – (£1,400,000 / 20,000) = £70 per unit. So, the value carried forward into the next period under absorption costing is 1,200 units x (£145 + £80 + £70) = £354,000.

Under marginal costing the value of closing inventory is only based on the marginal costs alone (£145 + £80) = £225 per unit x 1,200 = £270,000. All of the fixed overheads of £1,400,000 are treated as period costs and deducted from profit in this period, rather than carrying forward (1,200 x £70) = £84,000 of the cost to the next period, as is the case with absorption costing.

### Activity 6.11

D. Melly Ltd commenced trading on 1$^{st}$ January 20X5. It manufactures a single product, an infra-red lamp which eases muscular injuries. The following information about the business's first year of trading has been collated:

| | |
|---|---|
| Selling price per machine | £380 |
| Direct materials | £75 per machine |
| Direct labour | £15 per machine |

Fixed production overheads for the year were £2,000,000.

During the year to 31$^{st}$ December 20X5, 12,500 machines were made and 12,200 were sold.

# Chapter 6: Marginal Costing

Using the templates provided, calculate the profit for the year using both the absorption costing and marginal costing methods.

| Absorption Costing | |
|---|---|
| Sales Revenue | |
| | |
| Opening Inventory | |
| Variable Costs | |
| - Direct Materials | |
| - Direct Labour | |
| - Fixed Production Overheads | |
| Less Closing Inventory | |
| Cost of Goods Sold | |
| **Profit** | |

| Marginal Costing | |
|---|---|
| Sales Revenue | |
| | |
| Opening Inventory | |
| Variable Costs | |
| - Direct Materials | |
| - Direct Labour | |
| Less Closing Inventory | |
| Cost of Goods Sold | |
| **Contribution** | |
| Less Fixed Production Overheads | |
| **Profit** | |

## Chapter 6: Marginal Costing

### Advantages and Disadvantages of Absorption Costing and Marginal Costing

You may be wondering how there can be two different costing systems which produce different profit figures for the same period, and yet both are valid methods. There are in fact several different costing methods, and we shall look at another one - Activity Based Costing – in the next chapter.

For now, let us examine the advantages and disadvantages of both absorption costing and marginal costing.

|  | Advantages | Disadvantages |
| --- | --- | --- |
| **Absorption Costing** | Is used as the most acceptable way to calculate profits and the valuation of inventory for inclusion in the business's financial statements.<br><br>Is an acceptable method under IAS 2 *Inventories.* | It may 'overprice' products which may lead to potentially profitable orders being rejected.<br><br>May be difficult to establish an appropriate way to allocate fixed costs between different products.<br><br>Not as useful for short term decision making. |
| **Marginal Costing** | Focuses particularly on the **contribution** which allows managers to focus on the ways in which changes in sales revenue (e.g. a price reduction) will impact on profits.<br><br>Is particularly useful for short-term decision making. | Not acceptable under IAS 2 *Inventories*<br><br>May lead to lower prices being charged and may reduce profitability |

Absorption costing is perhaps most appropriate for use in *'traditional'* industries such as manufacturing, where there is a relatively high proportion of direct costs (labour and material). It may be less useful in modern industries where there is a higher proportion of fixed costs. Further consideration of this point is given in Chapter 7, where we consider Activity Based Costing.

### Ethical Considerations

Management may wish to exert some influence over the declared levels of profit for a period. For example, they may wish to see a high profit figure if they are being judged on their performance, such as when payment of a bonus is dependent upon achieving a given level of profit. Alternatively, they may wish to declare a lower profit to ensure the organisation pays less tax, or to 'hold back' some profit to a future period. Clearly, as absorption costing and marginal costing give different profit figures for a period (so long as there has been a change in inventory levels), this provides an opportunity for the manipulation of profits. This behaviour is, of course, unethical as it lacks integrity. The management of the organisation should adopt the consistent use of its preferred method of costing, and should not be tempted to manipulate inventory figures or other valuations to create a false or inaccurate profit figure.

Profits issued through the financial statements must be produced in line with the relevant accounting standards. IAS 2 *Inventories* prohibits the use of marginal costing as a means of establishing the profit for the period; therefore, any organisation which uses marginal costing for its management accounting must make necessary adjustments when preparing its financial statements to ensure they are compliant with the standards.

## Assessment 6

You are now required to log in to your ROGO account to complete your online assessment before progressing on to the next chapter.

This page is left intentionally blank.

# Chapter 7: Activity Based Costing

**At the end of this chapter, you should be able to:**

- Identify why Activity Based Costing developed as an alternative to more traditional costing methods

- Define cost pools and cost drivers

- Share overheads between products using ABC principles

# Chapter 7: Activity Based Costing

## Introduction

Activity Based Costing (ABC) is a development of absorption costing rather than marginal costing, in that it attempts to include the full cost of fixed overheads in the cost of each unit of product. However, it attempts to apportion costs on a much more accurate basis than traditional absorption costing, which uses a relatively straightforward basis of either direct labour hours or machine hours.

Activity Based Costing (ABC) was developed in the 1980s and became extremely popular for a period of time. Developed by two academics, Kaplan and Cooper, ABC seeks to recognise the fact that the typical cost structure of many businesses has changed since absorption costing was developed over 100 years earlier.

Traditionally, the majority of most products' costs comprised direct costs (materials and labour). Production was labour intensive, and materials were relatively expensive. The rise in mechanisation (initially through production line technology and increasingly through computerisation) and the development of new materials such as plastics have reduced the proportion of direct costs. At the same time, fixed costs have (proportionately) increased; new machinery must be depreciated and insured, there are greater levels of salaried managerial staff and increased expenditure on marketing. Although every business is different, there has undoubtedly been an increase in the proportion of expenditure on fixed costs.

This has made it more important than ever to accurately cost these fixed overheads into the full cost of products. Management needs to understand what causes costs to occur – in other words what activities drive the costs. This means examining the way the business operates in a lot more detail than is necessary in traditional absorption costing.

 **Example 7.1**

Alpha Ltd operates a factory which is highly mechanised. It has been identified that a significant cost during the year is maintenance (which is a fixed cost). Using traditional absorption costing, the business has always apportioned the cost of maintenance between the three production departments on the basis of the carrying value of the machinery in each department. However, the manager of the assembly department has complained this year that she thinks it is unfair that her department is charged with a significant cost for maintenance when she knows that the maintenance staff are rarely called upon to work on the machines in

# Chapter 7: Activity Based Costing

the assembly department. This has led the senior management to investigate whether there is a more accurate way to apportion overheads to production departments and, ultimately, to the cost of the products.

## Activity Based Costing – the Basics

In Activity Based Costing (ABC), the organisation must first identify its major activities – the things it does on a regular basis. This may not be the same as its cost centres, as the focus here is on activities.

Then the organisation must identify the costs caused by these activities. Carrying out an action will cause costs to be incurred – and conversely not carrying out that action will not cause costs to be incurred.

 **Example 7.2**

Rosie runs a small business which embroiders T-shirts and other items for local businesses, sports clubs, dance troupes etc. Rosie has identified that the vast majority of the cost that she incurs in completing a job for a customer is the set-up; this is the activity of discussing the client's needs, designing the logo, programming her computer to translate the logo into an embroidery pattern and setting up the correct threads on the embroidery machine. This activity can take several hours but is essential to being able to complete the work for the client. Once these activities have been carried out, the next activity of embroidering the logo onto the T-shirts can take place – and this is relatively quick and machine intensive.

Rosie has therefore set her pricing to clients as follows:

| | | |
|---|---|---|
| Order size | 1-10 | £4.00 per item |
| | 11-30 | £3.00 per item |
| | 31+ | £2.50 per item |
| Set-up charge | | £50 (regardless of number of items) |

Without necessarily realising it, Rosie has introduced a (very simple) form of Activity Based Costing to her business. She has recognised that once her embroidery machine is running, it actually incurs very little cost. However, the real cost to her business is the set-ups – the more of these she has the greater her costs. It is much cheaper for Rosie to print 50 T-shirts with the same logo than 50 different individual T-shirts.

Of course, the example above is very simple but it helps to illustrate the basic premise of ABC – that a business must understand what causes it to incur costs. A cost driver is *a factor which causes a change in the cost of an activity.* These cost drivers will form the basis for an activity based costing system.

# Chapter 7: Activity Based Costing

| Examples of Activities and Possible Cost Drivers | |
|---|---|
| **Activity** | **Possible Cost Driver** |
| Ordering materials from suppliers | Number of orders placed |
| Handling materials (e.g. issuing from inventory to production) | Number of production runs |
| Production scheduling | Number of production runs |
| Dispatch (delivery of goods to customer) | Number of dispatches |

Costs are collected into cost pools; these are similar to cost centres but are linked to the cost drivers. Once all costs have been allocated to the cost pools, these are then apportioned to products on the basis of how often they have caused an activity to happen.

 **Example 7.3**

Pentastic Ltd makes a range of coloured ballpoint pens. In 20X7 the company expect to make 10,000,000 pens, as follows:

    6,000,000 blue
    2,000,000 black
    1,000,000 red
    750,000 green
    250,000 lilac

Pens are made in continuous production runs – that is, the 6,000,000 blue pens are made, then the 2,000,000 black pens and so on. All pens take the same amount of time to manufacture. Whenever a new colour pen is made, the production line has to be cleaned and new ink installed in the feeder tanks above the production line. This is a lengthy and costly process which must be completed to the highest level of accuracy. Any ink left in the feeder tanks or any of the tubing which feeds the production line would taint the colour of the ink and cause the new pens to be rejected at the quality assurance stage of the production process.

The annual cost of these set-ups has been established as £100,000, for five set-ups.

Under traditional absorption costing, the £100,000 expense would be apportioned on the basis of either labour or machine hours. As all pens take the same amount of time to go through the production process, this would be:

    £100,000 / 10,000,000 = **£0.01 per pen (i.e. 1p per pen).**

All pens would be charged with the same amount of this overhead.

Under ABC, however, each colour of a pen would be charged with the set-up costs they caused to be incurred. In this example, each colour of pen caused one set-up to be incurred, so that is (£100,000 / 5) = £20,000 per pen colour.

The cost per pen is therefore:

Blue:   £20,000/6,000,000   = **0.33p**
Black:  £20,000/2,000,000   = **1p**
Red:    £20,000/1,000,000   = **2p**
Green:  £20,000/750,000     = **2.67p**
Lilac:  £20,000/250,000     = **8p**

Under ABC, more of the overhead is charged to smaller production runs. The lilac pens are charged with 8p each, whereas blue pens are only charged with one third of a penny. This reflects modern manufacturing techniques which are largely designed to minimise the cost of large production runs.

Activity based costing has grown in importance in recent decades because:

(1) manufacturing overhead costs have increased significantly

(2) the manufacturing overhead costs no longer correlate with machine hours or direct labour hours

(3) the diversity of products and the diversity in customers' demands have grown

(4) some products are produced in large batches, while others are produced in small batches.

 **Example 7.4**

Winton College has two teaching departments – hairdressing and beauty therapy. Information about each is shown below:

Hairdressing

No of teaching staff = 6

Annual teaching labour costs £210,000

No of rooms = 4

Beauty Therapy

No of teaching staff = 10

Annual teaching labour cost £330,000

No of rooms = 12

The annual cost of cleaning the rooms is £20,000

Traditionally, this overhead cost of £20,000 has been allocated between the two departments on the basis of their annual salary cost:

Hairdressing: £210,000/£540,000 x £20,000    = £ 7,778
B. Therapy:   £330,000/£540,000 x £20,000    = **£12,222**
                                               £20,000

# Chapter 7: Activity Based Costing

Under ABC, the cost driver can be assumed to be the number of rooms cleaned:

| Hairdressing | 4/16 x £20,000 | = £ 5,000 |
| B. Therapy | 12/16 x £20,000 | = £15,000 |
| | | £20,000 |

Using Activity Based Costing has resulted in a different allocation of the cleaning overhead. This could be fairer; after all, the beauty therapy department has three times as many rooms as hairdressing. However, care must be taken to ensure that the correct cost driver is used. In this example, the hairdressing salons may be much larger than the rooms used for beauty therapy, or perhaps hairdressing students are typically messier than beauty therapy students. Hence the number of rooms may not be the best cost driver after all.

Using ABC allows managers to gain a better understanding of how the costs in their business behave, and what activities cause costs to be incurred. It highlights costly aspects of the process, which encourages managers to focus on how these aspects can be improved or made more efficient.

## Example 7.5

Polycellic Ltd manufactures three products, D12, K11 and P33. All of the products use similar processes. Polycellic Ltd is using activity-based costing to calculate the total cost per unit. John has identified that there are two main overhead activities, **production setups** and **maintenance checks**.

The budgeted cost of production setups for the following period is £887,040.

The budgeted cost of maintenance checks for the following period is £521,465.

The following budgeted information has also been given to you.

| | D12 | K11 | P33 |
| --- | --- | --- | --- |
| Budgeted production (units) | 39,600 | 79,200 | 118,800 |
| Number of setups | 660 | 1,056 | 1,452 |
| Number of maintenance checks | 86 | 165 | 66 |

**Step 1: Calculate the cost driver for the setups and maintenance checks.**

| Cost driver per setup | £280 |
| --- | --- |
| Cost driver per maintenance check | £1,645 |

To find the cost driver per setup will divide the total budgeted overhead attributable to the production setups by the total number of setups to find the **cost driver per setup.**

# Chapter 7: Activity Based Costing

We will use the same process for the **cost driver per maintenance check**.

£887,040 overhead / 3,168 total setups = £280

£521,465 overhead / 317 total maintenance checks = £1,645

**Step 2: Calculate how much fixed overhead should be charged to each of the products.**

|  | D12 | K11 | P33 |
|---|---|---|---|
| Total cost - Production setups | £184,800 | £295,680 | £406,560 |
| Total cost - Maintenance checks | £141,470 | £271,425 | £108,570 |
| **Total Overhead per product** | £326,270 | £567,105 | £515,130 |

We will use the cost driver to calculate the total overhead cost of each product. For example, product D12 requires 660 setups and the cost driver per setup is £280.

660 setups multiplied by £280 = £184,800. This means that £184,800 of the total production overhead for setups of £887,040 is attributable to D12. This has shared a fair proportion of the overhead to how many setups D12 uses.

Now we will look at K11. This product requires 1,056 setups for the amount of required budgeted production of units. We will use the same process to share the overhead to be charged to the products. The cost driver is £280 multiplied by the 1,056 sets ups equals £295,680. We can see a larger proportion of the total overhead has been apportioned to K11 as it requires more setups than product D12.

Lastly, we have P33, again, using the same process £280 multiplied by 1,452 setups we have a total of £406,560 allocated to P33. P33 uses the most amount of setups so using this process we can see that each of the products has been allocated a fairer proportion of the total overheads associated with the cost pool of setups.

We will complete the table using the same process for the maintenance checks to calculate the total overhead that should be charged to each of the products.

**Step 3: Calculate the overhead recovery rate per unit.**

|  | D12 | K11 | P33 |
|---|---|---|---|
| Total Overhead per product | £326,270 | £567,105 | £515,130 |
| Total units | 39,600 | 79,200 | 118,800 |
| **Overhead recovery rate per unit** | £8.24 | £7.16 | £4.34 |

We can see that the overhead recovery for D12 is much higher than for P33. This is because although the total overhead is lower for D12, it is spread over less units than for P33, whose overheads are spread over three times as many units.

Now we have calculated the total overhead recovery rate for each product we can calculate how much overhead should be charged to each unit.

**Step 4: Calculate the budgeted total cost per unit using the information given in the table below.**

| Direct costs | D12 | K11 | P33 |
|---|---|---|---|
| Direct materials | £36.00 | £54.00 | £84.00 |
| Direct labour | £14.40 | £22.20 | £26.40 |
| Direct expenses | £5.52 | £6.48 | £5.04 |
| Overhead per unit | £8.24 | £7.16 | £4.34 |
| **Total cost per unit** | **£64.16** | **£89.84** | **£119.78** |

Once we have calculated the amount of overhead to be charged to each unit, we can add them together to calculate the total cost of each unit.

## Activity 7.1

State whether the following statements are true or false.

| | True/False |
|---|---|
| Activity based costing is a costing method that has been developed to deal with the perceived weaknesses of traditional absorption costing. | |
| A cost pool is an activity that uses resources. | |
| A cost driver is a factor that causes (or drives) the level of cost. | |

## Activity 7.2

Parcore Packing Ltd manufactures three products, Jump, Drop and Reach. All of the products are labour intensive and use similar processes. Parcore Packing Ltd is using activity-based costing to calculate the overhead recovery rate.

Mark has identified that there are two main overhead activities. Production setups and maintenance checks.

The budgeted cost of production setups for the following period is £118,800.
The budgeted cost of maintenance checks for the following period is £276,000.

The following budgeted information has also been given to you.

## Chapter 7: Activity Based Costing

|  | Jump | Drop | Reach |
|---|---|---|---|
| Budgeted production (units) | 10,000 | 20,000 | 16,000 |
| Number of setups | 40 | 80 | 60 |
| Number of maintenance checks | 25 | 60 | 30 |
| Direct labour hours per unit | 2 | 4 | 5.5 |

Calculate the cost driver for the setups and maintenance checks.

| Cost driver per setup | |
|---|---|
| Cost driver per maintenance check | |

Calculate how much fixed overhead should be charged to each of the products.

|  | Jump | Drop | Reach |
|---|---|---|---|
| Total cost - Production setups | | | |
| Total cost - Maintenance checks | | | |
| Total Overhead per product | | | |

Calculate the overhead recovery rate per unit under activity based costing.

|  | Jump | Drop | Reach |
|---|---|---|---|
| Total Overhead per product | | | |
| Total units | 10,000 | 20,000 | 16,000 |
| Overhead recovery rate per unit (2dp) | | | |

Calculate the overhead recovery rate under <u>absorption costing</u>.

| Total overheads | |
|---|---|
| Total labour hours | |
| Overhead recovery rate per labour hour | |

Calculate the overhead recovery rate per labour hour.

|  | Jump | Drop | Reach |
|---|---|---|---|
| Overhead recovery rate per labour hour | | | |

# Chapter 7: Activity Based Costing

 **Activity 7.3**

In an estate agent's office, there are overhead costs incurred relating to the cost of office support for the conveyancing centre. There are two departments. Dept A has dealt with 15 property transactions with an average value of £100,000 each, whilst Dept B has dealt with 5 transactions with an average value of £1,000,000 each.

The amount of office support overheads is £100,000. This has traditionally been apportioned on the basis of the total property value dealt with by each department.

You have been asked to investigate the impact of switching to an ABC approach, with a number of transactions as the cost driver. Write an email to the manager of the estate agency explaining how a switch to Activity Based Costing will impact the two departments. You should include figures to support your answer.

| To: Manager | |
|---|---|
| From: AAT Student | **Impact of Switch to ABC** |

# Assessment 7

You are now required to log in to your ROGO account to complete your online assessment before progressing on to the next chapter.

This page is left intentionally blank.

# Chapter 8: Types of Costing Systems

**At the end of this chapter, you should be able to:**

- Choose an appropriate choice of costing system for different business sectors and individual organisations

- Record cost information using different costing systems, job, batch, contract and service costing systems

- Calculate the unit cost

# Chapter 8: Types of Costing Systems

## Introduction

Even within the manufacturing sector, there are many different types of business. Each of these will use costing systems which best reflect the nature of the business and the production process.

We will consider the following:

- Unit costing
- Job costing
- Batch costing
- Contract costing
- Service costing

Whichever method is chosen, the end objective remains to calculate the cost of a single unit of output.

## Unit costing

One of the main purposes of costing is to determine the cost incurred to produce one unit of output. Unit costing is the most common type of costing and is used in industries where the output is identical or has very few variants.

The unit cost of production is calculated as:

$$\frac{\text{Total production cost}}{\text{Number of units produced}} = \text{Unit Cost}$$

The total cost of production will include direct costs and indirect costs. However, non-production costs such as administration, selling and distribution costs may also be included to calculate an overall total cost per unit.

The appropriate cost unit will depend on the type of the organisation, for example for manufacturing it may be per product or item. Industries that produce chemicals, paper, cement or breweries may use per kilogram or litre, transport industries may use per mile and restaurants may use per meal.

## Job Costing

Job Costing is used when every job that is carried out in the business is likely to incur different costs.

Examples of businesses which are likely to use a job costing systems include:

- Engineers producing 'one-off' jobs to customer requirements
- Printers
- Web-site designers
- Accountants and solicitors
- Vehicle repairs
- Decorators, plumbers etc

## Chapter 8: Types of Costing Systems

The main steps of a job costing system can be thought of as follows:

```
Customer asks for estimate
         ↓
Job cost sheet prepared
  showing total cost
         ↓
Profit added to total cost and
 estimate sent to customer
         ↓
Customer accepts estimate
         ↓
Actual costs charged to job
          sheet
         ↓
Job completed and
dispatched to customer
         ↓
Variance between actual and
 budgeted cost is analysed
         ↓
Action take to overcome
problems highlighted by
        variances
```

The most important document is the job cost sheet; this is prepared in advance to provide an estimate to the customer. It is then also used to record the actual costs as they are incurred. Each job is given a separate Job Number, to identify it, and a separate job cost sheet is prepared for each job to estimate the costs that will be incurred.

It is usual for the estimate to be the final price charged to the customer, so if this is too low the business will bear the extra cost. This is why the variance (difference) between the actual and the budgeted costs should be analysed and, if necessary, action taken to prevent similar under-pricing in the future.

 **Example 8.1**

Glenda's Garage offers a repair service to local motorists. When the car is presented at the garage, Glenda examines the car and completes a number of checks which help to identify

## Chapter 8: Types of Costing Systems

any faults or issues. She then estimates the cost of repairs and advises the client of the likely cost (which includes an element for profit).

The job cost card for repairs to Mr Young's Vauxhall is shown below:

| Customer: Mr Young     Vehicle: Vauxhall Astra<br>Reg: TG65 5DT | *Estimated Cost* | *Actual Cost* |
|---|---|---|
| Work Required: | | |
| Replace damaged nearside wing – parts | £289 | |
| Replace damaged nearside bulbs - parts | £76 | |
| Repair minor scratches to bodywork – parts | £25 | |
| Labour – 8 hours @ £45 per hour | £360 | |
| Total direct costs | £750 | |
| Profit margin (30% of direct costs) | £225 | |
| **Total Estimated Cost to Customer** | **£975** | |

The client is advised that the cost will be £975, and agrees to go ahead with the repairs. Unfortunately, the work takes Glenda slightly longer than she expected and she also dropped and smashed a bulb before she could fit it. The cost of the parts needed to repair the minor bodywork scratches was £10 higher than Glenda expected.

The job cost card after completion was, therefore:

| Customer: Mr Young     Vehicle: Vauxhall Astra<br>Reg: TG65 5DT | *Estimated Cost* | *Actual Cost* |
|---|---|---|
| Work Required: | | |
| Replace damaged nearside wing – parts | £289 | £289 |
| Replace damaged nearside bulbs - parts | £76 | £98 |
| Repair minor scratches to bodywork – parts | £25 | £35 |
| Labour – 9 hours @ £45 per hour | £350 | £405 |
| Total direct costs | £750 | £827 |
| Mark-up (30% of direct costs) | £225 | £148 |
| **Total Estimated Cost to Customer** | **£975** | **£975** |

Glenda does not want to suddenly increase the price to the client, so must charge the same price as quoted (£975). This means that the actual profit earned on this job falls from £225 to £148, and the mark-up falls from 30% (£225 / £750) to 18% (£148 / £827). The profit margin also falls, from 23% (£225 / £975) to 15% (£148 / £975).

## Chapter 8: Types of Costing Systems

Although Glenda made a profit on this job, it was considerably lower than she expected. She will need to review this job (and others like it) to ensure she is accurately estimating the costs she includes to her customers.

### Batch Costing

Batch costing is used where the output consists of a number of identical items produced together as a batch. Examples include:

- Baking – white loaves, then croissants, then brown rolls
- Clothing – men's shirts, then trousers then jackets

Batch costing is virtually identical to job costing – except a number of identical units are produced in each batch. The batch is costed as a job and the costs collected. This will consist of a number of inputs to achieve the required output. Upon completion, a cost per unit can be calculated by dividing the cost of the batch by the number of units within that batch.

It should be noted that the number of inputs may sometimes be higher than the output achieved. This could be due to normal or expected losses in the process of production. For example, when manufacturing liquids there may be an element of evaporation when the product is heated and then cooled. For other processes, some materials may be wasted, for example, stamping circles out of square sheets, or other irregular shapes, there may be offcuts that might be of no other use and scrapped or even a number of inevitable defective units. When using this type of costing system, the total cost of inputs per batch is determined and then shared out over the number of outputted units, to give an average production cost per unit.

 **Example 8.2**

Eatwell Ltd is a catering company which makes a range of desserts for outside events such as weddings, sporting events and corporate events.

This week, Eatwell Ltd is making a batch of 1,200 individual trifles for a major sporting event. The cost of the batch is expected to be:

| Direct materials | £384 |
| --- | --- |
| Direct labour 12 hrs @ £16/hr | £192 |
| Variable production overheads per batch | £120 |
| Fixed production overheads per batch | £60 |
| Administration, selling and distribution costs per batch | £95 |
| **Total costs** | **£851** |

# Chapter 8: Types of Costing Systems

Calculate:

a) The prime cost per batch
b) The marginal cost per batch
c) The absorption cost per batch
d) The marginal cost per trifle
e) The absorption cost per trifle
f) Total overall cost per trifle

**Answer**

a) <u>Prime cost</u>

| | |
|---|---|
| Direct Materials | £384 |
| Direct Labour | £192 |
| **Total Prime Cost** | **£576** |

b) <u>Marginal cost</u>

| | |
|---|---|
| Direct Materials | £384 |
| Direct Labour | £192 |
| Variable Production Overheads | £120 |
| **Total Marginal Cost** | **£696** |

c) <u>Absorption cost</u>

| | |
|---|---|
| Direct Materials | £384 |
| Direct Labour | £192 |
| Variable Production Overheads | £120 |
| Fixed Production Overheads | £ 60 |
| **Total Absorption Cost** | **£756** |

d) <u>The marginal cost per trifle</u>

£696 / 1,200 = **£0.58**

e) <u>The absorption cost per trifle</u>

£756 / 1,200 = **£0.63**

f) <u>Total overall cost per trifle</u>

£851 / 1,200 = **£0.71**

# Chapter 8: Types of Costing Systems

 **Activity 8.1**

Webster & Weaver Ltd manufacture cans of fence and shed paint and is planning to launch a new colour called 'Urban Grey'. This will be manufactured in batches of 20,000 cans.

The following cost estimates have been produced for each batch of 20,000 cans.

|  | £ |
|---|---|
| Direct materials | 10,000 |
| Direct labour | 11,000 |
| Variable production overheads | 6,000 |
| Fixed production overheads | 4,000 |
| Administration selling and distribution costs per batch | 2,000 |
| Total costs | 367,000 |

Calculate:

a) The prime cost per batch.   £

b) The marginal cost per batch.   £

c) The absorption cost per batch.   £

d) The marginal cost per can.   £

e) The absorption cost per can.   £

## Contract Costing

Some businesses will have contracts with customers or clients which last many months or even years. For example, a civil engineering company may have contracts to build roads or bridges which last over two, three or more years. These contracts are worth many millions of pounds, and it is essential that they are costed carefully to avoid overspends.

Contract costing is essentially very similar to job costing but on a much larger and longer scale. The whole contract is usually split into 'sub-jobs' to make costing and financial control easier. Many costs which may normally be considered to be indirect, may become direct in nature as they are based entirely on site and for the purposes of that particular contract. For example, security costs for the site can be directly attributed to the contract, and so would be treated as direct costs.

Where a contract 'straddles' the organisation's year-end, it is necessary to include a value for the work-in-progress in the financial statements. Guidance on this is given in IAS 2 *Inventories* (or SSAP 9 *Stocks and long-term contracts* for organisations following UK GAAP).

Contract costing can be extremely complex, and you do not require knowledge of how to complete contract costings at this level, but you do need an awareness of the issues it raises.

## Service Costing

The focus so far has largely been on costing in the manufacturing sector. However, there are many organisations which do not operate in the manufacturing sector that still need to be able to cost their outputs.

Service sector organisations include public sector organisations such as the National Health Service and local authorities, and commercial sector businesses such as hotels or bus and rail companies.

Unlike manufacturing, where there are a series of 'inputs' (such as materials and labour) which result in a number of 'outputs' (finished products), there is no easily measurable, comparable or tangible output in the service sector.

 **Example 8.3**

Sunshine Transport Company operate a bus and coach service between Leeds and a number of different destinations, ranging from seaside resorts to local villages. They need to know how much to cost each journey at, but are having difficulty determining the costs involved and therefore establishing a 'cost per unit'.

The key problem is that there is no standard unit of output. It would be meaningless to talk about a 'cost per journey', as some journeys may be several hundred miles whereas others may only be a few miles.

The company could consider a 'cost per mile', however, this does not take into account how many passengers use each service. For example, the company might establish that its overheads for the year are £200,000 and that in total its coaches cover 500,000 miles a year. This means that the overhead absorption rate is 40p per mile. A trip to the seaside, which incurs a round trip of 150 miles, would therefore be charged with (150 x £0.40) = £60. This would then be incorporated into the selling price per ticket – so if there were 30 passengers this would be £2 per passenger (in addition to direct costs and profit margin). However, a rural service which calls at a number of local villages may entail a round trip of 60 miles, and therefore be charged with (60 x £0.40) = £24 of overheads. However, there may only be a handful of passengers, none of which would complete the full trip. At times, the coach may even be running empty of passengers between certain villages. Hence it is much harder to incorporate this cost into the ticket price. This can have the effect of making rural services

## Chapter 8: Types of Costing Systems

(which are vital for residents and businesses in the rural areas) very expensive to run, and with no guarantee of being profitable.

A more common measure used is therefore 'cost per passenger mile'. This is calculated by measuring the total number of passenger miles in the year.

For example, a particular bus route, which operates three services a week, has been measured over a year and found to have had the following passenger numbers:

| From | To | Miles | Total Passengers | Passenger Miles |
|---|---|---|---|---|
| Leeds | Fringley | 11 | 1,200 | 13,200 |
| Fringley | Gilberthwaite | 18 | 860 | 15,480 |
| Gilberthwaite | Heckley | 7 | 840 | 5,880 |
| Heckley | Rotherwick | 12 | 630 | 7,560 |
| Rotherwick | Bintly | 4 | 450 | 1,800 |
| Bintly | Leeds | 18 | 1,850 | 33,300 |
| | **Totals** | **70** | **5,830** | **77,220** |

*Note: Passenger miles are calculated as total passengers x miles*

The total number of passenger miles for this service is therefore 77,220. If this calculation was made for every route operated by the business, a 'cost per passenger mile' could be established and applied to each route, which would give a more accurate indication of the costs incurred.

Similar measures are established in other service sector organisations. Common measures include:

- Cost per passenger mile
- Cost per student hour
- Cost per resident night

# Chapter 8: Types of Costing Systems

 **Example 8.4**

A hotel has 30 rooms which are let on a 'bed & breakfast, per room per night' basis. The hotel's occupancy rate is 86%. Costs for last year were:

*Direct Costs*
| | |
|---|---|
| Cleaning and laundry | £163,300 |
| Food | £254,200 |
| Other direct costs | £ 81,300 |

*Indirect Costs*
| | |
|---|---|
| Overheads | £346,800 |
| | £845,600 |

a) Calculate the cost per room per night.

b) The hotel currently charges £120 per room per night. It wishes to increase its profits next year. Identify three different strategies which could lead to an increase in profits, and for each strategy identify one possible difficulty in implementing it.

**Answer**

a) The total number of occupied bed nights is:

   30 x 365 x 86% = **9,417 nights**

   Cost per room night is, therefore:

   £845,600 / 9,417 = **£89.80 to 2 decimal places**

b) There are three ways the hotel could improve profitability next year. These are:

   i. Reduce costs
   ii. Increase prices
   iii. Increase the room occupancy rate (i.e. attract more customers)

However, each of these will be difficult to achieve:

i. Costs can be reduced in a number of ways – the hotel could use cheaper ingredients for the breakfast, reduce the number of staff or turn the heating off. Some of these measures may be achievable without affecting customer satisfaction (e.g. by eliminating wastage) but the hotel must be careful not to cut costs in such a way that it leads to customers being dissatisfied, which could lead to a deterioration in the hotel's reputation and future visitor numbers.

ii. The hotel could increase prices, but this may be difficult if there is strong local competition. There is a danger that if the hotel increases prices potential guests may choose to stay in a cheaper local alternative.

# Chapter 8: Types of Costing Systems

iii. The occupancy rate could be increased by stronger marketing or reducing prices. However, these both carry risks. Increased expenditure on marketing will increase overhead costs, and this increase in expenditure must be more than covered by the increased number of guests it attracts. Reducing prices may increase occupancy rates but will reduce contribution per bed night and may not necessarily increase profit. However, if the marketing and/or reduced prices are directed specifically at times when the hotel knows its occupancy is likely to be low (e.g. midweek or winter) then this is likely to be a successful alternative.

## Activity 8.2

You work for a small accounting firm called Barnes & Co. You are responsible for advising a number of clients.

a) One client is Paris Ltd, a company which re-upholsters furniture. They have asked you to provide a quotation for a contract to re-upholster all the chairs and sofas in a local hotel.

The materials required have been estimated at 320 metres of fabric at £8 per metre, and 280 square metres of leather, at £24 per square metre. The work is estimated to take 60 hours, with the relevant rate of pay of £12 per hour.

Paris Ltd absorbs overheads at a rate of £5 per labour hour.

Calculate the total estimated cost of the job, and the selling price if Paris Ltd wish to make a profit of 30% of the total cost.

b) Another customer is Healthyman Clinic Ltd, a small private hospital. For the year ending 31st December 20X6, the following data is available:

- Lease costs for premises    £210,000
- Depreciation expense        £180,000
- Maintenance costs           £ 95,000
- Salaries and wages          £845,000
- Drugs and dressings         £680,000
- Administration              £380,000
- Other costs                 £585,000

The hospital has twenty beds and has an average occupancy rate of 95%.

Calculate the cost per patient bed night to two decimal places.

## Assessment 8

You are now required to log in to your ROGO account to complete your online assessment before progressing on to the next chapter.

# Chapter 9: Budgeting

**At the end of this chapter, you should be able to:**

- Flex an original budget to take into account changes in the level of output/sales
- Calculate variances against the flexed budget
- Identify reasons why variances may occur

# Chapter 9: Budgeting

## Introduction

You will learn more about the process and techniques of budgeting at the Professional Diploma level (Level 4). However, in this unit we will be looking at a number of different aspects of budgeting, including why they are important in business and how they can be used to monitor performance and identify areas where the business can improve.

## What is a Budget?

A budget is a financial plan for the future. This means it must be prepared in advance, and so by definition is guesswork based on a series of assumptions. In preparing a budget the accountant must make assumptions about:

- Activity levels in the future – how much will be produced?
- Sales levels in the future – how much will you be able to sell and at what price?
- Future costs – how much will materials, labour and overheads cost?
- Changes in strategy – will the business continue in the same markets with the same products, or will there be changes in direction?
- External factors – how will the business be affected by possible changes in legislation, politics, technology, the economy, economics and ethical issues?

It is extremely difficult to make accurate predictions about the future – and the further into the future we try to predict the harder it gets! Most budgets are produced for a period of no more than twelve months, with more detailed budgets being produced for perhaps the next three months. Hence budgeting is an ongoing process for the organisation.

Budgeting is a useful process because it can help the organisation improve the following:

- **Planning**
  Organisations use budgeting as part of the planning process. Although organisations must always be reactive to issues when they happen, it is always preferable where possible to plan activities and operations in advance. Budgeting is the financial plan which supports all the other organisational plans.

- **Communication**
  The budgeting process requires staff within different departments to communicate with each other. This can help to ensure that different departments are aware of difficulties and opportunities faced by their colleagues.

- **Co-ordination**
  This in turn supports '**goal congruence**'- the idea that everybody in the organisation is working towards the same end goals and objectives. Individuals, or departments, may sometimes be tempted to pursue their own personal objectives, which can be damaging if they differ from the organisation's goals.

# Chapter 9: Budgeting

- **Control**

  An important aspect of managing a business is to control the resources which it has available to it. Resources such as labour and materials are expensive so it is important that they are not wasted or used in ways which are not profitable to the business.

- **Performance Evaluation**

  An organisation will usually wish to understand how its managers and departments are operating. By giving managers the responsibility for keeping within the assigned budget for expenditure or income, the organisation is then able to analyse how effectively they have done this.

- **Motivation**

  Budgets can be used to motivate managers. The budget should be challenging to achieve – if it is too easy managers will not feel challenged, whilst if it is impossible to achieve then managers will simply give up. Managers who achieve their targets may receive extra rewards such as bonuses or promotions.

## What Budgets are Needed?

The organisation needs to budget all items of income and expenditure that it expects to receive or incur over the forthcoming period. Most organisations will start by producing a **sales budget**, based on the projections of the sales team. Once this has been produced, the next stage is to produce a **production budget** which forecasts how many units the business will need to make in order to meet the sales demand, along with any required changes to inventory levels. Once the production budget is agreed upon, separate **materials, labour and overhead budgets** can be produced, identifying both the quantity and the cost of each. Further **cash budgets** (showing the flows of cash in and out of the business) and **capital budgets** (showing planned expenditure on non-current assets) can then also be produced.

 **Example 9.1**

Your manager has provided you with a standard cost card. This is a breakdown of the costs of producing the budgeted output for March based on each classification of the cost. Many of these areas were covered in your Level 2 Principles of Costing.

The standard cost card is used for internal reporting and calculates the total cost to produce one unit or a number of units.

A standard cost card can be produced for one unit or the planned level of product for a particular period. Here will look at the planned production for the period.

| Direct Costs | £ |
|---|---|
| Direct Material | 120,000 |
| Direct Labour | 85,000 |
| Direct Expenses | 18,000 |
| **= Prime cost (total direct costs)** | **223,000** |
| Variable production overheads | 25,000 |
| **= Marginal production costs** (total of direct and variable costs) | **248,000** |
| Fixed production overheads | 35,000 |
| **= Absorption cost** (total production cost) | **283,000** |
| Non-production overheads (period costs e.g. selling and admin costs) | 48,000 |
| **= Total cost** | **331,000** |

Because budgets are usually produced on a departmental basis, they are often particularly concerned with showing how each department is expected to contribute towards meeting the overall fixed costs of the business.

 **Example 9.2**

Barnsley Ltd has prepared some forecast figures relating to the following month. It expects to produce and sell 40,000 units, with a forecast total sales revenue of £280,000. Direct materials are forecast to be £140,000, and direct labour to be £50,000. The budgeted fixed overheads are £60,000. Budgeted non-manufacturing overheads are £14,000.

Complete the following table showing the budgeted contribution per unit and the budgeted profit for the next period.

**Answer**

| Selling price per unit | £7.00 | (£280,000 / 40,000) |
|---|---|---|
| Less: Variable Costs per Unit | | |
|   Direct Materials | £3.50 | (£140,000 / 40,000) |
|   Direct Labour | £1.25 | (£50,000 / 40,000) |
| **Contribution per Unit** | **£2.25** | (£7.00 - £3.50 - £1.25) |
| Sales Volume (units) | 40,000 | (from question) |
| Total Contribution | £90,000 | (40,000 x £2.25) |
| Less: Fixed Costs | £60,000 | (from question) |
| **Budgeted Operating Profit** | **£30,000** | |
| Non-Manufacturing Overheads | £14,000 | (from question) |
| **Budgeted Net Profit** | **£16,000** | |

## Chapter 9: Budgeting

**Variances**

As we have seen, a budget is a financial plan, which looks forward into the future. It directs management as to how much they are able to spend on goods and services and is a reflection of the organisation's plans.

However, a budget also serves another, equally important, purpose. It allows the organisation to monitor whether it is remaining on track against its plans, by providing a benchmark against which the actual income or expenditure can be compared.

The difference between the actual expenditure (or income) and the budgeted expenditure (or income) is called the **variance.**

A **favourable variance** occurs when actual expenditure is **less** than the budget, or alternatively, when actual income is **more** than the budget. A favourable profit variance occurs when the business makes **more** profit than expected.

An **adverse variance** occurs when actual expenditure is **more** than the budget, or when actual income is **less** than the budgeted income. An adverse profit variance occurs when the business makes **less** profit than expected.

 **Example 9.3**

Rothwell Ltd has prepared the following information, showing the budgeted and actual figures for June.

Calculate the variances for each item, and identify whether it is a favourable or adverse variance.

|  | Budgeted | Actual | Variance | Adv/Fav |
|---|---|---|---|---|
| Sales Revenue | 1,250,000 | 1,274,250 |  |  |
|  |  |  |  |  |
| Direct Materials | 614,500 | 621,070 |  |  |
| Direct Labour | 204,360 | 201,850 |  |  |
| Variable Overheads | 18,580 | 20,635 |  |  |
| Fixed Overheads | 352,400 | 337,890 |  |  |
| Profit | 60,160 | 92,805 |  |  |

# Chapter 9: Budgeting

**Answer**

|  | Budgeted | Actual | Variance | Adv/Fav |
|---|---|---|---|---|
| Sales Revenue | 1,250,000 | 1,274,250 | **24,250** | **Fav** |
|  |  |  |  |  |
| Direct Materials | 614,500 | 621,070 | **6,570** | **Adv** |
| Direct Labour | 204,360 | 201,850 | **2,510** | **Fav** |
| Variable Overheads | 18,580 | 20,635 | **2,055** | **Adv** |
| Fixed Overheads | 352,400 | 337,890 | **14,510** | **Fav** |
| Profit | 60,160 | 92,805 | **32,645** | **Fav** |

## Causes of Variances

Variances can occur for many reasons. However, it is possible to think of any variance as resulting from one of two core reasons:

- A difference between the budgeted activity and the actual activity
- A difference between the budgeted cost per unit and the actual cost per unit

The following table shows some common causes of variances.

|  | Favourable Variance | Adverse Variance |
|---|---|---|
| Sales Revenue | More units sold than expected, or the selling price per unit was higher than expected. | Fewer units sold than expected, or the selling price per unit was lower than expected. |
| Direct Materials | Less materials used than expected, or the cost per kg of material is lower than expected. | More materials used than expected, or the cost per kg of material is higher than expected. |
| Direct Labour | Fewer hours used than expected, or the labour cost per hour is lower than expected. | More hours used than expected, or the labour cost per hour is higher than expected. |
| Variable Overheads | Fewer units produced (or hours worked) than expected, or the cost per unit of the variable overheads is lower than expected. | More units produced (or hours worked) than expected, or the cost per unit of the variable overheads is higher than expected. |
| Fixed overheads | Because these are fixed, they are not affected by changes in activity. Therefore, the variance must simply be caused by spending less on overheads than expected. | Because these are fixed, they are not affected by changes in activity. Therefore, the variance must simply be caused by spending more on overheads than expected. |

# Chapter 9: Budgeting

 **Example 9.4**

Match the following variances to the possible causes:

| Variance | Cause |
|---|---|
| Favourable Direct Labour | The business obtained a new order from a large customer. |
| Adverse Direct Materials | The business had budgeted to give staff a 10% pay rise but only actually gave a 3% pay rise. |
| Adverse Fixed Overheads | The business held a sale, with all prices reduced by 25%, because of unexpected competition. |
| Favourable Direct Materials | The cost of a particular material imported from Spain rose due to the weakening £ against the €. |
| Favourable Sales Revenue | The monthly rent of the business's offices unexpectedly rose by 5%. |
| Adverse Sales Revenue | The business switched to a cheaper supplier for one of its main materials. |

**Answer**

| Variance | Cause |
|---|---|
| Favourable Direct Labour | The business had budgeted to give staff a 10% pay rise but only actually gave a 3% pay rise. |
| Adverse Direct Materials | The cost of a particular material imported from Spain rose due to the weakening £ against the €. |
| Adverse Fixed Overheads | The monthly rent of the business's offices unexpectedly rose by 5%. |
| Favourable Direct Materials | The business switched to a cheaper supplier for one of its main materials. |
| Favourable Sales Revenue | The business obtained a new order with a large customer. |
| Adverse Sales Revenue | The business held a sale, with all prices reduced by 25%, because of unexpected competition. |

# Chapter 9: Budgeting

## Types of Budget

There are three main types of budgets. Rolling budgets, fixed budgets and flexed budgets.

### Rolling Budgets

A **rolling budget** is continually updated throughout the year. This update may be done monthly or quarterly.

 **Example 9.5**

Ben produces his budget for the three forthcoming months, so he can anticipate and prepare for any fluctuations in demand and production.

In January he prepares his budget for January through to March.

At the end of January Ben will review his budget and perform a variance analysis by comparing the budgeted and actual figures and revise and amend his figures for February and March if needed. Ben will then add another month to the budget for April, using his findings from the variance analysis, therefore keeping the budget to the three month scale.

Ben will continue this process throughout the year comparing and revising his figures and adding another month to his budget as the current one expires. This continuous process keeps the budget 'rolling' month on month and provides a plan and a picture of what to expect for future periods to come.

### Fixed Budgets

You will already be familiar with fixed budgets from your studies at Level 2 Principles of Costing and in the previous Example 9.3. Fixed budgets do not change with any change in activity level or output level. This type of budget assumes one sales level with no flexibility.

### Flexed Budgets

So far, we have assumed that the budgeted output (the number of units planned to be produced in the period) and the actual output (the number of units actually produced) have been the same. However, it will often be the case that actual production may be higher, or lower, than the budgeted figure. This can have a significant impact when considering the variances which arise. A **flexed budget** is in effect a reworked budget, based on the same original forecasts for costs but updated to take into account any change in activity. Fixed costs will remain the same in the flexed budget as in the original, but variable costs will need to be updated to reflect the change in activity. The flexed budget is the budget that would have been produced had the organisation known how many units would actually be sold during the period at the time when they produced the original budget.

# Example 9.6

Peregrine Ltd budgeted to make 50,000 units of output, using 100,000kg of material, in June and 2,800 direct labour hours. However, the actual production was 70,000 units. The budgeted cost per kg of material is £2 and the hourly labour cost is £16. The actual total cost of materials was £254,000 and the actual total labour cost was £52,500 for 3,000 actual hours worked. Budgeted fixed overheads are £127,500 and the actual fixed overheads are £133,900. The selling price per unit is £18.

The original budget (based on 50,000 units) is shown below, along with the actual figures.

|  | Original Budget | Flexed Budget | Actual | Variance | Adverse / Favourable |
|---|---|---|---|---|---|
| Number of units | 50,000 |  | 70,000 |  |  |
|  | £ |  | £ | £ |  |
| Sales Revenue | 900,000 |  | 1,260,000 |  |  |
| Less Costs |  |  |  |  |  |
| Direct Materials | 200,000 |  | 254,000 |  |  |
| Direct Labour | 44,800 |  | 52,500 |  |  |
| Fixed Overheads | 127,500 |  | 133,900 |  |  |
| **Profit from Operations** | 527,700 |  | 819,600 |  |  |

This would suggest that the company has made a much larger profit than originally budgeted. However, we are not comparing like with like, due to the differences in the volumes between the original budget and the actual situation. To flex the budget, we need to recalculate each figure in the original budget to take into account the revised activity level.

# Chapter 9: Budgeting

Calculate the flexed budget and the variances for June.

|  | Original Budget | Flexed Budget | Actual | Variance | Adverse / Favourable |
|---|---|---|---|---|---|
| Number of units | 50,000 | 70,000 | 70,000 |  |  |
|  | £ |  | £ | £ |  |
| Sales Revenue | 900,000 | **1,260,000** | 1,260,000 |  |  |
| Less Costs |  |  |  |  |  |
| Direct Materials | 200,000 | **280,000** | 254,000 |  |  |
| Direct Labour | 44,800 | **62,720** | 52,500 |  |  |
| Fixed Overheads | 127,500 | **127,500** | 133,900 |  |  |
| **Profit from Operations** | 527,700 | **789,780** | 819,600 |  |  |

Variable costs and revenues are flexed by dividing the original budget by the original activity (to calculate the budgeted cost per unit) and then multiplying by the actual activity level. So, in this example:

Sales Revenue    £900,000 / 50,000 x 70,000 = £1,260,000

Direct Materials    £200,000 / 50,000 x 70,000 = £280,000

Direct Labour    £44,800 / 50,000 x 70,000 = £62,720

Any fixed costs however remain fixed (as they do not change with changes in activity), and so the flexed fixed costs are the same as the original budgeted fixed costs. Care must be taken with stepped costs because where the change in activity causes a stepped cost to increase or decrease this must be shown in the flexed budget.

Having flexed the budget we can now calculate the variances:

|  | Original Budget | Flexed Budget | Actual | Variance | Adverse / Favourable |
|---|---|---|---|---|---|
| Number of units | 50,000 | 70,000 | 70,000 |  |  |
|  | £ |  | £ | £ |  |
| Sales Revenue | 900,000 | **1,260,000** | 1,260,000 | 0 | N/A |
| Less Costs |  |  |  |  |  |
| Direct Materials | 200,000 | **280,000** | 254,000 | **26,000** | F |
| Direct Labour | 44,800 | **62,720** | 52,500 | **10,220** | F |
| Fixed Overheads | 127,500 | **127,500** | 133,900 | **6,400** | A |
| **Profit from Operations** | 527,700 | **789,780** | 819,600 | **29,820** | F |

# Chapter 9: Budgeting

## Activity 9.1

Rockhopper Ltd had budgeted to manufacture and sell 100,000 bottles of "Whizzy", a fizzy drink, in the third quarter of the year. However, the actual output and sales figure was only 90,000 bottles.

All manufacturing costs are variable, except power which is a semi-variable cost with a fixed element of £15,000 per quarter, and fixed overheads.

a) Complete the table below to show a flexed budget and the resulting variances against the budget for 'Whizzy' for quarter 3, and whether each variance is Adverse or Favourable. Enter 0 where any figure is zero.

|  | Original Budget | Flexed Budget | Actual | Variance | Adverse / Favourable |
|---|---|---|---|---|---|
| Number of bottles | 100,000 |  | 90,000 |  |  |
|  | £ |  | £ | £ |  |
| Sales Revenue | 150,000 |  | 144,000 |  |  |
| Less Costs |  |  |  |  |  |
| Direct Materials | 35,000 |  | 33,500 |  |  |
| Direct Labour | 18,000 |  | 16,900 |  |  |
| Variable Overheads | 1,200 |  | 1,400 |  |  |
| Power | 20,000 |  | 24,000 |  |  |
| Fixed Overheads | 38,000 |  | 46,700 |  |  |
| **Profit from Operations** | 37,800 |  | 21,500 |  |  |

b) Referring to your figures in part a), answer the following:

i. Which of these is a possible reason for the Direct Labour Variance?

|  | ✓ |
|---|---|
| Fewer hours were worked as the number of units produced was lower |  |
| The production labour force had undertaken some training and so were more efficient |  |
| There was an unforeseen increase in the hourly rate of pay for production workers |  |
| A scheduled strike was called off at the last minute, with production workers coming in to work instead |  |

# Chapter 9: Budgeting

ii. Which of these explains the variance in power costs?

|  | ✓ |
|---|---|
| The fixed cost increased from £12,000 to £14,000, but the variable cost remained the same |  |
| The fixed cost remained the same, but the variable cost increased by 5p per unit |  |
| The fixed cost and variable cost were both the same as budgeted |  |
| The fixed cost increased by £1,000 and the variable cost increased by 5p per unit |  |

## Calculating variances as a percentage flexed budget

In order to highlight the significance of a variance it is possible to express each variance as a percentage of its flexed budget amount.

### Example 9.7

Materials were budgeted to be £500,000 for output of 20,000 units. Actual production was 24,000 units and the cost of materials at that level was £648,000.

Firstly we need calculate the flexed budget cost for material based on the actual level of output.

£500,000 ÷ 20,000 units = £25.00 per unit x 24,000 units = £600,000.

Actual cost of material £648,000 – flexed budget cost of £600,000 = £48,000 adverse

To express this as a percentage divide the variance by the flexed budget and multiply by 100.

**Workings: £48,000 ÷ £600,000 x 10 = 8%**

### Activity 9.2

a) The budget for production supervisors' costs for a period for a business at an activity level of 180,000 units is £18,000. One production supervisor is required for every 40,000 units of production. If actual production is 220,000 units, what figure would appear in the flexed budget for production supervisors' costs?

# Chapter 9: Budgeting

b) The budgeted production overhead for a business is £15,800 at an activity level of 2,000 units and £19,950 at an activity level of 3,000 units. If the actual activity level is 2,600 units what is the flexed budget figure for production overhead?

c) The following operating statement has been prepared using marginal costing and a flexed budget. Calculate the variance for each line in the operating statement in £ (showing whether it is favourable or adverse) and as a percentage of the flexed budget. Show your percentage to 2 decimal places.

| Operating Statement for November | Flexed Budget £ | Actual £ | Variance £ (F/A) | Variance % |
|---|---|---|---|---|
| Turnover | 144,000 | 132,000 | | |
| **Variable Costs** | | | | |
| Materials | 48,000 | 45,000 | | |
| Labour | 24,000 | 28,500 | | |
| Packaging | 12,000 | 12,000 | | |
| Power | 9,000 | 8,850 | | |
| Contribution | 51,000 | 37,650 | | |
| **Fixed Costs** | | | | |
| Power | 3,750 | 4,500 | | |
| Depreciation | 5,250 | 4,950 | | |
| Sales & Marketing | 7,500 | 7,500 | | |
| Administration | 9,750 | 9,750 | | |
| **Operating Profit** | 24,750 | 10,950 | | |

 **Activity 9.3**

The operating statement that forms part of the following table has been produced using the original fixed budget (based on production and sales of 90,000 units) and the actual costs which occurred when 80,000 units were produced and sold.

a) Using the data in the operating statement, together with the notes shown below, complete the flexed budget and variances in the appropriate columns in the table.

|  | Original Budget | Actual | Flexed Budget | Variance (F / A) |
|---|---|---|---|---|
| **Volume (units)** | 90,000 | 80,000 | 80,000 |  |
|  | £ | £ | £ | £ |
| **Turnover** | 1,440,000 | 1,320,000 | 1,280,000 | 40,000 F |
| **Costs** |  |  |  |  |
| **Materials** | 472,500 | 432,000 | 420,000 | 12,000 A |
| **Labour** | 270,000 | 232,000 | 240,000 | 8,000 F |
| **Distribution** | 135,000 | 100,000 | 120,000 | 20,000 F |
| **Energy** | 71,000 | 67,000 | 64,000 | 3,000 A |
| **Equipment hire** | 8,000 | 7,400 | 7,000 | 400 A |
| **Depreciation** | 16,000 | 19,400 | 16,000 | 3,400 A |
| **Marketing** | 27,000 | 15,000 | 27,000 | 12,000 F |
| **Administration** | 18,900 | 21,200 | 18,900 | 2,300 A |
| **Total Costs** | 1,018,400 | 894,000 | 912,900 | 18,900 F |
|  |  |  |  |  |
| **Operating Profit** | 421,600 | 426,000 | 367,100 | 58,900 F |

**Notes**
- Material, labour and distribution costs are variable
- The budget for energy is semi-variable. The fixed element is £8,000
- Equipment hire budget is based on a cost of £1,000 for every 12,000 units or fewer
- Depreciation, marketing and administration costs are fixed

b) Write a short note to the finance director identifying **one** possible reason for each variance you have calculated.

# Chapter 9: Budgeting

## Using Flexed Budgets for Different Scenarios

Using flexed budgets to calculate alternative or 'best case' and 'worst case' scenarios can be a very valuable technique for businesses to use when planning for future periods. This can be particularly useful when considering different outcomes such as if sales are expected to increase or decrease.

## Example 9.8

Your manager has given you the following information on the expected outcomes of product ST100 for the following month. You have completed a budgeted operating statement for 30,000 units which has resulted in a budgeted profit of £16,500. Your manager has asked you to prepare the same budget but based on a 'worst case' scenario by selling 10,000 units and a 'best case' scenario of 50,000 units.

### Required

Flex the budgeted operating statement to reflect the different sales of units.

| Units | 10,000 | 30,000 | 50,000 |
|---|---|---|---|
| Sales revenue | | £240,000 | |
| **Variable costs:** | | | |
| Material | | £12,000 | |
| Labour | | £195,000 | |
| **Contribution** | | **£33,000** | |
| | | | |
| Fixed costs | | £16,500 | |
| **Total costs** | | **£223,500** | |
| | | | |
| **Profit** | | **£16,500** | |

### Answer

| Units | 10,000 | 30,000 | 50,000 |
|---|---|---|---|
| Sales revenue | £80,000 | £240,000 | £400,000 |
| **Variable costs:** | | | |
| Material | £4,000 | £12,000 | £20,000 |
| Labour | £65,000 | £195,000 | £325,000 |
| **Contribution** | **£11,000** | **£33,000** | **£55,000** |
| | | | |
| Fixed costs | £16,500 | £16,500 | £16,500 |
| **Total costs** | **£85,500** | **£223,500** | **£361,500** |
| | | | |
| **Profit** | **-£5,500** | **£16,500** | **£38,500** |

Using flexed budgets for different scenarios can be a vital tool to ensure the business is profitable. We can see that in the worst case scenario of 10,000 units, the business will make a **loss** of £5,500. When we look at the best case scenario, the profit has increased to £38,500 which is three times the amount of profit for the standard budgeted units of 30,000 units.

## Activity 9.4

Your manager has given you the following information on the expected outcomes of product T980 for the following quarter. You have completed a budgeted operating statement for 40,000 units which has resulted in a budgeted profit of £67,600. Your client has asked you to prepare the same budget but based on a 'worst case' scenario by selling 20,000 units and a 'best case' scenario of 65,000 units.

Flex the budgeted operating statement to reflect the different sales of units.

| Units | 20,000 | 40,000 | 65,000 |
|---|---|---|---|
|  |  |  |  |
| Sales revenue |  | £480,000 |  |
|  |  |  |  |
| **Variable costs:** |  |  |  |
| Material |  | £104,000 |  |
| Labour |  | £240,000 |  |
|  |  |  |  |
| **Contribution** |  | £136,000 |  |
|  |  |  |  |
| Fixed costs |  | £68,400 |  |
|  |  |  |  |
| **Total costs** |  | £412,400 |  |
|  |  |  |  |
| **Profit** |  | £67,600 |  |

# Chapter 9: Budgeting

 **Example 9.9**

You have already prepared a draft operating budget for 2,000 units of Product MW1 for the following month.

|  | 2,000 units |
|---|---|
| Revenue | £80,000 |
| Variable material costs | £24,000 |
| Variable labour costs | £20,000 |
| **Contribution** | **£36,000** |
| Fixed costs | £15,000 |
| **Forecast profit / (loss)** | **£21,000** |

Sales volume for this month is expected to increase by 500 units. You have been asked by your manager to prepare a further draft budget for 2,500 units.

**Flex the current budget of 2,000 units to the new budgeted volume of 2,500 units to calculate the forecast profit or loss.**

|  | 2,000 units | 2,500 units |
|---|---|---|
| Revenue | £80,000 | £100,000 |
| Variable material costs | £24,000 | £30,000 |
| Variable labour costs | £20,000 | £25,000 |
| **Contribution** | **£36,000** | **£45,000** |
| Fixed costs | £15,000 | £15,000 |
| **Forecast profit / (loss)** | **£21,000** | **£30,000** |

We can see that if we produce 2,500 units then the budgeted profit will increase from £21,000 to £30,000.

Your manager has recently reviewed the product MW1 and has found some potential savings on materials and labour when the production reaches 3,000 units. This would allow the business to potentially sell the product at a lower selling price to compete with a rival company and attract more customers. It has been proposed that:

- Revenue per unit will decrease by 10%
- Material costs will decrease by £2 per unit
- Labour costs will decrease by 5%
- Fixed costs will increase by £2,000

# Chapter 9: Budgeting

You have completed the table below to show the forecast profit or loss for the manufacture and sale of 3,000 units, taking into account the information given above.

|  | 2,000 units | 2,500 units | 3,000 units |
|---|---|---|---|
| Revenue | £80,000 | £100,000 | £108,000 |
| Variable material costs | £24,000 | £30,000 | £30,000 |
| Variable labour costs | £20,000 | £25,000 | £28,500 |
| **Contribution** | **£36,000** | **£45,000** | **£49,500** |
| Fixed costs | £15,000 | £15,000 | £17,000 |
| **Forecast profit / (loss)** | **£21,000** | **£30,000** | **£32,500** |

*Current selling price per unit: £40 less 10% = £36 new selling price per unit*
*Current material cost per unit: £12 - £2 = £10 new material cost per unit*
*Current labour cost per unit: £10 less 5% = £9.50 new labour cost per unit*

Overall, we can see that although we have decreased the costs of material and labour, by decreasing the selling price per unit and taking into account the additional fixed costs this has quite a significant impact on the forecasted profit when we compare the increase in profit from producing 2,000 units and 2,500 units.

 **Activity 9.5**

The management accountant of SYK Ltd has been looking at revising some of the costs and the selling price of product WH88.

At 4,000 units product WH88 is showing a forecasted loss. The management accountant has estimated the following changes.

At 6,000 units:

- The revenue will decrease by 8%
- The material cost will decrease by £2
- The labour cost will decrease by 5%
- The fixed costs will decrease by £3,000

# Chapter 9: Budgeting

Complete the table to show the forecast profit / loss for the 5,000 units and 6,000 units. Enter your answers to the nearest whole pound. Enter any loss as a minus figure.

|  | 4,000 units | 5,000 units | 6,000 units |
|---|---|---|---|
| Revenue | £200,000 | £250,000 | £300,000 |
| Variable material costs | £80,000 | £100,000 | £120,000 |
| Variable labour costs | £64,000 | £80,000 | £96,000 |
| **Contribution** | **£56,000** | **£70,000** | **£84,000** |
| Fixed costs | £58,000 | £58,000 | £58,000 |
| **Forecast profit / (loss)** | -£2,000 | £12,000 | £26,000 |

 **Assessment 9**

You are now required to log in to your ROGO account to complete your online assessment before progressing on to the next chapter.

# Chapter 10: Cash Management

**At the end of this chapter, you should be able to:**

- Understand the difference between cash and profit
- Produce a cash budget
- Understand the different funding methods for the acquisition of non-current assets
- Understand the importance of liquidity and actions to be taken to improve cash flow
- Calculate working capital using ratios

# Chapter 10: Cash Management

## Introduction

Cash is one of the most important elements of any business. In fact, it could even be considered the single most important aspect to remain solvent. Solvency means having enough cash to pay current liabilities - in other words, being able to pay for raw materials, pay the bills and wages etc and continue to make a profit.

Without cash, a business is unable to meet its financial obligations; it will be unable to pay its employees, suppliers, rent or other obligations such as interest and taxation. In this situation, the business may become insolvent.

There have been many large, well-known companies in recent years going out of business as a result of not being able to pay their debts as they fall due, for example, Thomas Cook, Toys R Us, Blockbusters and Maplins.

When an organisation becomes insolvent (i.e., doesn't have sufficient cash to pay its bills) it must cease trading, meaning staff lose their jobs and owners of the business often suffer severe financial losses. Many businesses that cease trading are in fact profitable, but fail because of solvency issues – i.e., they have insufficient cash in the business to support their activities. Remaining solvent at all times is important for any organisation.

To ensure the business does not run out of cash it is important to:

- Monitor trade receivable balances to ensure all customers pay the money they owe on or before the date they are due.
- Complete bank reconciliations regularly so they know exactly how much money there is in the bank and to ensure records are correct.
- Plan for the short term and monitor liquidity risks.
- Reduce interest and debt.

Businesses need to look forward and plan what is happening in the future to ensure that there is enough cash available for the day to day running of the business. A business would plan its cash flow over a period of time to foresee any potential problem in the coming months or near future. For example, if the business knows that there will be a month coming up when there will not be much cash coming into the business, then it knows that it will need to be careful what it spends that month or plan for that event by way of an overdraft or a form of short term lending to keep it going.

The key issue here is that cash flows do not necessarily occur at the same time as the transaction to which they relate. In the functional budgets, an organisation will budget for the sales and purchases it expects to make in a given period. Similarly, expenses are also budgeted for on an accrual basis – matched to the period in which the expense is incurred, rather than when it is paid for. This can lead to an organisation encountering cash flow difficulties in certain periods, even though they appear to be very profitable.

## Chapter 10: Cash Management

### The Cash Budget

A **cash budget** is an estimation of cash inflows and outflows over a specific period, for example, weekly, monthly, or quarterly. A cash budget enables management to monitor likely periods where the business may have a cash surplus (which could then be used to pay off debts or be invested) and when it will have a cash shortfall. If a cash shortfall can be predicted, the organisation may be able to take alternative action (such as arranging an overdraft with the bank or delaying a capital acquisition) to minimise the impact of the deficit.

The cash budget is usually prepared after the functional budgets have been produced. This is because it will be based on information contained within the functional budgets, such as sales, material purchases, labour costs etc.

In a cash budget, we are only looking at the actual movements (in and out) of cash – which introduces the issue of '**lagging**' – where payment or receipt of cash takes place in a different period to the transaction itself.

The cash budget will also record expected cash inflows and outflows for items such as overhead costs, sale or purchase of non-current assets (e.g. equipment or vehicles), new loans taken out (which is a cash inflow) or loans repaid (a cash outflow), taxation payments and interest payments. In fact, anything which leads to cash entering or leaving the business should be included.

### Including the Bank Balance in the Cash Budget

As well as seeing when the cash flows are forecast to happen, management also needs to know what the overall impact of these cash flows will be on the company's bank balance. In particular, they will be interested in identifying periods where there are likely to be significant cash surpluses (so that more efficient use of the cash can be made) and cash deficits (to avoid potentially being unable to meet financial obligations).

The change in an organisation's bank balance between the start of the period and the end can be measured in terms of its cash inflows and outflows. Every time cash flows into the business (receipts) the bank balance will increase, whilst every time a payment is made (a cash outflow) the bank balance will decrease.

Therefore:

| | |
|---|---|
| **Bank Balance at Start of Period** | X |
| *Plus* **Receipts** | X |
| *Minus* **Payments** | (X) |
| **Bank Balance at End of Period** | X |

> **Cash Inflows *minus* Cash Outflows = Net Cash Flow.**
>
> If receipts are more than payments, net cash flow is positive. If payments are more than receipts, net cash flow is negative

This is incorporated into the cash budget by including the bank balances at the start and the end of the month at the bottom. The net cash flow (total receipts *less* total payments) is also often shown.

The cash budget therefore looks like this:

|  | January | February | March | April |
|---|---|---|---|---|
| **Cash Receipts (inflows)** |  |  |  |  |
| - From Cash Sales |  |  |  |  |
| - From Credit Customers |  |  |  |  |
| - New Loans |  |  |  |  |
| - Sale of Non-Current Asset |  |  |  |  |
| **Total Receipts** |  |  |  |  |
| **Cash Payments (outflows)** |  |  |  |  |
| - Cash Purchases |  |  |  |  |
| - Credit Purchases |  |  |  |  |
| - Salaries and Wages |  |  |  |  |
| - Overhead Costs |  |  |  |  |
| - Purchase of Non-Current Assets |  |  |  |  |
| - Repayment of Loans |  |  |  |  |
| - Dividends / Drawings |  |  |  |  |
| **Total Payments** |  |  |  |  |
|  |  |  |  |  |
| **Opening Bank Balance** |  |  |  |  |
| **Net Cash Flow** |  |  |  |  |
| **Closing Bank Balance** |  |  |  |  |

 **Example 10.1**

Erika runs a profitable small business. She has some plans for the next few months and wants to see the effect it will have on her cash flow. She has asked you to complete the cash flow forecast for January to April. She has provided you with the following budgeted information.

| Cash receipts | January | February | March | April |
|---|---|---|---|---|
| Cash sales | 58,600 | 63,000 | 66,400 | 68,600 |

| Cash payments | January | February | March | April |
|---|---|---|---|---|
| Cash purchases | 43,500 | 42,500 | 44,500 | 46,300 |

Salaries and wages are £8,800 per month.

General Overheads are expected to be £7,800 per month.

In January Erika will pay an annual insurance premium of £4,400. This is to be included in general overheads.

In February Erika expects to take out a loan of £30,000 to purchase a new drilling machine. She will repay £2,500 per month starting the following month.

In March Erika will purchase the new drilling machine for £35,000.

In April Erika will purchase a second hand delivery van for £15,000. She expects to sell the old van for £2,500 in the same month.

Erika plans to take £2,500 per month as drawings.

The closing bank balance in December was £20,000.

|  | January | February | March | April |
|---|---|---|---|---|
| **Cash Receipts** | £ | £ | £ | £ |
| From Cash Sales | 58,600 | 63,000 | 66,400 | 68,600 |
| Capital / New Loans |  | 30,000 |  |  |
| Sale of Non-Current Asset |  |  |  | 2,500 |
| **Total Receipts** | **58,600** | **93,000** | **66,400** | **71,100** |
|  |  |  |  |  |
| **Cash Payments** |  |  |  |  |
| Cash purchases | 43,500 | 42,500 | 44,500 | 46,300 |
| Salaries and Wages | 8,800 | 8,800 | 8,800 | 8,800 |
| General Overhead Costs | 12,200 | 7,800 | 7,800 | 7,800 |
| Purchase of Non-Current Assets |  |  | 35,000 | 15,000 |
| Repayment of Loans |  |  | 2,500 | 2,500 |
| Drawings | 2,500 | 2,500 | 2,500 | 2,500 |
| **Total Payments** | **67,000** | **61,600** | **101,100** | **82,900** |
|  |  |  |  |  |
| **Opening Bank Balance** | 20,000 | 11,600 | 43,000 | 8,300 |
| **Net Cash Flow** | - 8,400 | 31,400 | - 34,700 | - 11,800 |
| **Closing Bank Balance** | 11,600 | 43,000 | 8,300 | - 3,500 |

## Chapter 10: Cash Management

**Notes:**

The opening bank balance of £20,000 at the start of January will be the closing bank balance from the end of December. The closing bank balance at the end of January will be the opening balance for the beginning of February and so on.

General Overhead costs are to be £7,800 per month however, in January there is the additional cost of the annual insurance premium of £4,400 making the total general overhead costs that month £12,200.

Closing balance in April: we can see that the balance is negative. This would mean that in April Erika will not have enough cash coming into the business to cover the payments going out. This allows us to foresee that in April Erika would need to plan or prepare for the shortfall during this month. Erika could delay the purchase of the van or she would need to use her overdraft, if she has one, or speak with her bank.

## Example 10.2

Johann runs a successful electrical goods business, with various outlets in the local region. Johann has a mixture of sales to the public and trade customers. Trade customers are given credit terms and pay in the following month. Purchases are made by cash and on credit. Purchases made on credit are also paid for in the month after purchase.

Due to shortages and problems with importing goods from China, he believes that the cost of purchasing goods for resale will increase until the importing issues are resolved in April. Johann has found a temporary supplier who is much more expensive but is based in the UK. This has raised some concerns for Johann and he wants to see what effect these additional short-term costs will have on his cash flow over the next few months. He has asked you to complete the cash flow forecast for January to April. He has provided you with the following budgeted information.

| Cash receipts | January | February | March | April |
| --- | --- | --- | --- | --- |
| Cash sales | 40,000 | 42,000 | 45,000 | 48,000 |
| Credit customers | 77,200 | 84,000 | 87,800 | 89,200 |

| Cash payments | January | February | March | April |
| --- | --- | --- | --- | --- |
| Cash purchases | 12,200 | 14,600 | 16,200 | 17,300 |
| Credit purchases | 79,600 | 80,600 | 59,100 | 58,400 |

Sales to credit customers in December were £78,000.

Purchases made on credit in December were £75,100.

Salaries and wages are £24,200 per month.

## Chapter 10: Cash Management

General Overheads are expected to be £17,500 per month.

In January Johann will pay an annual insurance premium of £1,600. This is to be included in general overheads.

Johann plans to take £2,700 per month as drawings.

The closing bank balance in December was £45,000.

|  | January | February | March | April |
|---|---|---|---|---|
| **Cash Receipts** | £ | £ | £ | £ |
| From Cash Sales | 40,000 | 42,000 | 45,000 | 48,000 |
| From Credit Customers | 78,000 | 77,200 | 84,000 | 87,800 |
| Capital / New Loans |  |  |  |  |
| Sale of Non-Current Asset |  |  |  |  |
| **Total Receipts** | **118,000** | **119,200** | **129,000** | **135,800** |
|  |  |  |  |  |
| **Cash Payments** |  |  |  |  |
| Cash purchases | 12,200 | 14,600 | 16,200 | 17,300 |
| Credit purchases | 75,100 | 79,600 | 80,600 | 59,100 |
| Salaries and Wages | 24,200 | 24,200 | 24,200 | 24,200 |
| General Overhead Costs | 19,100 | 17,500 | 17,500 | 17,500 |
| Purchase of Non-Current Assets |  |  |  |  |
| Repayment of Loans |  |  |  |  |
| Drawings | 2,700 | 2,700 | 2,700 | 2,700 |
| **Total Payments** | **133,300** | **138,600** | **141,200** | **120,800** |
|  |  |  |  |  |
| **Opening Bank Balance** | 45,000 | 29,700 | 10,300 | - 1,900 |
| **Net Cash Flow** | - 15,300 | - 19,400 | - 12,200 | 15,000 |
| **Closing Bank Balance** | 29,700 | 10,300 | - 1,900 | 13,100 |

**Notes:**

The information tells us that the sales to credit customers are paid in the **following month**. This means that the sales to credit customers in December, will not be received until January. Sales made to credit customers in January will not be received until February, and so on.

Purchases made on credit are **also paid the following month**. This means that the credit purchases made in December will not be paid until January. Credit purchases made in January

# Chapter 10: Cash Management

will not be paid until February, and so on. This is an example of '**lagging**' – where payment or receipt of cash takes place in a different period to the transaction itself.

As we have seen in the previous example, the opening bank balance of £45,000 at the start of January will be the closing bank balance from the end of December. The closing bank balance at the end of January will be the opening balance for the beginning of February and so on.

General Overhead costs are to be £17,500 per month however, in January there is the additional cost of the annual insurance premium of £1,600 making the total general overhead costs that month £19,100.

Closing balance in March: we can see that the balance is negative. This would mean that in March, Johann will not have enough cash coming into the business to cover the payments going out. This allows us to foresee that in March Johann would need to plan or prepare for the shortfall during this month. We can also see that Johann has a large shortfall of cash each month whilst using the new supplier, but this increases in April when trading is expected to return to normal. This significant increase in costs is concerning and Johann should re-evaluate the situation and consider finding an alternative UK supplier.

 **Activity 10.1**

Your manager has asked you to complete the cash flow forecast for a client called Jane from April to July. She runs a small catering business and has provided you with the following information.

Salaries and wages are £7,500 per month.

General Overheads are expected to be £3,500 per month.

During May the business will renew the annual insurance premium for vehicles and pay £300. This is to be included in general overheads.

In May the business expects to take out a loan of £10,000 to purchase a new van. The repayments for the loan will start from the following month at £230 per month.

In June the business will purchase the new van for £10,000 and sell the old van for £2,500.

Jane expects to take £2,000 per month as drawings.

The closing bank balance in March was £12,000.

Complete the cash flow forecast on the following page using the information above.

|  | April | May | June | July |
|---|---|---|---|---|
| Cash Receipts | £ | £ | £ | £ |
| - From Cash Sales | 2,500 | 2,600 | 2,400 | 2,500 |
| - From Credit Customers | 24,500 | 26,200 | 27,100 | 29,100 |
| - New Loans |  |  |  |  |
| - Sale of Non-Current Asset |  |  |  |  |
| Total Receipts |  |  |  |  |
| Cash Payments |  |  |  |  |
| - Purchases | 17,600 | 20,800 | 19,600 | 22,500 |
| - Salaries and Wages |  |  |  |  |
| - Overhead Costs |  |  |  |  |
| - Purchase of Non-Current Assets |  |  |  |  |
| - Repayment of Loans |  |  |  |  |
| - Drawings |  |  |  |  |
| Total Payments |  |  |  |  |
|  |  |  |  |  |
| Opening Bank Balance |  |  |  |  |
| Net Cash Flow |  |  |  |  |
| Closing Bank Balance |  |  |  |  |

 ## Activity 10.2

Samara runs a profitable interior design business. She is planning to purchase a new embroidery machine in July for £20,000. She has asked you to complete a cash flow forecast to help her decide whether or not she will need to take out a small loan to help pay for the purchase of the new machine. She has provided you with you following information.

| Cash receipts | June | July | August | September |
|---|---|---|---|---|
| Cash sales | 13,800 | 16,200 | 15,800 | 16,100 |
| Credit customers | 41,200 | 48,300 | 43,600 | 46,300 |

# Chapter 10: Cash Management

| Cash payments | June | July | August | September |
|---|---|---|---|---|
| Credit purchases | 36,200 | 25,600 | 26,400 | 27,400 |

Samara makes a mixture of cash and credit sales. Credit sales are received in the following month. All purchases are made on credit and are paid in the month after purchase.

Sales to credit customers in May were £40,500.

Purchases made on credit in May were £27,500.

Salaries and wages are £16,500 per month.

General Overheads are expected to be £3,560 per month. This is expected to increase by £200 per month from the start of August onwards, to allow for the extra maintenance of the new machine.

Samara plans to take £2,200 per month as drawings.

The closing bank balance in May was £25,600.

Complete the cash flow forecast on the following page using the information above.

|  | June | July | August | September |
|---|---|---|---|---|
|  | £ | £ | £ | £ |
| **Cash Receipts** | | | | |
| From Cash Sales | | | | |
| From Credit Customers | | | | |
| Capital / New Loans | | | | |
| **Total Receipts** | | | | |
|  | | | | |
| **Cash Payments** | | | | |
| Credit purchases | | | | |
| Salaries and Wages | | | | |
| General Overhead Costs | | | | |
| Purchase of Non-Current Assets | | | | |
| Repayment of Loans | | | | |
| Drawings | | | | |
| **Total Payments** | | | | |
|  | | | | |
| **Opening Bank Balance** | | | | |
| **Net Cash Flow** | | | | |
| **Closing Bank Balance** | | | | |

# Chapter 10: Cash Management

## The Working Capital Cycle

The working capital cycle, sometimes known as the operating cycle, is the amount of time between the **outflow of cash** to pay for materials or stock and **the inflow of cash** from customers.

### The Working Capital Cycle

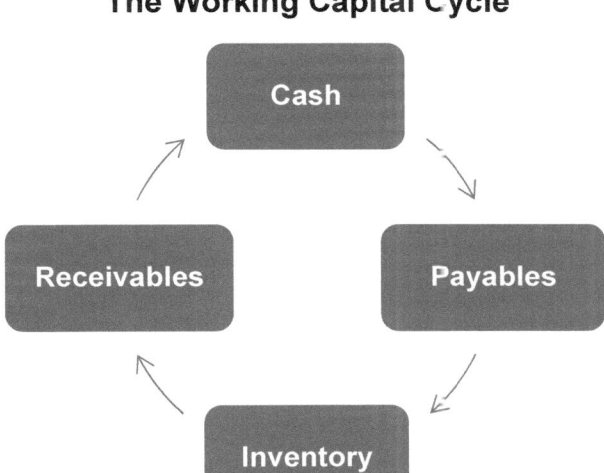

**Working capital** is the capital available for the day to day operations of the business. This is the value of the business's current assets (cash, inventory and receivables) less the value of the current liabilities (payables, overdrafts and loans – repayable in less than one year).

> **Working Capital = Current Assets – Current Liabilities**

Managing the working capital of a business is essential to minimise the risk of insolvency and maximise the return on assets and profits. In reality, many businesses fail and it is not because they are not profitable, it is because they do not have enough cash to pay their debts as they fall due.

The higher the level of working capital, the greater the level of cash and funds are readily available in the short term. This means that there is sufficient cash available to pay the business's short-term obligations (e.g. creditors, wages, loans), have spare cash as a precaution for any unforeseen circumstances that may arise and the ability to invest in more stock.

On this basis, the main objective of managing the working capital of the business is to increase the profits of the business and ensure there is sufficient cash to pay short term obligations as they fall due.

The following ratios can be used to identify how efficiently a business uses its resources on a day to day basis. They are concerned with the company's management of its **working capital – the balance between the money coming in and the money going out** (the balance of the company's current assets and current liabilities). Using the ratios, we can calculate the

# Chapter 10: Cash Management

working capital cycle. This will show us how many days it takes from the outflow of cash for inventory to receiving our payment from our customers.

For retail and wholesale businesses the working capital cycle formula would be:

> **Working Capital Cycle =**
> **Inventory Holding days + Trade Receivable days – Trade Payables days**

We would calculate the working capital cycle as:

| Inventory holding days | X |
|---|---|
| Trade receivables days | X |
| Less: Trade payables days | (X) |
| Working capital cycle (days) | X |

**Inventory holding period**

To calculate the inventory holding period we would use the following formula. This number indicates how long the inventory is held from purchase to being sold.

$$\frac{\text{Inventory}}{\text{Cost of Sales}} \times 365$$

This shows how efficiently the company sells its products. It is expensive to hold high volumes of inventories – they have to be paid for (which affects liquidity), but also must be stored, and insured and may suffer deterioration. Therefore, this ratio calculates how long it takes the company (on average) to sell its goods – in other words, how long an item is held in inventory before it is sold. Ideally, it will be as low as possible – but the ratio will very much depend on the type of business. A bakery should have a much shorter inventory turnover period than a jewellery shop.

**Trade Receivables Collection Period**

To calculate the trade receivables days, we would use the following formula. This measures how long (on average) the business's customers take to pay. This will depend largely on the credit terms it gives to its customers.

$$\frac{\text{Trade Receivables}}{\text{Revenue}} \times 365$$

An important aspect of working capital management is the way in which the organisation manages its trade receivables – customers who owe it money. If the business offers credit terms to customers (e.g. 30 days) it must ensure it has appropriate systems in place to chase and collect payments in a timely manner.

The higher the receivables collection period, the longer it takes the company to collect its debts. This has a negative impact on the company's cash flow and liquidity. Ideally, the

## Chapter 10: Cash Management

calculation should be in line with the credit period offered to customers, and if it significantly exceeds this the company should take steps to reduce it.

**Trade Payables Payment Period**

To calculate the trade payables days, we would use the following formula. This measures how long (on average) the business takes to pay its suppliers. This will depend largely on the credit terms the business receives from its suppliers.

$$\frac{\text{Trade Payables}}{\text{Cost of Sales}} \times 365$$

In many ways, this is the opposite of the receivables collection period – this measures how long (on average) it takes the company to pay its debts. This will depend largely on the credit terms that it can secure from its suppliers.

The longer the company takes to pay its bills, the better it is for its cash flow and liquidity. However, taking too long to pay bills risks suppliers becoming disgruntled, perhaps removing credit facilities or taking legal action. Furthermore, any potential discounts may be lost.

## Activity 10.3

You have been given the following extract of the company's financial statements.

| Extract of financial statements | £000 |
| --- | --- |
| Sales revenue | 38,000 |
| Cost of sales | (13,980) |
| Profit from operations | 4,800 |
| **Assets** | |
| Inventory | 4,055 |
| Trade receivables | 4,545 |
| **Liabilities** | |
| Trade payables | 3,200 |
| Tax liabilities | 850 |

Calculate the working capital cycle to the nearest day assuming all purchases and sales are on credit. (Roundup to the nearest whole day.)

| | Days |
| --- | --- |
| Inventory holding Period | |
| Trade Receivables Collection Period | |
| Trade Payables Payment Period | |
| Working Capital Cycle | |

# Chapter 10: Cash Management

## The Working Capital Cycle and Improving Cash Flow

The working capital cycle uses the results of the three efficiency ratios to provide a measure of how well an organisation manages its working capital.

The working capital cycle reflects that most organisations must **finance** the period of time from when they **first pay for goods** or materials to the time when they **receive payment from customers**.

The shorter the working capital cycle is, the less likely it is that the company will suffer cash shortages. Improvements in the working capital cycle can be made by making improvements in one or more of the three ratios. For example, reducing inventory days or receivable days, or increasing payable days, will all lead to an improvement in the working capital cycle.

The faster a business can move items around the cycle, the less the business will need to invest in the working capital. Therefore, a business needs to carefully consider, when making decisions, the level of investment it puts into the working capital of the business.

The working capital / operating cycle can vary from business to business. For example, a manufacturing company will have a longer operating cycle than wholesale or retail, whereas a sandwich shop or a supermarket would have a short cycle. Therefore, manufacturing businesses would need to take great care in making decisions with working capital to ensure there is enough cash to cover any outgoings and keep costs under control.

### The Costs of Holding Current Assets (Inventory)

Inventory is the main investment for most businesses, especially those in manufacturing. Manufacturing businesses will hold levels of inventory to meet customer demand but this comes at a price. This could be the amount of cash tied up in the inventory, paying for that inventory and also the cost of storing it.

It is important for a business to consider the associated risks of holding too much inventory and also the risks of not holding enough for example when a 'stock out' arises.

There are a number of costs associated with holding stock / inventory that need to be considered.

| Holding Costs | Stock shortage Costs | Purchase Costs |
|---|---|---|
| Storage | Loss of sales | Ordering costs |
| Insurance | Loss of contribution | Delivery costs |
| Theft | Loss of customers | Administration |
| Deterioration / damage | Production stoppages | |
| Obsolete stock | Increased purchase costs | |

## Cost of high levels of inventory

There can be potential problems with holding high volumes of inventory. There is a large investment of working capital which means cash is tied up in that stock, or even the possibility that the inventory had to be financed to purchase it. This capital could be invested elsewhere in the business where it could create a return. There is the cost of storage and employing staff to manage the warehouse and control the inventory systems, increased insurance and the risk of that stock becoming obsolete, stolen or damaged.

## Cost of low levels of inventory

In contrast, if stock levels are too low there are other potential risks. The business could run out of stock (stock out) which could lead to a stop on production. This would cause possible idle time of the production and staff and missed orders. This would lead to dissatisfied customers and it is possible some customers would be lost and use an alternative supplier. If it is foreseen that a stock out is imminent then it might be possible to purchase emergency stock from a different supplier, which could be of course more expensive or of a poorer quality. This, therefore, leads to more problems with increased costs, more wastage and more dissatisfied customers.

## Managing the Working Capital Cycle by Reducing Investment in Inventory

The problem facing businesses is therefore one of balancing the quantities of materials ordered in each purchase to ensure that it is holding sufficient inventories at all times to cover the risk of stock-outs (taking into account the lead times involved in purchasing replenishment inventory) whilst not holding excessive inventory which leads to increased costs.

There are a number of techniques which can help organisations maintain the optimum levels of inventory.

Before being able to determine the best quantities to order an organisation must first identify the best level of inventories to hold. This will be determined by a number of factors, including available storage space, demand and price, which we considered in Chapter 3.

## Managing the Working Capital Cycle by Reducing Investment in Receivables

When a business offers credit to its customers the business hopes this will attract customers and increase the level of sales and therefore profit. In certain industries, it is expected that credit is given and if no credit is given, they will go elsewhere.

When offering credit to customers a business must create a credit policy that outlines the terms and conditions and procedures to be adopted. A number of factors need to be considered when establishing a credit policy.

- Credit terms, for example, payment due within 30 days.
- Early settlement discounts.
- The method of payment, (BACS, CHAPS, cash, bankers draft, cheque).
- Risk of irrecoverable debts.
- Credit terms offered by competitors.
- Cost of credit control.
- Financing costs.

# Chapter 10: Cash Management

It is important that businesses are able to find a balance between how much profit will increase from sales by allowing credit and the cost of allowing that credit.

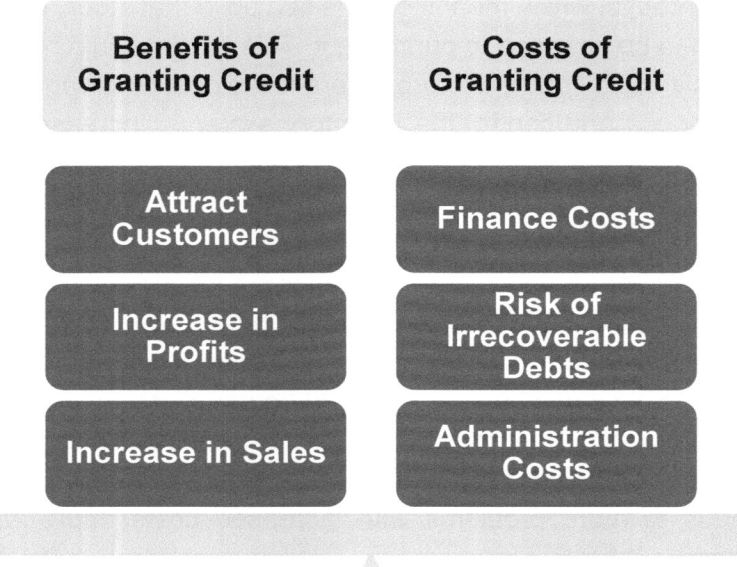

The main cost to a business when offering credit terms to its customers is the **finance cost**. Although the trade receivables appear on the balance sheet as an asset, they are not cash in the bank or part of the working capital needed by the business to run day to day. This may lead to the business needing to raise finance to cover the day to day running of the business until the payment is received. For example, a bank overdraft.

When offering credit to customers the following factors should be taken into consideration.

- **Creditworthiness** of the customer - credit scoring / rating, trade references, published information, visit to the premises, CCJ's.
- **Credit limits** – the amount of credit given to the customer.
- **Invoicing without delay** – the period of credit starts from the day of the invoice.
- **Credit control** – collecting overdue debts, policies and follow up procedures.
- **Review of credit system** - ensure it is working efficiently for the overall working capital - using age debtor analysis and ratios to decide if action is needed.

As with the costs associated with investing in inventory, giving credit to customers also incurs costs.

The two main costs associated with offering credit to customers are:

- Interest costs
- Early settlement discount costs.

## Chapter 10: Cash Management

**Interest Costs**

The business would have invested and most likely financed the inventory it had purchased, however by extending the period to receive payment from the customers by allowing them credit terms to pay at a later date, the trade receivables balance may need to be financed, commonly by short term finance. Any finance will incur an interest cost. If the balance increases then the cost to business will also increase. Over the period of a year, this could be quite substantial.

**Prompt Payment Settlement Discounts.**

Early settlement discounts or cash discounts are often given to customers to encourage early payment. This can help increase liquidity, decrease the receivables balance, and therefore reduce any interest charge on financing and also reduce irrecoverable debts. The cost of the discount is balanced against any savings made by the business from having less capital tied up and any interest costs.

It is important to consider the impact and costs of offering early settlement discounts and any savings on financing the trade debtor balance to improve the management of the working capital. Here we have two conflicting influences to consider. Would it be more cost effective for the business to offer a settlement discount or would continuing to finance the debtor balance by the overdraft or short-term loan be the better option, and what the overall effect would be on the profit of the business?

### Funding Methods for the Acquisition of Non-Current Assets

Financing is a way that businesses can fund new projects, new non-current assets (for example machinery, vehicles and premises) and grow without using their own cash or waiting until they have enough cash to do so. If the business had to wait to have enough money then the opportunity may no longer be available, therefore, financing is an ideal way to raise capital to invest with the view that the new business venture will be successful and the business can repay the money borrowed.

Purchasing non-current assets usually entails a significant outlay by the organisation – property, equipment and vehicles usually cost several thousands of pounds, if not more. The organisation may not have sufficient cash in the bank to pay for the new asset, and so must consider different sources of finance to enable the purchase to take place.

Different possible sources of finance include:

- **Cash** – some organisations may be able to simply purchase the asset directly from their own funds.

- **Credit** – alternatively, the organisation may be able to secure credit from the supplier (in the same way as other purchases can be made on credit). The supplier will issue an invoice, with payment to be made within an agreed period of time.

- **Part Exchange** – sometimes the business may be able to 'trade-in' an old asset in part exchange for the new one. When this happens, an allowance is made by the supplier for the old asset; this will have the impact of reducing the cost of the new asset. The remaining balance must then be financed by the business.

- **Loans** – loans are a contractual agreement between the business and (most commonly) a bank. The bank will lend the business a specific amount that is repayable over a fixed period and interest is charged at a fixed or variable rate. Some banks will offer low interest rates, depending on the credit score of the business, however, the process of applying can be long and time consuming. In many cases, some banks may also require a source of security by way of a personal guarantee (personal assets are at risk) and/or a fixed or floating charge over the business's assets.

- **Hire Purchase** – this is an alternative to borrowing money from an external source such as a bank. Hire purchase (HP) is usually arranged with the supplier; the business takes delivery of the asset and can start using it, but legal ownership of the asset is retained by the supplier. The business makes a regular (monthly) payment to the supplier over a fixed number of periods, and at the end of this time, legal ownership of the asset passes to the business.

- **Finance Lease** – this is a similar arrangement to Hire Purchase; however, although legally the ownership of the asset is retained by the lessor (i.e. the supplier), the lessee (the business) records the asset in their financial statements as if they owned it. There are a number of conditions attached to a finance lease; the benefits (and risks) of ownership must pass from the lessor to the lessee. This means that obligations such as repairs, maintenance and insurance costs are borne by the business; however, they will also generally have more freedom to use the asset as they wish.

The management of a business must evaluate which funding method is most appropriate for each acquisition of non-current assets. This may be different depending on the financial conditions of the business at the time. The following considerations should be taken into account before any decision is made:

- **Overall cost of finance** – taking into account interest, charges and other costs.

- **Expected life of the asset** – any finance arrangement should ideally not be for longer than the expected life of the asset; for example, if a new car has an expected useful life of four years, then any bank loan taken out to finance the purchase should not be for a period of longer than four years.

- **Liquidity** – a business may have sufficient funds in the bank to finance the purchase of a non-current asset. However, any reduction in the bank balance will make the business less solvent; any large liabilities which have to be met in the near future could take the business into an overdraft which would have significant charges.

## Improving Cash Flow

As we have seen in this chapter, it is important that a business also has enough working capital for the day to day running of the business and remain solvent. If a business has insufficient cash to pay its bills as they fall due then the business is insolvent. The business

## Chapter 10: Cash Management

needs enough money to purchase inventory to sell, whilst the business waits for credit customers to pay to continue to trade.

If the business does not have enough working capital, then the business can take action to increase liquidity quickly.

This can be in the form of:

- **Raising additional finance from the owners in the form of capital:** for example, investing money into the business, introducing new partners or issuing shares.

- **Raising additional finance in the form of debt:** for example, short term bank loans and overdrafts. An overdraft is flexible because it can be paid off early and is a continuous source of finance that can be used as and when it is needed, therefore the business will only pay interest on what is used.

There are other methods of improving cash flow which a business can utilise. We have already considered some of these earlier in this chapter when we looked at managing the working capital cycle.

Here are some of the most common methods businesses can use:

- Prompt payments discounts
- Chasing receivables
- Delay supplier payments
- Disposal of non-current assets
- Reduce inventory

**Prompt Payment discounts**

Early settlement discounts or cash discounts are often given to customers to encourage early payment. This can help to encourage customers to pay earlier and bring more cash into the business.

**Chasing receivables**

Customer payments are integral to any business's cash flow and the working capital cycle, as without customers there would be no cash flow to manage. Most businesses will offer credit terms to other businesses in the range of 14 – 60 days and for larger businesses could be as much as 90 days. Ideally, all invoices would be paid on time and there would not be a need to chase customers, unfortunately, that is never quite the case. Chasing customers for payment of overdue invoices is a common practice in businesses of all sizes all over the world.

**Trade Creditors**

Trade credit from suppliers is one of the most important and straightforward means of short-term finance for most businesses. It is a free source of finance as it has no interest or fees charged.

By having credit to pay suppliers, the business is able to delay the payment to suppliers, which means the business can fund its inventory free of charge through its supplier. This allows the business more time to sell and receive payment from its customers and therefore improves the working capital of the business.

A business should aim to pay as late as possible to gain the full benefit of this free finance but should also stay within its credit terms with suppliers because purposely delaying payments can cause problems. Disgruntled suppliers may refuse to continue to supply the business with goods in the future or move to a cash upfront basis. There is also the loss of reputation to be considered and also the possibility of a price increase to give the supplier security or new suppliers may need to be used.

In contrast, early settlement discounts may also be offered so it is important that a business considers the benefit (saving), the cost of accepting the discount if borrowing is required and the negative impact this can have on a business's cash flow.

### Disposal of non-current assets

Selling assets can raise a considerable sum of money to help improve cash flow or help fund a particular project, particularly in the case of a large asset such as a property. If a particular asset is no longer used, for example, plant and machinery or vehicles, the sale of the assets will not only ease the cash flow problem or help fund a new project but also enhance the overall profitability of the business.

Assets such as property and machinery can be difficult to sell quickly and when trying to make a quick sale a business will usually have to accept a much lower price than its true value.

### Reduce Inventory

It is important for the business to keep track of inventory and find the optimal level of inventory to hold. Holding large amounts of inventory has a significant effect on cash flow. If unused inventory is being held unnecessarily this means cash is tied up in that inventory so it would be more cash efficient to sell that inventory, even at a discounted price. This could also potentially lower holding and storage costs.

## Cash Flow and Software

Accounting software and the use of automation and visualisation can provide insight and aid cash flow planning.

In recent years the use of software and artificial intelligence (AI) has grown at a significant rate. Cash flow forecasting can be produced within various software and add-on apps. Cash flow forecasts require the collection of data from various sources to calculate expected cash inflows and outflows. In the past, this will have been performed manually by a person and then entered into a spreadsheet or even on paper. With the advanced technology available today businesses that use accounting software can use the information recorded in the software to perform a cash flow forecast almost at the click of a button. Information and data can be pulled from within the system to create an accurate forecast of payments due in and due out to predict periods of cash shortfalls, assist with business decision making, and plan for actions needed to be taken to prevent potential events from becoming insolvent.

Many accounting software platforms now also include dashboards that give an overview of the current real-time position of the business. Dashboards are great tools that are used to

# Chapter 10: Cash Management

present data visualisations within accounting packages for insights and data analytics including cash flow.

Here is an example of an accounting software dashboard. We can see in the example how data visualisations presented on a dashboard can include different formats e.g. graphs, charts and infographics.

**Milstead Ltd**

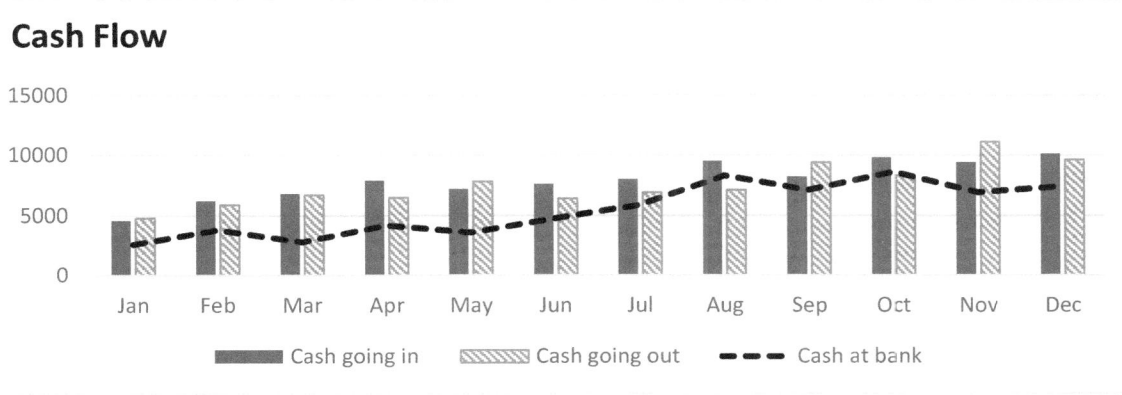

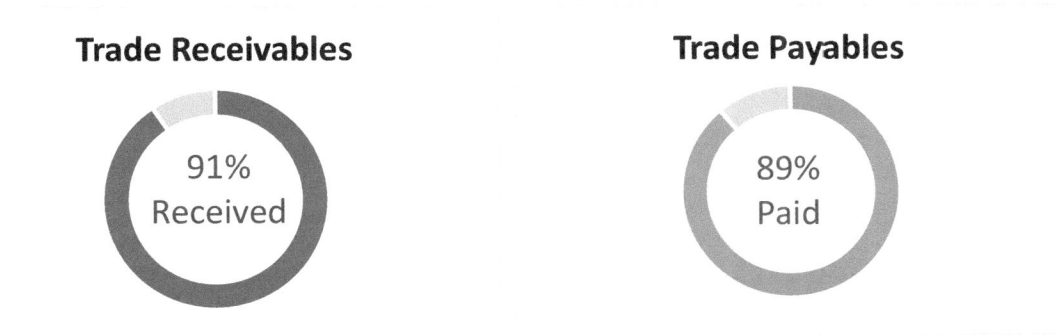

| Cash at bank | Cash inflows | Cash outflows | Profit / Loss |
|---|---|---|---|
| £7,400 | £95,300 | £90,500 | £2,600 |

# Chapter 10: Cash Management

As the role of the accountant is changing with the current advancements in technology it is important for students to be familiar with data presented in different formats and be able to interpret data.

Interpreting data and data analytics can provide accountants with valuable insights, identify process improvements that increase efficiency, help manage risk and aid decision making.

## Example 10.3

The management accountant is currently on annual leave and the director has asked you to assist with the cash flow forecast for the following six months.

You have used the accounting software of the business to predict the cash flow at the end of each of the following months. The software has given the following results.

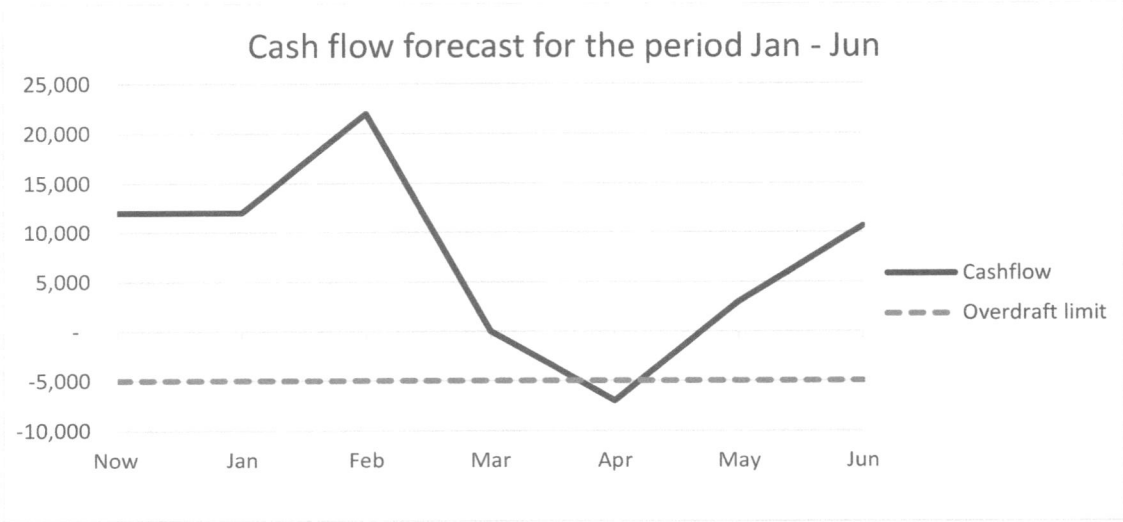

Identify to the director the point where the company will go into its overdraft.

Identify to the director the point where the company will exceed its overdraft limit and will need to raise additional finance or capital.

**Answer:**

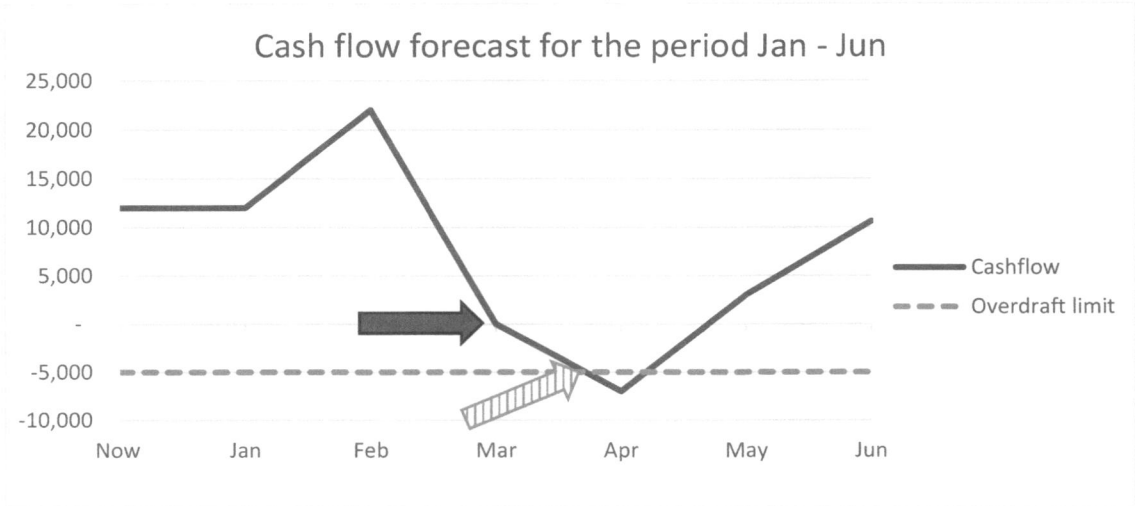

# Chapter 10: Cash Management

Here we can see that the business is expected to reach the overdraft at the start of March. This is indicated by the solid arrow where the cash balance reaches zero.

We can see that during April the business will exceed its overdraft limit. The striped arrow indicates the point where the business's cash balance reaches the overdraft limit of £5,000 towards the end of March. This means the business will run out of money to pay its outgoings and will need to make a plan to correct this or raise additional finance (e.g. increase overdraft if the bank will allow) or further capital into the business to cover this shortfall. It should be noted that the graph shows that towards April, the business will have a positive cash balance and this increases further during June, therefore indicating the shortfall of cash is possibly only a short-term problem.

## Reconciling Profit and Cash

Not all payments and receipts are involved in the calculation of profit or loss, for example, the purchase of a non-current asset, the introduction of new capital/equity, or increasing/reducing other long-term debt. Additionally, some figures used when calculating profit or loss are non-cash transactions, for example, depreciation. It is therefore these types of transactions that need to be considered when reconciling profit and cash.

 **Example 10.4**

Your business has sales of £250,000 with revenue expenditure (including depreciation) of £180,000, therefore there is a profit of £70,000 during its first year. The depreciation expense for the year was £5,000.

You have introduced £68,000 and take out a bank loan of £32,000 at the start. Loan repayments are £1,000 per month with total payments to date of £12,000. You have purchased equipment in the period of £35,000. The closing cash balance at the end of the period is £128,000.

**Reconcile the recorded the recorded profit to the recorded cash balance.**

| Profit | 70,000 | Action |
|---|---|---|
| Depreciation | 5,000 | add |
|  |  |  |
|  |  |  |
|  |  |  |
| Cash | 128,000 |  |

Depreciation is a non-cash expense to the business showing the reduction in the value of an asset and will have reduced the net profit recorded. However, because this does not affect the cash balance, it must be added back to profit.

# Chapter 10: Cash Management

| Profit | 70,000 | Action |
|---|---|---|
| Depreciation | 5,000 | add |
| **Capital** | **68,000** | **add** |
|  |  |  |
|  |  |  |
|  |  |  |
| **Cash** | **128,000** |  |

An introduction of new capital will increase the cash balance but will not be reflected in the recorded profit of the business. Therefore, to reconcile the figures this must be added to profit.

| Profit | 70,000 | Action |
|---|---|---|
| Depreciation | 5,000 | add |
| Capital | 68,000 | add |
| **Bank loan** | **32,000** | **add** |
|  |  |  |
|  |  |  |
| **Cash** | **128,000** |  |

Like an injection of new capital, taking out a bank loan will increase the cash balance, but this is not recorded in the profit or loss account so will be added to the profit figure in order to reconcile the two figures.

| Profit | 70,000 | Action |
|---|---|---|
| Depreciation | 5,000 | add |
| Capital | 68,000 | add |
| Bank loan | 32,000 | add |
| **Loan repayments** | **12,000** | **deduct** |
|  |  |  |
| **Cash** | **128,000** |  |

Loan repayments are in a way the opposite of taking out the bank loan. These are also not recorded in the SPL, they simply have transactions recorded been the Bank Loan Account (Liability) and the Bank Account (Asset) which are shown in the SFP. This represents cash that has been paid out of the business but not represented by profit. This is therefore deducted from the profit figure.

## Chapter 10: Cash Management

| Profit | 70,000 | Action |
|---|---|---|
| Depreciation | 5,000 | add |
| Capital | 68,000 | add |
| Bank loan | 32,000 | add |
| Loan repayments | 12,000 | deduct |
| **Purchase of new equipment** | 35,000 | deduct |
| **Cash** | 128,000 | |

Finally, there is the purchase of a non-current asset. The transactions to record the purchase of a new non-current asset are only recorded in the SFP. It will simply reduce the bank account for any payments made, and the increase in value in the Asset account. Therefore, this needs to be deducted from the Profit figure.

By adding and deducting these figures as appropriate, you will be able to reconcile. The profit to cash

 **Activity 10.4**

Indicate whether the figures below should be added or deducted and calculate the cash figure when allowing for these adjustments.

| Profit | 80,800 | Add / Deduct |
|---|---|---|
| New Bank Loan | 32,000 | |
| Bank Loan repayments | 17,500 | |
| Capital | 40,000 | |
| Purchase of new equipment | 55,000 | |
| Depreciation | 4,700 | |
| **Cash** | | |

 **Assessment 10**

You are now required to log in to your ROGO account to complete your online assessment before progressing on to the next chapter.

**Once you have completed Assessment 10 you should continue on to Book 2.**

This page is left intentionally blank.

# Chapter 1: Activity Answers

 **Activity Answer 1.1**

a) Decide whether the following statements are true or false:

|  | True | False |
|---|---|---|
| Operational decision making looks at the long-term future of the business. |  | ✓ |
| Information for management accounting comes from different sources than that used in financial accounting. |  | ✓ |
| Management accounting is used for forecasting and budgeting for future periods. | ✓ |  |
| Financial accounting is used for forecasting and budgeting for future periods. |  | ✓ |
| Management accounts are used externally only. |  | ✓ |

b) Which of the following are characteristics of useful information for management accounting purposes?

|  | ✓ |
|---|---|
| Relevant | ✓ |
| Computerised |  |
| Complete | ✓ |
| Cost effective | ✓ |
| Absolute accuracy |  |

# Chapter 2: Activity Answers

 Activity Answer 2.1

Classify the following costs of a manufacturing company into fixed, variable or semi-variable:

| Cost | Fixed | Variable | Semi-Variable |
|---|---|---|---|
| Annual salary of the finance manager. | ✓ | | |
| Cost of cooling fluid which keeps machinery cool during the production process. | | ✓ | |
| Labour cost of production staff paid an amount for each unit of production they make. | | ✓ | |
| Cost of power used to run the machines in the production process. | | | ✓ |

 Activity Answer 2.2

Jeffrey Ltd has identified the following costs at different levels of activity. Identify the type of cost behaviour shown by each of the costs.

| | Variable | Fixed | Semi-Variable |
|---|---|---|---|
| At 2,000 units the total cost is £9,000. At 3,000 units the total cost is £13,000. | | | ✓ |
| At 5,000 units the cost per unit is £2.25. At 8,000 units the total cost is £18,000. | ✓ | | |
| At 4,000 units the cost per unit is £6. At 3,000 units the cost per unit is £8. | | ✓ | |

# Chapter 2: Activity Answers

 Activity Answer 2.3

Francis Ltd has identified the following costs associated with a number of different activity levels over the past six months. Use the high-low method to identify:

| Fixed element of the cost | £12,000 |
|---|---|
| Variable element of the cost (cost per unit) | £3.20 |
| Forecast cost at activity level of 5,500 units | £29,600 |

High        5,800 units = £30,560
Low         3,800 units = £24,160

   2,000 units = £ 6,400 so the variable cost is £6,400 / 2,000 = **£3.20**

   The fixed cost is therefore £30,560 – (5,800 x £3.20) = **£12,000**

If activity is 5,500 units the cost will be (5,500 x £3.20) + £12,000 = **£29,600**

 Activity Answer 2.4

Complete the table below by inserting all costs for the activity levels of 2,500 and 2,800 units.

|  | 2,000 Units | 2,500 Units | 2,800 Units | 3,100 Units |
|---|---|---|---|---|
| Variable Cost (£) |  | 24,750 | 27,720 |  |
| Fixed Cost (£) |  | 16,800 | 16,800 |  |
| Total Cost (£) | 36,600 | 41,550 | 44,520 | 47,490 |

High        3,100 units = £47,490
Low         2,000 units = £36,600

   1,100 units = £10,890 so the variable cost is £10,890 / 1,100 = **£9.90**

   The fixed cost is therefore £47,490 – (3,100 x £9.90) = **£16,800**

If activity is 2,500 units the cost will be £16,800 + (2,500 x £9.90) = **£41,550**

If activity is 2,800 units the cost will be £16,800 + (2,800 x £9.90) = **£44,520**

##  Activity Answer 2.5

Use the high-low method to determine:

i. The variable cost per unit.

£6.00 per unit

ii. The fixed cost.

£22,500

iii. The forecast cost for November, when the activity level is estimated to be 10,630 units.

£86,280

High  12,800 units = £99,300
Low   9,420 units = £79,020
      3,380 units = £20,280

So, the variable cost is £20,280 / 3,380 **£6.00 per unit**

The fixed cost is therefore £99,300 − (12,800 x £6.00) = **£22,500**

The total cost for an activity level of 10,630 units is £22,500 + (10,630 x £6) = **£86,280**

# Chapter 3: Activity Answers

## Activity Answer 3.1

Use the FIFO method to complete the inventory record card below for mushrooms.

**Inventory record card for mushrooms**

| Date | Receipts | | | Issues | | | Balance | |
| --- | --- | --- | --- | --- | --- | --- | --- | --- |
| | Quantity | Cost per tonne | Total cost | Quantity | Cost per tonne | Total cost | Quantity | Total cost |
| | tonnes | £ | £ | tonnes | £ | £ | tonnes | £ |
| Balance as at: 1 June | | | | | | | 72 | 10,512 |
| 2 June | 70 | 150.00 | 10,500 | | | | 142 | 21,012 |
| 3 June | | | | 90 | 72 x £146<br>18 x £150 | £13,212 | 52 | £7,800 |
| 4 June | 50 | 152.00 | 7,600 | | | | 102 | £15,400 |
| 5 June | | | | 70 | 52 x £150<br>18 x £152 | £10,536 | 32 | £4,864 |

## Activity Answer 3.2

Identify the valuation method described in the statements below. Indicate which is which by selecting the relevant column of the table below.

| Statement | FIFO | AVCO |
| --- | --- | --- |
| The closing inventory is valued at £51,900. | | ✓ |
| The closing inventory is valued at £52,200. | ✓ | |

|  | *Issue: 8,500 units* | *Balance: 25,500 units* |
| --- | --- | --- |
| **FIFO** | 8,500 units @ £2.00 = £17,000 | (19,500 units @ £2.00) + (6,000 units x £2.20) = £52,200 |
| **AVCO** | 8,500 units @ (£69,200 / 34,000) = £17,300 | 25,500 units @ (£69,200 / 34,000) = £51,900 |

# Chapter 3: Activity Answers

 Activity Answer 3.3

Identify whether the following statements are true or false by selecting the relevant column of the table below.

| Statement | True | False |
|---|---|---|
| If using AVCO it is necessary to recalculate the weighted average cost every time there is a new receipt of goods. | | ✓ |
| FIFO values all issues at the most recent price. | | ✓ |
| LIFO can be used for internal use, but not for the valuation of inventory in the financial statements. | ✓ | |

 Activity Answer 3.4

Complete the table below for the issue costs and the closing inventory value. Show all answers as whole numbers.

| Method | Cost of issues on 18th April £ | Value of inventory on 26th April £ |
|---|---|---|
| FIFO | £6,050 | £6,390 |
| AVCO | £6,189 | £6,251 |

 **Activity Answer 3.5**

a) Complete the inventory record card shown below (to 2 dp).

| Date | Receipts | | | Issues | | | Balance | |
|---|---|---|---|---|---|---|---|---|
| | Quantity | Cost per unit | Total cost | Quantity | Cost per unit | Total cost | Quantity | Total cost |
| | units | £ | £ | units | £ | £ | units | £ |
| Balance as at: 1 May | | | | | | | 2,100 | 1,050 |
| 5 May | 2,000 | 0.55 | **1,100** | | | | 4,100 | 2,150 |
| 18 May | | | | 2,500 | 2,000 @ 0.55<br>500 @ 0.50 | 1,350 | 1,600 | 800 |
| 24 May | 200 | 0.50 | **100** | | | | 1,800 | 900 |
| 28 May | | | | 300 | 200 @ 0.50<br>100 @ 0.50 | 150 | 1,500 | 750 |

b) Prepare the bookkeeping entries in the table below using the relevant cost codes.

| Date | Cost Code | Debit (£) | Credit (£) |
|---|---|---|---|
| 5 May | 3500 | 1,100 | |
| 5 May | 8618 | | 1,100 |
| 18 May | 4150 | 1,350 | |
| 18 May | 3500 | | 1,350 |
| 24 May | 3500 | 100 | |
| 24 May | 8618 | | 100 |
| 28 May | 4150 | 150 | |
| 28 May | 3500 | | 150 |

## Activity Answer 3.6

a) Calculate the value of raw materials at 30th April 20X7.

£3,200 + £1,565 + £400 = £5,165

b) Calculate the value of finished goods at 30th April 20X7.

230 x £19* = £4,370

c) Calculate the value of work-in-progress at 30th April 20X7.

50 x £19* = £950

*Cost per unit = £28,900 + £41,250 + £30,550 = £100,700 / (5,000 + 250 + (150/3)) = £100,700 / 5,300 = £19 per unit*

## Activity Answer 3.7

a) Complete the table below to calculate the cost per equivalent unit.

|  | Completed Units | WIP equivalent units | Total equivalent units | Total cost | Cost per equivalent unit |
|---|---|---|---|---|---|
| Material | 2,000 | 150 | 2,150 | £75,250.00 | £35.00 |
| Labour | 2,000 | 80 | 2,080 | £99,840.00 | £48.00 |
| Overheads | 2,000 | 110 | 2,110 | £28,485.00 | £13.50 |

b) What was the total value of finished goods in inventory?   £ 1,930.00

c) What was the total value work-in-progress (WIP)?   £ 10,575.00

*FGS = 20 x (£35+£48+£13.50) £96.50 = £1,930*

*WIP = (150 x £35) + (80 x £48) + (110 x £13.50) = £10,575*

# Chapter 3: Activity Answers

 **Activity Answer 3.8**

Calculate the optimum re-order level (in reams) and quantity to be ordered (in reams) for A4 paper.

Reorder Level = (40 x 6) + 200 = **440 reams**

Reorder Quantity = 2,400 – 200 = **2,200 reams**

 **Activity Answer 3.9**

Calculate the economic order quantity for this chemical.

$$EOQ = \sqrt{\frac{2 \times 90{,}000 \times 25}{2}} = \textbf{1{,}500 litres}$$

How many orders a year the company should place?

90,000 / 1,500 = **60 orders per year**

 **Activity Answer 3.10**

a) Complete the stock record card below. Show cost per litre to 3dp.

| Date | Receipts | | | Issues | | | Balance | |
|---|---|---|---|---|---|---|---|---|
| | Quantity (litres) | Cost per Litre £ | Total Cost £ | Quantity (litres) | Cost per Litre £ | Total Cost £ | Quantity (litres) | Total Cost £ |
| 1 May | | | | | | | 10,000 | 24,500 |
| 5 May | 8,000 | 2.50 | | | | | 18,000 | 44,500 |
| 12 May | | | | 5,000 | 2.472 | 12,361 | 13,000 | 32,139 |
| 19 May | | 2.58 | 23,220 | | | | 22,000 | 55,359 |
| 28 May | | | | 8,400 | 2.516 | 21,137 | 13,600 | 34,222 |

# Chapter 3: Activity Answers

b) The policy of ordering BG56 in quantities of at least 8,000 litres has been complied with:

|  | ✓ |
|---|---|
| On the 5th May but not on the 19th May |  |
| On the 19th May but not on the 5th May |  |
| On both the 5th May and the 19th May | ✓ |
| On neither the 5th May nor the 19th May |  |

c) The policy of ordering when the inventory balance falls below 12,000 litres has been complied with:

|  | ✓ |
|---|---|
| On the 5th May but not on the 19th May | ✓ |
| On the 19th May but not on the 5th May |  |
| On both the 5th May and the 19th May |  |
| On neither the 5th May nor the 19th May |  |

d) Assuming component KK88 can only be ordered in batches of 100 units, which of these is the most economic order quantity for Spangles Ltd?

|  | ✓ |
|---|---|
| 200 units |  |
| 5,600 units |  |
| 5,657 units |  |
| 5,700 units | ✓ |
| 32,000,000 units |  |

## Activity Answer 3.11

a) Which IAS deals with Inventory?  IAS 2

b) Calculate the cost of issues and also the value of the balance of remaining inventory on August 31st using:

- First In First Out (FIFO)
- Weighted Average Cost (AVCO)

Round your answers to the nearest whole £.

# Chapter 3: Activity Answers

|  | Cost £ |
|---|---|
| FIFO Cost of Issues | 41,725 |
| AVCO Cost of Issues | 41,850 |
| FIFO Balance - kg | 14,500 |
| AVCO Balance - kg | 14,500 |
| FIFO – Balance (£) | 46,275 |
| AVCO – Balance (£) | 46,150 |

c) In times of rising prices, which of the following inventory valuation methods would you expect to result in the **highest** profit for the period?

|  | ✓ |
|---|---|
| First In First Out (FIFO) | ✓ |
| Last In First Out (LIFO) |  |
| Average Cost (AVCO) |  |

d) Assuming screws can only be ordered in multiples of 1,000 at a time, calculate how many screws should be purchased at a time, and approximately how many orders should be placed a year.

| Economic Order Quantity | 22,000 |
|---|---|
| Approximate Number of Orders per Year | 18 |

e) Identify **four** advantages and **four** disadvantages to a business of holding high levels of inventory.

| Four Advantages |
|---|
| Risk of 'Stock-Out' reduced |
| Supplier Unreliability minimised |
| Bulk discounts may be earned |
| Reduced costs if prices are rising |

| Four Disadvantages |
|---|
| Storage and Handling Costs increased |
| Increased Risk of Obsolescence |
| Cash tied up in inventory |
| Failure to take advantage of falling prices |

This page is left intentionally blank.

# Chapter 4: Activity Answers

 Activity Answer 4.1

Calculate the gross wages of the following employees:

**Note:** If no overtime is paid you should enter 0 into the overtime column

| Employee | Hours Worked | Basic Wage | Overtime Premium | Gross Wage |
|---|---|---|---|---|
| | | £ | £ | £ |
| A Toal | 46 | 552 | 24 | 576 |
| B Fewster | 39 | 468 | 0 | 468 |
| C Tindall | 36 | 432 | 0 | 432 |
| D Hall | 42 | 504 | 8 | 512 |

A Toal – 46 hours x £12.00 + 6 hours x (£12 x 1/3)

D Hall – 42 hours x £12.00 + 2 hours x (£12 x 1/3)

 Activity Answer 4.2

Identify whether the following statements are true or false by selecting the relevant column of the table below.

| Statement | True | False |
|---|---|---|
| If during a 40 hour week, the employee produces 4,600 units a bonus of £1,840 will apply.<br>*The bonus will be (4,600 – (40 x 100)) = 600 x £0.40 = £240* | | ✓ |
| An employee who works 35 hours and produces 3,450 units will not be entitled to a bonus.<br>*In 35 hours he should produce 3,500 units to receive a bonus* | ✓ | |
| An employee who works 42 hours and produces 4,475 units will be due a total payment of £740<br>*Bonus = (4,475 – (42 x 100) = 275 x £0.40 = £110*<br>*So total payment is (42 x £15) = £630 + £110 = £740* | ✓ | |

# Chapter 4: Activity Answers

 Activity Answer 4.3

Complete the table below for the two methods, showing the gross wage for the time rate with bonus and the piecework wage.

Note: If no bonus is paid, you should enter 0 as the bonus for that employee in the table.

| Hours worked | Unit Output | Basic Wage | Bonus Pay | Gross Wage | Piecework Wage |
|---|---|---|---|---|---|
| | | £ | £ | £ | £ |
| 36 | 9,200 | 432.00 | 120.00 | 552.00 | 552.00 |
| 40 | 9,950 | 480.00 | 0 | 480.00 | 597.00 |
| 38 | 9,780 | 456.00 | 168.00 | 624.00 | 586.80 |
| 42 | 10,860 | 504.00 | 216.00 | 720.00 | 651.60 |

 Activity Answer 4.4

Calculate the amount to be paid to each employee and complete the table below.

| Name | Amount £ | Workings |
|---|---|---|
| Alan Adams | £725.00 | (39 x £15) + (7 x £20) |
| Barney Brown | £691.70 | (39 x £12.50) + (10 x £16.67) + (2 x 18.75) |
| Cheetan Chauna | £610.00 | (11,200 x £0.05) + £50 |
| Daisy Dawson | £497.50 | 9,950 x £0.05 |
| Edgar Ellis | £637.53 | (39 x £12.50) + (9 x £16.67) |
| Faisal Fakir | £1,575.00 | £18,900 / 12 |
| Gary Gibson | £557.00 | (10,140 x £0.05) + £50 |
| Hamid Haseef | £2,485.00 | (£28,400 / 12) x 105/100 |
| Ivory Ilonga | £2,241.67 | (£26,900 / 12) |
| Jimmy Jones | £456.65 | (39 x £10.00) + (5 x £13.33) |
| Karen Keith | £495.00 | (9,900 x 0.05) |
| Larry Long | £1,541.67 | (£18,500 / 12) |

# Chapter 4: Activity Answers

 Activity Answer 4.5

a) Complete the wages control account entries in the account shown below:

| Wages control account | | | |
|---|---|---|---|
| **Debit** | **£** | **Credit** | **£** |
| Bank (net wages/salaries) | 10,000 | Direct Labour | 7,000 |
| HMRC (income tax and NIC) | 2,000 | Production Overhead | 4,000 |
| Pension contributions | 1,000 | Non-Production Overhead | 2,000 |
| | 13,000 | | 13,000 |

b) Complete the table below to show how the gross payroll cost for the week is charged to the various cost accounts of the business:

| Date | Code | Debit | Credit |
|---|---|---|---|
| 30 April | 8200 | £7,000 | |
| 30 April | 9100 | | £7,000 |
| 30 April | 8400 | £4,000 | |
| 30 April | 9100 | | £4,000 |
| 30 April | 8600 | £2,000 | |
| 30 April | 9100 | | £2,000 |

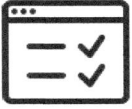 Activity Answer 4.6

a) Prepare the wages control account at 31st July

| Wages Control Account | | | |
|---|---|---|---|
| | **£** | | **£** |
| Bank | 9,130 | Production / Direct Labour | 8,690 |
| HMRC | 2,075 | Production Overheads | 2,017 |
| Pension Company | 854 | Non-Production Overheads | 1,352 |
| | | | |
| | 12,059 | | 12,059 |

# Chapter 4: Activity Answers

b) Prepare the bookkeeping entries in the table below using the relevant cost codes, showing how the total cost of payment is split between the different cost centres of the organisation.

| Date | Cost Code | Debit (£) | Credit (£) |
|---|---|---|---|
| 31st July | 8880 | £8,690 | |
| 31st July | 1850 | | £8,690 |
| 31st July | 8920 | £2,017 | |
| 31st July | 1850 | | £2,017 |
| 31st July | 8960 | £1,352 | |
| 31st July | 1850 | | £1,352 |

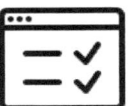 **Activity Answer 4.7**

a) Complete the timesheet below for the week ended 24th April.

| Employee Name – Benny Rich | | | | Cost Centre - Machining | | |
|---|---|---|---|---|---|---|
| | Hours spent on production | Hours spent on indirect work | Notes | Basic Pay £ | Overtime Premium £ | Total Pay £ |
| Monday | 8 | 0 | | 112 | 0 | 112 |
| Tuesday | 8 | 0 | | 112 | 0 | 112 |
| Wednesday | 6 | 2 | Compulsory Staff Meeting | 112 | 0 | 112 |
| Thursday | 9 | 0 | | 126 | 7 | 133 |
| Friday | 7 | 1 | Fire Evacuation | 112 | 0 | 112 |
| Saturday | 4 | 0 | | 56 | 56 | 112 |
| Sunday | 4 | 0 | | 56 | 56 | 112 |
| Total | 46 | 3 | | 686 | 119 | 805 |

How much should be charged to direct costs and how much to indirect costs?

| Direct Costs | £644 *(46 x £14)* |
|---|---|
| Indirect Costs | £161 *(3 hrs on indirect work + £119)* |

© Accountext

## Chapter 4: Activity Answers

b) Complete the cost journal entries to record the four payroll payments made last week using the following information for the 'code' section of the table.

| Date | Code | Dr £ | Cr £ |
| --- | --- | --- | --- |
| Nov 15th | 9001 | 8,550.00 | |
| Nov 15th | 9800 | | 8,550.00 |
| Nov 16th | 9002 | 4,695.00 | |
| Nov 16th | 9800 | | 4,695.00 |
| Nov 17th | 9301 | 1,032.48 | |
| Nov 17th | 9800 | | 1,032.48 |
| Nov 18th | 9302 | 6,611.25 | |
| Nov 18th | 9800 | | 6,611.25 |

This page is left intentionally blank.

# Chapter 5: Activity Answers

## Activity Answer 5.1

Complete the following table to show how overheads are allocated and apportioned between the four centres.

|  | Basis Used | Total | Assembly | Painting | Admin | Stores |
|---|---|---|---|---|---|---|
| Heat & Light | Floor Area | 60,000 | 20,000 | 24,000 | 10,000 | 6,000 |
| Power | Floor Area | 48,000 | 16,000 | 19,200 | 8,000 | 4,800 |
| Insurance Buildings | Floor Area | 10,000 | 3,333 | 4,000 | 1,667 | 1,000 |
| Insurance Machinery | Value | 6,500 | 3,250 | 1,788 | 812 | 650 |
| Depreciation Machinery | Value | 12,000 | 6,000 | 3,300 | 1,500 | 1,200 |
| Canteen | Staff | 15,000 | 5,000 | 7,500 | 1,667 | 833 |
| Supervisor Salary | 60:40 | 32,000 | 19,200 | 12,800 | - | - |

*Note that the apportionment for the Machinery Insurance costs have been rounded to £1,788 and £812. This is to ensure that the table cross-casts and to therefore ensure the total is £650. It would be equally correct to round these to £1,787 and £813.*

# Activity Answer 5.2

Use the following table to allocate or apportion the overheads between the profit/cost centres, using the most appropriate basis.

| | Basis of apportionment | Scheduled services £000 | Charter flights £000 | Aircraft maintenance and repairs £000 | Fuel and parts store £000 | General admin. £000 | Totals £000 |
|---|---|---|---|---|---|---|---|
| Depreciation of aircraft | NBV of aircraft | 21,840 | 14,560 | | | | 36,400 |
| Aviation fuel and other variable costs | No of planned miles | 23,210 | 18,990 | | | | 42,200 |
| Pilots and aircrew salaries | Allocated | 5,250 | 4,709 | | | | 9,959 |
| Rent and rates and other premises costs | Floor space | | | 6,300 | 3,780 | 2,520 | 12,600 |
| Indirect labour | Allocated | | | 9,600 | 3,200 | 7,800 | 20,600 |
| Totals | | 50,300 | 38,259 | 15,900 | 6,980 | 10,320 | 121,759 |
| Reapportion Aircraft maintenance and repairs | | 9,540 | 6,360 | (15,900) | | | |
| Reapportion Fuel and parts store | | 3,839 | 3,141 | | (6,980) | | |
| Reapportion General admin. | | 5,160 | 5,160 | | | (10,320) | |
| Total overheads to profit centres | | 68,839 | 52,920 | | | | 121,759 |

# Chapter 5: Activity Answers

 ## Activity Answer 5.3

Allocate or apportion the budgeted overhead costs between the four departments, using the most appropriate basis. Then reapportion the two service departments' costs to the two production departments using the additional data. (Round to the nearest £ throughout).

| Overhead | Basis of allocation | Ingredients mixing | Canning | Stores | Factory maintenance | Total |
|---|---|---|---|---|---|---|
| | | £ | £ | £ | £ | £ |
| Rent and rates | Floor | 176,000 | 80,000 | 32,000 | 32,000 | 320,000 |
| Insurance | Floor | 9,900 | 4,500 | 1,800 | 1,800 | 18,000 |
| Light, heat and power fixed cost | Even Split | 7,500 | 7,500 | 7,500 | 7,500 | 30,000 |
| Light, heat and power variable cost | Floor | 33,000 | 15,000 | 6,000 | 6,000 | 60,000 |
| Supervision | Direct Lab | 32,000 | 48,000 | | | 80,000 |
| Stores wages | Allocated | | | 68,000 | | 68,000 |
| Factory maintenance wages | Allocated | | | | 96,000 | 96,000 |
| Depreciation of fixed assets | NBV | 22,400 | 16,800 | 5,600 | 11,200 | 56,000 |
| Other overhead costs | 30:40:15:15 | 19,200 | 25,600 | 9,600 | 9,600 | 64,000 |
| | | | | | | |
| Totals | | 300,000 | 197,400 | 130,500 | 164,100 | 792,000 |
| Reapportion Factory maintenance | Equal | 54,700 | 54,700 | 54,700 | (164,100) | |
| Reapportion Stores | Stores Reqs | 111,120 | 74,080 | (185,200) | | |
| Total production department overheads | | 465,820 | 326,180 | | | |

© Accountext

# Chapter 5: Activity Answers

 **Activity Answer 5.4**

What would be the budgeted overhead absorption rate for each department if:

a) Both rates were set based on direct labour hours?

b) Both rates were set based on machine hours?

|  | Direct Labour Hour | Machine Hour |
|---|---|---|
| **Assembly Department** | £8 per d/l hr<br>*£205,600 / 25,700* | £12.50 per m/c hr<br>*£205,600 / 16,448* |
| **Painting Department** | £25 per d/l hr<br>*£452,500 / 18,100* | £20 per m/c hr<br>*£452,500 / 22,625* |

 **Activity Answer 5.5**

Using the most appropriate absorption rate;

The Budgeted Overhead Absorption Rate for Machining is £ 8 per m/c hr

The Budgeted Overhead Absorption Rate for Assembly is £ 4 per lab hr

 **Activity Answer 5.6**

Calculate the under or over absorption of fixed overheads in January 20X4.

£6,448    ~~under absorbed~~ / *over absorbed*.

# Chapter 5: Activity Answers

 Activity Answer 5.7

Use the following table to allocate or apportion the overheads between the production departments, using the most appropriate basis. Round to the nearest £ throughout.

| Overhead | Basis of allocation | Plastics Moulding | Labelling | Stores | Equipment Maintenance | Total |
|---|---|---|---|---|---|---|
| | | £ | £ | £ | £ | £ |
| Heat and lighting fixed cost | Equal | 6,000 | 6,000 | 6,000 | 6,000 | 24,000 |
| Heat and lighting variable cost | Floor area | 19,200 | 10,800 | 4,800 | 1,200 | 36,000 |
| Power for machinery | Percentages given | 19,600 | 8,400 | | | 28,000 |
| Supervision | Direct labour costs | 50,000 | 70,000 | | | 120,000 |
| Stores wages | Allocated | | | 72,000 | | 72,000 |
| Equipment Maintenance salaries | Allocated | | | | 188,200 | 188,200 |
| Depreciation of fixed assets | Net book value of fixed assets | 48,000 | 24,000 | 9,000 | 3,000 | 84,000 |
| Other overhead costs | Percentages given | 76,800 | 25,600 | 12,800 | 12,800 | 128,000 |
| | | | | | | |
| Total of primary apportionments | | 219,600 | 144,800 | 104,600 | 211,200 | 680,200 |
| Reapportion Equipment Maintenance | Equal charges | 70,400 | 70,400 | 70,400 | (211,200) | |
| Reapportion Stores | Material requisitions | 130,200 | 44,800 | (175,000) | | |
| Total production department overheads | | 420,200 | 260,000 | | | |

# Chapter 5: Activity Answers

Using the above information and your calculations from above, calculate the budgeted overhead recovery (absorption) rate for:

a) The Plastics Moulding department: £420,200 / 8,404 = £50/machine hour

b) The Labelling department: £260,000 / 16,250 = £16/direct labour hour

c) Calculate the under or over absorption of fixed overheads for each department.

| | | |
|---|---|---|
| **Plastics Moulding:** | £ 13,900 | ~~over~~ / **under** absorbed |
| **Labelling:** | £ 23,880 | ~~over~~ / **under** absorbed |

*Plastics Moulding: Absorbed (8,612 x £50) – Actual £444,500 = £13,900 under absorbed*

*Labelling: Absorbed (16,620 x £16) – Actual £289,800 = £23,880 under absorbed*

# Chapter 6: Activity Answers

 **Activity Answer 6.1**

Calculate the **contribution per unit** for each of the following:

| Selling Price | Variable Cost | Contribution per Unit |
|---|---|---|
| £35.00 | £14.00 | £21.00 |
| £480.00 | £225.00 | £255.00 |
| £9.99 | £6.75 | £3.24 |
| £249.49 | £109.80 | £139.69 |

*Contribution per unit = Selling Price – Variable Cost*

 **Activity Answer 6.2**

Calculate the **total contribution** and the **profit (or loss) for the period** for each of the following:

| Contribution per unit | Total Fixed Overheads | Number of Units sold | Total Contribution | Profit (or loss) for period |
|---|---|---|---|---|
| £12.00 | £90,000 | 9,800 | £117,600 | £27,600 |
| £25.00 | £220,000 | 12,600 | £315,000 | £95,000 |
| £28.50 | £304,200 | 9,900 | £282,150 | (£22,050) |
| £2.20 | £65,000 | 36,500 | £80,300 | 15,300 |

*Total Contribution = Contribution per Unit x Number of Units Sold*

*Profit for Period = Total Contribution – Total Fixed Overheads*

# Chapter 6: Activity Answers

 **Activity Answer 6.3**

a) Which of these is the correct formula to calculate the contribution per unit?

| | ✓ |
|---|---|
| Selling Price – Total Cost | |
| Total Cost – Variable Cost | |
| Selling Price – Fixed Cost | |
| Selling Price – Variable Cost | ✓ |
| Selling Price + Variable Cost | |

b) Calculate:

i. The contribution per unit.   £17.00   (£32 - £15)

ii. The break-even point.   24,942   (£424,000 / £17)

If the selling price per unit was reduced from £32 to £30 per unit, and fixed costs increased by 5%, calculate:

iii. The contribution per unit.   £15.00   (£30 - £15)

iv. The revised break-even point.   29,680   (£424,000 + 5%) / £15

 **Activity Answer 6.4**

Calculate the **break-even point** in units for each of the following products. Round your answers up to the nearest whole number.

| Selling Price | Variable Cost | Total Fixed Overheads | Break-Even Point |
|---|---|---|---|
| £80.00 | £36.00 | £124,000 | 2,819 |
| £235.00 | £108.50 | £220,800 | 1,746 |
| £1,040.99 | £657.85 | £85,600 | 224 |
| £399.99 | £198.54 | £654,350 | 3,249 |

*Break-Even Point = Total Fixed Overheads / (Selling Price – Variable Cost)*

Chapter 6: Activity Answers

 Activity Answer 6.5

Calculate the break-even point for each of the three bicycles.

|  | Flyer | Ace | Whizzer |
|---|---|---|---|
| Break-even point (units) | 2,371 units | 1,875 units | 2,572 units |

Flyer: £320,000 / (£230 - £95) = 2,371 units

Ace: £150,000 / (£200 - £80) = 1,875 units

Whizzer: £540,000 / (£450 - £240) = 2,572 units

 Activity Answer 6.6

a) Calculate the break-even point for June.

£210,000 / (£51 - £26) = 8,400 units

b) Calculate the margin of safety in units for June.

11,300 – 8,400 = 2,900 units

c) Calculate the margin of safety (%) for June to 2 d.p.

2,900 / 11,300 x 100 = 25.66%

d) Identify three factors which would increase the margin of safety for Fleur Ltd.

Increasing the selling price

Reducing the cost per unit

Increasing the volume of actual sales

# Chapter 6: Activity Answers

 Activity Answer 6.7

a. Calculate the Budgeted Fixed Overheads for this product £ | 165,600

b. Calculate the Break-Even Volume for this product | 3,465 | units.

Using your answers from part b above, and assuming Brookes Ltd sells 11,000 units:

c. Calculate the Margin of Safety (Units) | 7,535 | units.

d. Calculate the Margin of Safety (%) | 68.5 | %

e. Due to civil unrest in the country of origin of one of the key components, Brookes Ltd faces an unavoidable 5% rise in the cost of raw materials. Assuming all other costs and revenue per unit stayed the same, which of the following statements is correct?

|  | ✓ |
|---|---|
| The breakeven point will decrease and the margin of safety will increase |  |
| The breakeven point will stay the same and the margin of safety will decrease |  |
| The breakeven point will stay the same and the margin of safety will increase |  |
| The breakeven point will increase and the margin of safety will decrease | ✓ |

f. The manager of the factory which produces the Jagstack wants to earn a profit in the next month of £80,000. Using your answers to parts a-d only (i.e. assuming there is no increase in materials costs), what is the required level of sales to earn a target profit of £80,000?

The required level of sales is | 5,139 | units.

# Chapter 6: Activity Answers

 Activity Answer 6.8

Complete the table below (in pence) to show the budgeted contribution per packet for both types of pasta, and the company's budgeted profit or loss for the year from these two products (in £).

|  | Spaghetti | Fusilli |  |
|---|---|---|---|
|  | pence | pence |  |
| Selling price per packet | 60 | 50 |  |
| Less: variable costs per packet |  |  |  |
| Direct materials | 7 | 6 |  |
| Direct labour | 6 | 7 |  |
| Variable overheads | 2 | 3 |  |
| Contribution per packet | 45 | 34 |  |
|  | No. of packets | No. of packets |  |
| Sales volume (packets) | 1,200,000 | 1,800,000 |  |
|  |  |  |  |
|  | £ | £ | Total (£) |
| Total contribution | 540,000 | 612,000 | 1,152,000 |
| Less: fixed costs |  |  | 652,000 |
| Budgeted profit or loss |  |  | 500,000 |

a) Calculate the sales revenue of penne pasta Bartholomew Ltd has to achieve break-even.

| £500,000 | £312,500 / 50p = 625,000 x £0.80 = £500,000 |

b) Calculate the sales revenue of penne pasta Bartholomew Ltd needs to achieve to make a profit of £200,000.

| £820,000 | £312,500 + £200,000 / 50p = 1,025,000 units x £0.80 = £820,000 |

c) If Bartholomew Ltd were to sell £875,000 worth of penne pasta, what would be the margin of safety (in units) and margin of safety (%)?

| 468,750 units | 42.86% % |

Margin of safety (MOS) = (£875,000 / 0.80) = 1,093,750 – 625,000 = 468,750  MOS % = 468,750 / 1,093,750 = 42.86%

# Chapter 6: Activity Answers

 **Activity Answer 6.9**

a) Calculate the marginal cost of producing each gnome.

£1.74

b) Calculate the contribution per gnome.

£4.26

c) Complete the marginal costing statement below to show the total contribution and the total profit each week.

|  | £ | Workings |
|---|---|---|
| Sales | 120,000 | 20,000 x £6.00 |
| *Less Variable Costs* |  |  |
| Direct Materials | 18,000 | In question |
| Direct Labour | 15,000 | In question |
| Variable Production Overheads | 1,800 | In question |
| Total Contribution | 85,200 | £120,000 – (£18,000 + £15,000 + £1,800) |
| *Less Fixed Costs* |  |  |
| Fixed Production Overheads | 6,200 | £8,000 - £1,800 |
| **Profit for the Week** | 79,000 | £85,200 - £6,200 |

d) Calculate the absorption cost of producing each gnome.   £2.05

*Total Cost = £18,000 + £15,000 + £8,000 = £41,000 / 20,000 = £2.05 per gnome*

# Chapter 6: Activity Answers

e) Complete the absorption costing statement below to show the total profit each week.

|  | £ |
|---|---|
| Sales | 120,000 |
| *Less Costs* |  |
| Direct Materials | 18,000 |
| Direct Labour | 15,000 |
| Production Overheads | 8,000 |
| **Profit for the Week** | 79,000 |

 **Activity Answer 6.10**

a) Calculate the marginal cost of producing each mug.

£1.17  £45,000 + £20,000 + £5,000 = £70,000 / 60 000 = £1.167

b) Calculate the contribution per mug.

£4.33  £5.50 – £1.17 = £4.33

c) Complete the marginal costing statement below to show the total contribution and the total profit for November.

|  | £ |
|---|---|
| Sales | 247,500 |
| *Less Variable Costs* |  |
| Direct Materials | 33,750 |
| Direct Labour | 15,000 |
| Variable Production Overheads | 3,750 |
| **Total Contribution** | 195,000 |
| *Less Fixed Costs* |  |
| Fixed Production Overheads | 25,000 |
| **Profit for the Month** | 170,000 |

d) Calculate the absorption cost of producing each mug.

£1.58    £45,000 + £20,000 + £30,000 = £95,000 / 60,000 = £1.58

e) Complete the absorption costing statement below to show the total profit for November.

|  | £ |
|---|---|
| Sales | 247,500 |
| Less Costs |  |
| Direct Materials | 33,750 |
| Direct Labour | 15,000 |
| Production Overheads | 22,500 |
| **Profit for the Month** | 176,250 |

 **Activity Answer 6.11**

Using the templates provided, calculate the profit for the year using both the absorption costing and marginal costing methods.

| Absorption Costing | |
|---|---|
| Sales Revenue | £4,636,000 |
|  |  |
| Opening Inventory | £0 |
| Variable Costs |  |
| -   Direct Materials | £937,500 |
| -   Direct Labour | £187,500 |
| -   Fixed Production Overheads | £2,000,000 |
| Less Closing Inventory | (£75,000) |
| Cost of Goods Sold | £3,050,000 |
| **Profit** | £1,586,000 |

# Chapter 6: Activity Answers

| Marginal Costing | |
|---|---:|
| Sales Revenue | £4,636,000 |
| | |
| Opening Inventory | £0 |
| Variable Costs | |
| - Direct Materials | £937,500 |
| - Direct Labour | £187,500 |
| Less Closing Inventory | (£27,000) |
| Cost of Goods Sold | £1,098,000 |
| **Contribution** | £3,538,000 |
| Less Fixed Production Overheads | £2,000,000 |
| **Profit** | £1,538,000 |

*The difference in profit (£48,000) represents the difference in the value of closing inventory carried forward to the next period. Under absorption costing this is 300 units at £250 = £75,000, whilst under marginal costing it is 300 units at £90 = £27,000. £75,000 - £27,000 = £48,000.*

This page is left intentionally blank.

# Chapter 7: Activity Answers

 ## Activity Answer 7.1

State whether the following statements are true or false.

|  | True/False |
|---|---|
| Activity based costing is a costing method that has been developed to deal with the perceived weaknesses of traditional absorption costing. | True |
| A cost pool is an activity that uses resources. | True |
| A cost driver is a factor that causes (or drives) the level of cost. | True |

 ## Activity Answer 7.2

Calculate the cost driver for the setups and maintenance checks.

| Cost driver per setup | £660 | £118,800 / (40+80+60) |
|---|---|---|
| Cost driver per maintenance check | £2,400 | £276,000 / (25+60+30) |

Calculate how much fixed overhead should be charged to each of the products.

|  | Jump | Drop | Reach |
|---|---|---|---|
| Total cost - Production setups | £26,400 | £52,800 | £39,600 |
| Total cost - Maintenance checks | £60,000 | £144,000 | £72,000 |
| Total Overhead per product | £86,400 | £196,800 | £111,600 |

Calculate the overhead recovery rate per unit under activity based costing.

|  | Jump | Drop | Reach |
|---|---|---|---|
| Total Overhead per product | £86,400 | £196,800 | £111,600 |
| Total units | 10,000 | 20,000 | 16,000 |
| Overhead recovery rate per unit (2dp) | £8.64 | £9.84 | £6.98 |

# Chapter 7: Activity Answers

Calculate the overhead recovery rate under <u>absorption costing</u>.

| Total overheads | £394,800 | £118,800+£276,000 |
|---|---|---|
| Total labour hours | 188,000 | See below |
| **Overhead recovery rate per labour hour** | £2.10 | £394,800/188,000 |

*Total hours: Jump 2 hrs x 10,000 units, Drop 4 hrs x 20,000 units, Reach 5.5 hrs x 16,000 units*

Calculate the overhead recovery rate per labour hour.

|  | Jump | Drop | Reach |
|---|---|---|---|
| Overhead recovery rate per labour hour | £4.20 | £8.40 | £11.55 |

*Jump = £2.10 x 2 hours, Drop = £2.10 x 4 hours, Reach = £2.10 x 5.5 hours*

 **Activity Answer 7.3**

You have been asked to investigate the impact of switching to an ABC approach, with a number of transactions as the cost driver. Write an email to the manager of the estate agency explaining how a switch to Activity Based Costing will impact on the two departments. You should include figures to support your answer.

| To: Manager | |
|---|---|
| From: AAT Student | **Impact of Switch to ABC** |

*If the estate agency were to switch from its present method of absorbing overheads on the basis of property value to a method where the driver of number of transactions is used, there would be a significant impact on how the business's overheads are shared between departments. Under the existing method overheads are shared:*

*Department A - £100,000 x 1,500,000/6,500,000 = £23,077*

*Department B - £100,000 x 5,000,000/6,500,000 = £76,923*

*Using the number of transactions as the driver, the split is:*

*Department A - £100,000 x 15/20 = £75,000*

*Department B - £100,000 x 5/20 = £25,000*

*A much greater share of the overheads will be charged to Department A than at present; this is because this department has a high number of (relatively) low value sales. As the overheads for office support mainly includes the costs of servicing each sale (e.g. completion of paperwork etc) it is fair to assume that the real driver for these costs is the number of sales rather than the value of the sales.*

# Chapter 8: Activity Answers

 **Activity Answer 8.1**

Calculate:

a) The prime cost per batch.  £10,000 + £11,000 = **£21,000**

b) The marginal cost per batch.  £21,000 + £6,000 = **£27,000**

c) The absorption cost per batch.  £27,000 + £4,000 = **£31,000**

d) The marginal cost per can.  £27,000 / 20,000 cans = **£1.35**

e) The absorption cost per can.  £31,000 / 20,000 cans = **£1.55**

 **Activity Answer 8.2**

a) Calculate the total estimated cost of the job, and the selling price if Paris Ltd wish to make a profit of 30% of the total cost.

| | | |
|---|---|---|
| Fabric | £ 2,560 | |
| Leather | £ 6,720 | |
| Labour | £ 720 | |
| O/Hs | £ 300 | |
| Total Cost | £10,300 | |
| Profit | £ 3,090 | *(30% of total cost)* |
| Price | £13,390 | |

b) Calculate the cost per patient bed night to two decimal places.

Total Cost = £2,975,000

Total Bed Nights = 20 x 365 x 95% = 6,935

Cost per bed night = £2,975,000 / 6,935 = **£428.98**

This page is left intentionally blank.

# Chapter 9: Activity Answers

## Activity Answer 9.1

a) Complete the table below to show a flexed budget and the resulting variances against the budget for 'Whizzy' for quarter 3, and whether each variance is Adverse or Favourable. Enter 0 where any figure is zero.

|  | Original Budget | Flexed Budget | Actual | Variance | Adverse / Favourable |
|---|---|---|---|---|---|
| Number of bottles | 100,000 | 90,000 | 90,000 |  |  |
|  | £ |  | £ | £ |  |
| Sales Revenue | 150,000 | 135,000 | 144,000 | 9,000 | Fav |
| Less Costs |  |  |  |  |  |
| Direct Materials | 35,000 | 31,500 | 33,500 | 2,000 | Adv |
| Direct Labour | 18,000 | 16,200 | 16,900 | 700 | Adv |
| Variable Overheads | 1,200 | 1,080 | 1,400 | 320 | Adv |
| Power | 20,000 | 19,500 | 24,000 | 4,500 | Adv |
| Fixed Overheads | 38,000 | 38,000 | 46,700 | 8,700 | Adv |
| **Profit from Operations** | 37,800 | 28,720 | 21,500 | 7,220 | Adv |

b) Referring to your figures in part a), answer the following:

i. Which of these is a possible reason for the Direct Labour Variance?

|  | ✓ |
|---|---|
| Fewer hours were worked as the number of units produced was lower |  |
| The production labour force had undertaken some training and so were more efficient |  |
| There was an unforeseen increase in the hourly rate of pay for production workers | ✓ |
| A scheduled strike was called off at the last minute, with production workers coming in to work instead |  |

ii. Which of these explains the variance in power costs?

| | ✓ |
|---|---|
| The fixed cost increased from £12,000 to £14,000, but the variable cost remained the same | |
| The fixed cost remained the same, but the variable cost increased by 5p per unit | ✓ |
| The fixed cost and variable cost were both the same as budgeted | |
| The fixed cost increased by £1,000 and the variable cost increased by 5p per unit | |

 **Activity Answer 9.2**

a) The budget for production supervisors' costs for a period for a business at an activity level of 180,000 units is £18,000. One production supervisor is required for every 40,000 units of production. If actual production is 220,000 units, what figure would appear in the flexed budget for production supervisors' costs?

> £21,600
>
> Workings:   180,000 / 40,000 = 4.5 rounded up to 5 supervisors
>
>   220,000 / 40,000 = 5.5 rounded up to 6 supervisors
>   £18,000 / 5 x 6 = £21,600

b) The budgeted production overhead for a business is £15,800 at an activity level of 2,000 units and £19,950 at an activity level of 3,000 units. If the actual activity level is 2,600 units what is the flexed budget figure for production overhead?

> £18,290
>
> Workings:    Units          Cost
>
>     3,000         19,950
>
>     2,000         15,800
>
>     1,000          4,150
>
> £4,150 / 1,000 = 4.15 Variable cost per unit  3,000 x £4.15 = £12,450
>
> £19,950 - £12,450 = £7,500 Fixed Cost
>
> 2,600 units x £4.15 = £10,790 + £7,500 Fixed Cost = £18,290

c) Calculate the variance for each line in the operating statement in £ (showing whether it is favourable or adverse) and as a percentage of the flexed budget. Show your percentage to 2 decimal places.

# Chapter 9: Activity Answers

| Operating Statement for November | Flexed Budget £ | Actual £ | Variance £ (F/A) | Variance % |
|---|---|---|---|---|
| Turnover | 144,000 | 132,000 | 12,000 Adv | 8.33% |
| **Variable Costs** | | | | |
| Materials | 48,000 | 45,000 | 3,000 Fav | 6.25% |
| Labour | 24,000 | 28,500 | 4,500 Adv | 18.75% |
| Packaging | 12,000 | 12,000 | n/a | n/a |
| Power | 9,000 | 8,850 | 150 Fav | 1.67% |
| Contribution | 51,000 | 37,650 | 13,350 Adv | 26.18% |
| **Fixed Costs** | | | | |
| Power | 3,750 | 4,500 | 750 Adv | 20% |
| Depreciation | 5,250 | 4,950 | 300 Fav | 5.71% |
| Sales & Marketing | 7,500 | 7,500 | n/a | n/a |
| Administration | 9,750 | 9,750 | n/a | n/a |
| Operating Profit | 24,750 | 10,950 | 13,800 Adv | 55.76% |

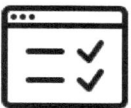 ## Activity Answer 9.3

a) Using the data in the operating statement, together with the notes shown below, complete the flexed budget and variances in the appropriate columns in the table.

| | Original Budget | Actual | Flexed Budget | Variance (F / A) |
|---|---|---|---|---|
| **Volume (units)** | 90,000 | 80,000 | 80,000 | |
| | £ | £ | £ | £ |
| Turnover | 1,440,000 | 1,320,000 | 1,280,000 | 40,000 (F) |
| Costs | | | | |
| Materials | 472,500 | 432,000 | 420,000 | 12,000 (A) |
| Labour | 270,000 | 232,000 | 240,000 | 8,000 (F) |
| Distribution | 135,000 | 100,000 | 120,000 | 20,000 (F) |
| Energy | 71,000 | 67,000 | 64,000 | 3,000 (A) |
| Equipment hire | 8,000 | 7,400 | 7,000 | 400 (A) |
| Depreciation | 16,000 | 19,400 | 16,000 | 3,400 (A) |
| Marketing | 27,000 | 15,000 | 27,000 | 12,000 (F) |
| Administration | 18,900 | 21,200 | 18,900 | 2,300 (A) |
| | | | | |
| Total Costs | 1,018,400 | 894,000 | 912,900 | 18,900 (F) |
| | | | | |
| Operating Profit | 421,600 | 426,000 | 367,100 | 58,900 (F) |

© Accountext

# Chapter 9: Activity Answers

b) Write a short note to the finance director identifying **one** possible reason for each variance you have calculated.

*Good morning*

*I have identified variances in the flexed budget, and the following are possible reasons for each variance:*

***Turnover*** *(£40,000 Fav) – the selling price was increased from £16.00 per unit to £16.50 per unit*

***Materials*** *(£12,000 Adv) – the cost per unit of materials was higher than expected, or there was more wastage of materials during production than expected.*

***Labour*** *(£8,000 Fav) – either fewer hours were worked than expected to produce the actual level of output, or the labour rate per hour was lower than budgeted.*

***Distribution*** *(£20,000 Fav) – the distribution cost per unit is lower than expected. This could be because fuel costs have fallen meaning delivery costs are lower than expected.*

***Energy*** *(£3,000 Adv) – the energy costs are higher than budgeted for the actual level of activity – this suggests that either more energy was used than expected or that the cost of energy has risen.*

***Equipment Hire*** *(£400 Adv) – this is a stepped cost. As the activity level has been flexed to 80,000 units we based the budget on requiring (80,000 / 12000) = 6.66 rounded up to 7 pieces of equipment being hired. The original budget was based on (90,000 / 12,000) = 7.5 rounded up to 8 pieces of equipment hired. The budgeted cost £1,000 per hire. The adverse variance is caused by the actual cost of hiring this equipment being higher than budgeted.*

***Depreciation*** *(£3,400 Adv) – the depreciation cost was higher than budgeted. It may be that the business has recently purchased new non-current assets which have been depreciated, thereby increasing the expense.*

***Marketing*** *(£12,000 Fav) – the favourable variance here indicates less was spent on marketing than forecast. Perhaps some advertising was cancelled, or fewer other marketing activities took place. This may in part explain why sales volume were lower than forecast.*

***Administration*** *(£2,300 Adv) – this could be caused by additional administration staff being employed or other costs being higher than expected.*

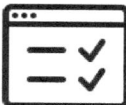

## Activity Answer 9.4

Flex the budgeted operating statement to reflect the different sales of units.

| Units | 20,000 | 40,000 | 65,000 |
|---|---|---|---|
| Sales revenue | £240,000 | £480,000 | £780,000 |
| **Variable costs:** | | | |
| Material | £52,000 | £104,000 | £169,000 |
| Labour | £120,000 | £240,000 | £390,000 |
| **Contribution** | £68,000 | **£136,000** | £221,000 |
| Fixed costs | £68,400 | £68,400 | £68,400 |
| **Total costs** | £240,400 | £412,400 | £627,400 |
| **Profit** | -£400 | **£67,600** | £152,600 |

## Activity Answer 9.5

Complete the table to show the forecast profit / loss for the 5,000 units and 6,000 units. Enter your answers to the nearest whole pound. Enter any loss as a minus figure.

|  | 4,000 units | 5,000 units | 6,000 units |
|---|---|---|---|
| Revenue | £200,000 | £250,000 | £276,000 |
| Variable material costs | £80,000 | £100,000 | £108,000 |
| Variable labour costs | £64,000 | £80,000 | £91,200 |
| **Contribution** | **£56,000** | £70,000 | £76,800 |
| Fixed costs | £58,000 | £58,000 | £55,000 |
| **Forecast profit / (loss)** | **-£2,000** | £12,000 | £21,800 |

This page is left intentionally blank.

# Chapter 10: Activity Answers

 ## Activity Answer 10.1

Complete the cash flow forecast on the following page using the information above.

|  | April | May | June | July |
|---|---|---|---|---|
| Cash Receipts | £ | £ | £ | £ |
| - From Cash Sales | 2,500 | 2,600 | 2,400 | 2,500 |
| - From Credit Customers | 24,500 | 26,200 | 27,100 | 29,100 |
| - New Loans |  | 10,000 |  |  |
| - Sale of Non-Current Asset |  |  | 2,500 |  |
| **Total Receipts** | 27,000 | 38,800 | 32,000 | 31,600 |
| Cash Payments |  |  |  |  |
| - Purchases | 17,600 | 20,800 | 19,600 | 22,500 |
| - Salaries and Wages | 7,500 | 7,500 | 7,500 | 7,500 |
| - Overhead Costs | 3,500 | 3,800 | 3,500 | 3,500 |
| - Purchase of Non-Current Assets |  |  | 10,000 | - |
| - Repayment of Loans |  |  | 230 | 230 |
| - Drawings | 2,000 | 2,000 | 2,000 | 2,000 |
| **Total Payments** | 30,600 | 34,100 | 42,830 | 35,730 |
|  |  |  |  |  |
| Opening Bank Balance | 12,000 | 8,400 | 13,100 | 2,270 |
| Net Cash Flow | - 3,600 | 4,700 | - 10,830 | - 4,130 |
| Closing Bank Balance | 8,400 | 13,100 | 2,270 | - 1,860 |

# Chapter 10: Activity Answers

 Activity Answer 10.2

Complete the cash flow forecast on the following page using the information above.

|  | June | July | August | September |
|---|---|---|---|---|
| **Cash Receipts** | £ | £ | £ | £ |
| From Cash Sales | 13,800 | 16,200 | 15,800 | 16,100 |
| From Credit Customers | 40,500 | 41,200 | 48,300 | 43,600 |
| Capital / New Loans |  |  |  |  |
| **Total Receipts** | 54,300 | 57,400 | 64,100 | 59,700 |
|  |  |  |  |  |
| **Cash Payments** |  |  |  |  |
| Credit purchases | 27,500 | 36,200 | 25,600 | 26,400 |
| Salaries and Wages | 16,500 | 16,500 | 16,500 | 16,500 |
| General Overhead Costs | 3,560 | 3,560 | 3,760 | 3,760 |
| Purchase of Non-Current Assets |  | 20,000 |  |  |
| Repayment of Loans |  |  |  |  |
| Drawings | 2,200 | 2,200 | 2,200 | 2,200 |
| **Total Payments** | 49,760 | 78,460 | 48,060 | 48,860 |
|  |  |  |  |  |
| **Opening Bank Balance** | 25,600 | 30,140 | 9,080 | 25,120 |
| **Net Cash Flow** | 4,540 | - 21,060 | 16,040 | 10,840 |
| **Closing Bank Balance** | 30,140 | 9,080 | 25,120 | 35,960 |

 Activity Answer 10.3

Calculate the working capital cycle to the nearest day assuming all purchases and sales are on credit.

|  | Days |  |
|---|---|---|
| Inventory holding days | 106 days | (4,055 / 13,980 x 365) |
| Trade Receivables Collection Period | 44 days | (4,545 / 38,000 x 365) |
| Trade Payables Payment Period | 84 days | (3,200 / 13,980 x 365) |
| Working capital cycle | 66 days | (106 + 44 – 84) |

© Accountext

# Chapter 10: Activity Answers

 **Activity Answer 10.4**

Indicate whether the figures below should be added or deducted and calculate the cash figure when allowing for these adjustments.

| Profit | 80,800 | Add / Deduct |
|---|---|---|
| New Bank Loan | 32,000 | add |
| Bank Loan repayments | 17,500 | deduct |
| Capital | 40,000 | add |
| Purchase of new equipment | 55,000 | deduct |
| Depreciation | 4,700 | add |
| **Cash** | **85,000** | |